Project Planning

A Guide for Practitioners

ALAN KIBBE GAYNOR
Boston University

JANE L. EVANSON
Alaska Pacific University

ALLYN AND BACON
Boston London Toronto Sydney Tokyo Singapore

Copyright © 1992 by Allyn and Bacon
A Division of Simon & Schuster, Inc.
160 Gould Street
Needham Heights, Massachusetts 02194

Library of Congress Cataloging-in-Publication Data

Gaynor, Alan K.
    Project planning : a guide for practitioners / Alan Kibbe Gaynor,
Jane L. Evanson.
        p.   cm.
    Includes bibliographical references (p.   ) and index.
    ISBN 0-205-13220-0
    1. Planning.   I. Evanson, Jane L.   II. Title.
HD30.28.G38   1992
    658.4′04 — dc20

91-20401
CIP

BK
$36.00

Printed in the United States of America
10   9   8   7   6   5   4   3   2   1   95   94   93   92   91

To our students

Contents

List of Figures

Foreword

Like most of my educator and community colleagues, I feel awash in paper these days—handbooks, textbooks, reports, proposals, journals, articles. So I respond eagerly when I come across material—in whatever format—that is readable, sensible, and directly useful. This volume by Alan Gaynor and Jane Evanson is all of those things.

There are two things that make this particular work so useful for me personally.

First, it is clearly and significantly framed by the authors' exploration of and acquaintance with important ideas—theory, research, and the assorted continuing debates among intellectuals and practitioners about the nature of organizations, goals, knowledge, and values. This "heavy" content is present here—but it is largely behind the scenes, and I don't have to wade through it once again. But that it is there is important in making this book sensible and useful. Most of the "how-to-do-it" papers that I see are without any real intellectual foundation, often being not much more than cookbooks or collections of "helpful hints." This book is rooted in sound theories about organizations and how they work, and in good research about effective organizational development.

Second, the book has a clear step-by-step workshop approach. It tells me and my students how to proceed in planning projects and writing proposals and it makes clear at every step what is vital in the process. It provides models, examples, and sample planning documents. These are all within the covers of the book so the reader doesn't have to go fishing through his or her files.

I spend a lot of time writing proposals (which, of course, are essentially planning documents) and trying to implement the proposal ideas when we are successful in obtaining funding. The mission hierarchy concept and its follow-up technology as described in the book are very useful to successful grantsmanship and project management. The approach helps me stay clear about what goals we can and cannot achieve. It helps to provide the specific focus and clear objectives that funders like to see.

Don Davies, *Professor, Boston University School of Education, President, Institute for Responsive Education, and former Deputy Commissioner, U.S. Office of Education*

Preface

This book is based on a course we have presented at Boston University, Alaska Pacific University, and to American military personnel in Germany and Italy. The course is about what we have come to call "Results-Oriented Planning and Management." The primary focus is on the planning and management of projects.

We wrote this book because, after many years of searching for a textbook for our students, we were unable to find one that explained the entire planning process. There are many books that discuss problem analysis or planning in broad or theoretical ways. Examples include Easton's *A Systems Analysis of Political Life* (1965), Lindblom's *The Intelligence of Democracy* (1965), Wildavsky's *The Politics of the Budgetary Process* (1983), and Peters and Waterman's *In Search of Excellence* (1982). Others, beyond counting, describe particular methods such as PERT or network analysis, flow charting, program planning and budgeting systems, and management information systems.

None of these has to our satisfaction described these micro-management tools in relation to planning as part of a broad management process. None of them takes you through the entire methodology of producing a finished plan or proposal. Yet people all over the world are writing plans and proposals all the time, to raise money and to get things done. In this book we present a sound method for comprehensive planning.

We wrote this book with the learner in mind. Several generations of our students have critiqued and shaped the writing of this book. One thing we have learned from our students is the importance of the right formats in helping people to think productively. And we have become aware of the importance of language in channeling design work into useful modes of thinking. We seek to assist you by providing appropriate formats and language models.

We have also come to understand the importance of providing good overviews, so that people understand the big picture within which the details make sense. Our whole planning model is based on the essential relationship between the big picture and the details. It emphasizes the connection between the values, purposes, and desired results, on the one hand, and the project activities, on the other.

Finally, our students have told us many times that a picture is worth a thousand words. Good examples really help. So we have included examples throughout the book, using the work of our former students to simplify your learning task.

Acknowledgments

We wish to express our gratitude to all the friends and colleagues who contributed to this publication in various ways. The intellectual roots of this work lie in the contributions of Gerald Nadler to the field of systems planning. The reading of his 1970 book, *Work Design: A Systems Concept* (Irwin, 1970), was seminal to our thinking about planning and has informed our teaching ever since. Discussions with Anatole Holt, former director of the Boston University Academic Computer Center, along with follow-up work done with Karl H. Clauset, Jr., were fundamental in developing the concepts in the book related to managing information for projects and programs in organizations. Clauset's contributions were also significant in the early planning stages of the book.

We are particularly indebted to George de George, Connecticut State Department of Education; Mardella Lower, Providence Hospital, Anchorage, Alaska; and Patrick T. Moran, Digital Equipment Corporation, for following our planning process meticulously and contributing their planning documents as models for those who use this text. Janet Buerklin, James Hayes, and George Watson graciously shared examples from their planning materials to illustrate selected concepts.

Special thanks go to the many participants in administrative planning courses and workshops in Boston, Europe, and Alaska who critiqued various versions of the manuscript, corrected errors, and suggested ideas for improvement. We would like to thank Kristin Hanson in particular for providing a detailed written critique of an early draft and Bob Lusignan and Charlene Reiss for their insights along the way. Yeoman work was done by Josephine J. (Jane) Pavese and Jo Ann Share, Boston University doctoral students, in reading a draft of the manuscript, along with the reviewers' comments, in the spring of 1990 and collaborating in the development of a plan for revising and reorganizing the manuscript. Our very special gratitude to Pavese for further reviewing the penultimate draft of the book during the fall of 1990 and for making detailed recommendations for final revision.

James W. Brown and his colleagues at Prentice-Hall were helpful in reading the manuscript and referring us to Allyn and Bacon. We feel fortunate to have worked with Ray Short of Allyn and Bacon. He guided us through the submission and review process and enthusiastically represented our project to his associates. We would also like to thank Carol Craig for her assistance throughout the review process.

We wish to acknowledge the contributions of our colleagues, who consulted with us, providing advice and encouragement at various times from the beginning to the end of the project. These include Karen Boatman, Don

Davies, Vivian Johnson, and Tim Weaver of the Department of Administration, Training, and Policy Studies, School of Education, Boston University; Jenny Quillien, Boston University Overseas Program; Mike Martin, University of Colorado; Mark R. Shibles, The University of Connecticut; Fred Frank and Muriel Mackett, Northern Illinois University; Lloyd DuVall, Nova University; Edward Hickcox and Richard Townsend, The Ontario Institute for Studies in Education; Patrick B. Forsyth, Executive Director, The University Council for Educational Administration; and Rosemary Cafferella, Virginia Commonwealth University. We extend our appreciation also to the department heads, plenary session representatives, and professors at twenty-three of the UCEA universities who responded to our survey of planning courses. Through their responses we were able to identity sixty professors within the UCEA network alone who are involved with the teaching of planning.

We are grateful to Boston University and Alaska Pacific University. We thank Dennis Berkey and Paul Warren for providing the sabbatical leave in 1984 that made it possible to give the book a running start. We are appreciative, too, of the support of Peter Greer, Joan Dee, Carole Greenes, and Boyd Dewey whose help and encouragement make serious writing possible, if not easy. This work would not have been completed without the support of former President Glenn A. Olds and President F. Thomas Trotter of Alaska Pacific University.

We are most grateful to our assistants, Rachel Harrington of Boston University and Vicki Gibbons of Alaska Pacific University, for their attention to detail in the preparation of parts of the manuscript and their ongoing support of our work.

We had the additional benefit of dear friends who either inspired us or provided insight, guidance, and editorial assistance along the way. These have included Lois Bender, Gretchen Bersch, Peggy Byrnes, LuAnne Dowling, Jan Ingram, Theodore Kessel, Kathleen Lynch, Bill Lytle, Luz Rivas McDade, Teri Mahaney, Lael Morgan, Kate O'Dell, Mary Rice, and Günter Sandscheper.

We also want to thank all our students and seminar participants, whose ideas, enthusiasm, and knowledge continue to stimulate our thinking and motivate us to write. We are grateful, as always, to our families for the inspiration and support they have given us all our lives. A special note of love, admiration, and appreciation in this regard to Lucy Warres Finkston. Then there is Chester, the constant and loving companion.

And, finally, our deepest gratitude and respect to great mentors, Jack A. Culbertson and Elazar J. Pedhazur.

Boston, Massachusetts   A.K.G.
August, 1991   J.L.E.

CHAPTER ONE

Introduction

Whether you work in business, government, or human services, you need to plan. The more care you take in developing your plans, the more effective your work is likely to be. Our purpose in this book is to show you how to develop good plans and to give you some models to use in planning a project or program of your own.

The way we view a project and the techniques we use for thinking through the procedures might be new to you. However, we believe you will find them valuable in any planning effort—large or small.

Planning is part of a problem-focused system of management. Such a system incorporates:

1. Scanning procedures for identifying possible problem situations
2. Follow-up data collection and analysis procedures for documenting problems, clarifying them, and developing ideas about what is causing them
3. Planning procedures for taking action to deal with problems and to move the organization toward a vision of effective performance
4. Management procedures for putting plans into action:
   a. Raising moneys and obtaining necessary approvals and authorizations
   b. Following up on planned project activities
   c. Implementing necessary subsystems dealing with personnel, materials, equipment, and facilities to support project activities
   d. Putting into place the information systems that support ongoing decision making and that are necessary for carrying out activities and decisions

Planning is crucial to:

1. Communicate to various audiences why the project is important to them
2. Clarify what the project will deliver

3. Describe the activities needed to achieve the desired results
4. Identify the subsystems needed to support project activities
5. Lay out timetables, job descriptions, work flow schedules, budgets, and managerial responsibilities
6. Avoid internal overload problems and external political, cultural, legal, financial, and technical problems

In the chapters that follow you will learn how to:

1. Place your project in a larger context
2. Write a clear statement describing your project
3. Specify your intended results
4. Analyze the existing conditions that can affect your project
5. Arrange a logical sequence of activities for the project, including activities to deal with and take advantage of existing conditions
6. Diagram patterns of information flow for making decisions and carrying out activities

This book is about putting together a planning document. Working on a planning document serves several valuable purposes:

1. Focusing the thinking of the planning team as you work through pieces of the plan
2. Clarifying ideas and rethinking issues as next steps are taken in the planning process
3. Producing evidence of careful thought as planning materials are produced
4. Communicating effectively to different audiences ideas that have been carefully thought out in the course of the planning process
5. Managing and evaluating the project based on the desired results and project activities described in the plan

The book takes you through sequential stages of planning. It provides you with step-by-step explanations of each format and planning process. It gives examples from a corporation, a hospital, and public education. You will follow these examples through the various stages of the planning process. An appendix at the end of the book includes complete sample planning documents. The diagram in Figure 1-1 provides an overview of the entire planning process and technical terms to be explained and illustrated as we move through the coming chapters.

In a certain sense, projects are different from programs. A project has a definite beginning and a definite end. It is a set of activities designed to accomplish specific results within a specified period of time. Projects are often

FIGURE 1-1 • *The Planning Process*

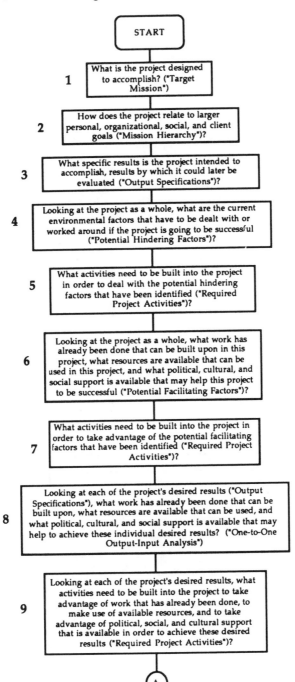

START

1 What is the project designed to accomplish? ("Target Mission")

2 How does the project relate to larger personal, organizational, social, and client goals ("Mission Hierarchy")?

3 What specific results is the project intended to accomplish, results by which it could later be evaluated ("Output Specifications")?

4 Looking at the project as a whole, what are the current environmental factors that have to be dealt with or worked around if the project is going to be successful ("Potential Hindering Factors")?

5 What activities need to be built into the project in order to deal with the potential hindering factors that have been identified ("Required Project Activities")?

6 Looking at the project as a whole, what work has already been done that can be built upon in this project, what resources are available that can be used in this project, and what political, cultural, and social support is available that may help this project to be successful ("Potential Facilitating Factors")?

7 What activities need to be built into the project in order to take advantage of the potential facilitating factors that have been identified ("Required Project Activities")?

8 Looking at each of the project's desired results ("Output Specifications"), what work has already been done that can be built upon, what resources are available that can be used, and what political, cultural, and social support is available that may help to achieve these individual desired results? ("One-to-One Output-Input Analysis")

9 Looking at each of the project's desired results, what activities need to be built into the project to take advantage of work that has already been done, to make use of available resources, and to take advantage of political, social, and cultural support that is available in order to achieve these desired results ("Required Project Activities")?

A

Continued

FIGURE 1-1 • *Continued*

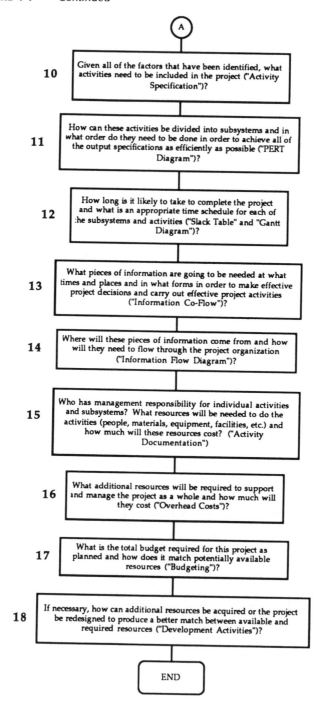

designed to accomplish results *within* programs, to get a program started, or to improve it at some point. While a project is a one-time-only entity, programs may go on year after year. Typically programs repeat what they do with new clients, students, patients, or customers.

What this book will teach you is how to use a set of designated techniques to plan, manage, and evaluate a project. However, you can also apply them to programs. In fact, our students often tell us that what is most valuable about our planning method is that it goes beyond any of the particular techniques it contains. What is likely to prove most useful to you over time is the way in which we have integrated these techniques in a planning, management, and evaluation *system*.

This book is a teaching tool and reference manual. We have also designed it as a workbook. It includes exercises to give you practice with each of the techniques taught. Answers given for these exercises provide feedback on your work. In addition, there is space (at least enough to get you started) for you to develop your own planning document as you go along. Just add pages as needed.

We use this format in "hands-on" workshops in which every student works on a plan for his or her own project. We build into the classes feedback sessions in which students display and critique their work. Students also turn in drafts of their work in progress for regular written feedback. At the end of the course, each one has produced a proposal. Many of our students have parlayed these documents into actual projects, job promotions, and new job opportunities.

We encourage instructors using this book as a text to adopt a workshop approach to teaching. We have found this to be an effective strategy. At the end of the course, student work is, with the rarest of exceptions, uniformly of professional quality. We also encourage those of you using this book on your own, outside a workshop situation, to do the exercises as a way of building and testing your technical skills. You can also use the book as a working guide in writing your own project proposals. Take advantage of the starter pages provided, and prepare a project proposal using the formats and techniques taught in the book. You will learn this subject best by doing it.

For more than a decade we have taught these formats to hundreds of students. It is clear that the method has broad applicability across different professions and organizations. Our students have included school teachers and administrators, corporate trainers and developers, and managers of universities and social agencies. We have also worked with private corporate consultants, foreign government ministry personnel, and international development personnel working for private voluntary agencies. Workshop participants have presented their proposals to corporate executives; military commanders; school, university, hospital, and agency administrators; along with public and private funding agencies. Students have frequently adapted the formats to meet the requirements of particular organizations or funding agencies. The basic content and organization of the work have always proved to be sound and easily modified to fit specific situational requirements.

Just recently one of our students reported an incident that well represents student responses over the years. The student, a corporate trainer, interviewed for a job with a major accounting and consulting firm. She showed them the planning work she had done for our course, which was clearly related to the job she was seeking. Her interviewer's response reflected the quality of her work and the power of the methodology. He said with surprise, "Where did you learn how to do this stuff?!" She got the job.

CHAPTER TWO

Clarifying Broad Goals— The Mission Hierarchy

No project is an end in itself. Curriculum projects in schools are designed to improve instruction, to enhance student learning—graduates should go out into the world knowing, believing, and doing things that make for better lives, a better country, and a better world. Staff training projects in hospitals improve health care, cure more patients, and lead to happier lives and a healthier society. They may even lead to cost savings, more efficient hospitals, and higher salaries and profits or lower hospital bills, insurance rates, and taxes. Similar human resource development projects in corporations may improve product quality and market share, or lower costs and increase profits.

It is important for you to think in terms of larger goals and agendas. It is important in part for pure design purposes. Knowing whether the long-range purpose is cost cutting, product quality, or safety, for example, helps to determine the content of a training project and may affect the training methodology, as well.

Being conscious of larger agendas is also important for selling the project. Projects often require support and cooperation from different constituencies. To gain support from diverse groups, each with its own agenda, you have to think about your project in their terms—that is, in terms of their agendas.

How often do people trumpet the benefits of a project in terms of their own interests and values? Who listens, other than politely? To gain support, talk to the other parties' interests! To do so, it is enormously helpful to imagine the long-range goals of other constituencies and to advocate your project from their perspectives. This is the politics of the planning process.

In this chapter you will learn an approach to describing your project in relationship to a larger agenda. You will learn how to create what we call a *mission hierarchy*. The mission hierarchy is a tool for thinking about and communicating your project as a part of a larger vision, a vision that others can share.

The Idea of a Mission Hierarchy

Meaning is a sense of context. It is only when I can see what I am doing in relation to other people and events that I give meaning to what I do. When you define your project as part of a larger agenda, you give a meaning to your project that you can communicate to others. Every project, no matter how technical it seems, is important because it contributes to larger values you and others believe in: products, profits, improved working and living conditions, human rights, and so on. It is your project's contribution to one or more of these larger values that makes it important and worthy of support.

It is important that you be clear about your purposes and the values behind them. It is also important that you clarify any mixed agendas that could create problems later on. One way to clarify your agenda is to build a mission hierarchy for the project. A mission hierarchy is a sequence of statements that defines a range of purposes—from those that are specific and clearly achievable to those that are very broad in scope. Figure 2-1 is an example of a mission hierarchy. Your project is actually one of the statements in your mission hierarchy. For example, you can see in Figure 2-1 that Moran's project was "to update product training books." It appears (underlined) as the third level in his mission hierarchy. Thus, anyone can see how his project fits into the larger agenda his hierarchy describes.

Moran's mission hierarchy illustrates four basic characteristics of mission hierarchies in general:

1. First, each succeeding level is broader in scope than the preceding level. The highest level of the mission hierarchy should be very broad in scope. The lowest level should be clearly feasible to do given existing

FIGURE 2-1 • *Pat Moran's Mission Hierarchy*

8. To contribute to company profitability
  7. To increase sales
    6. To maximize sales trainees' understanding of the products they sell
      5. To improve the company's sales training programs
        4. To improve instructional materials and methods for training sales people in the company
          3. To update product training books
            2. To gather information on the new products from experts who know them
              1. To identify new products the company has introduced since the existing product training books were written

constraints on time and resources. We recommend that the lowest mission statement in your mission hierarchy be very concrete, almost trivial. The idea is that your mission hierarchy should cover a broad range of project possibilities, from the narrowest in scope to some version of "save the world" at the top.

The schematic in Figure 2-2 illustrates how the levels of a mission hierarchy are logically embedded one within the other. Like a Chinese box puzzle, the lower levels of the hierarchy are progressively included in a series of larger and larger boxes until all are contained within the highest-level mission statement.

2. The second characteristic of a mission hierarchy is tht the levels of the hierarchy are logically connected from the lowest to the highest level. Each succeeding level stands as a rationale for the preceding level. If you asked, "Why?" about doing the project described at the first level of the mission hierarchy, you would find the answer in the statement at the second level—and so on up the hierarchy.

Question: Why identify new products the company has introduced since the existing product training books were written? (Level 1)

FIGURE 2-2 · *The Logical Structure of Moran's Mission Hierarchy*

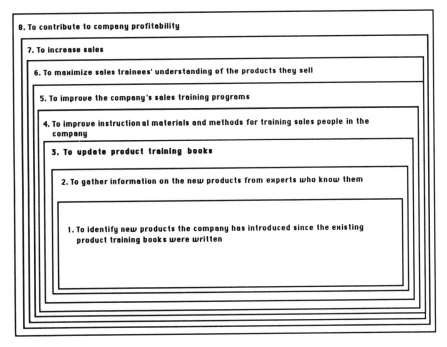

8. To contribute to company profitability

7. To increase sales

6. To maximize sales trainees' understanding of the products they sell

5. To improve the company's sales training programs

4. To improve instructional materials and methods for training sales people in the company

3. To update product training books

2. To gather information on the new products from experts who know them

1. To identify new products the company has introduced since the existing product training books were written

Answer: To gather information on the new products from experts who know them. (Level 2)

Question: Why gather information on the new products from experts who know them? (Level 2)

Answer: To update product training books (Level 3)

Question: Why update product training books? (Level 3)

Answer: To improve instructional materials and methods for training sales people in the company (Level 4) . . . and so on to the highest level in the mission hierarchy.

Thus, a mission hierarchy stands as as brief but comprehensive explanation of why the project or program is being undertaken. It suggests what immediate purposes it serves and to what larger purposes it contributes.

3. The third characteristic of a mission hierarchy is that the higher levels of the hierarchy clarify and delimit the meanings and implications of the lower levels. For example, do you think that you would update product training books the same way if you were using them to train customers instead of company sales personnel? Most likely, the content and style of the books would need to be different in the two cases. This illustrates how the upper levels of your mission hierarchy influence how you plan projects at the lower levels.

4. Finally, the project must seem likely to solve the problem you are dealing with. You want your mission statement to suggest exactly the results that you want, no more and no less. Look at the statement in the mission hierarchy you are thinking about for your project mission. Your mission statement may suggest results tht go beyond what you had in mind for your project. If so, you should choose a project mission that is at a lower level in the hierarchy (a smaller project). Your mission statement may suggest results that are narrower than what you had in mind. In this case choose a project at a higher level in the mission hierarchy (a bigger project). Choosing the project level is also a matter of feasibility. Presumably you want to engage in a project to achieve the most ambitious results you can within the limits of your skills, resources, and scope of authority and responsibility.

A Generic Mission Hierarchy

We have seen hundreds of mission hierarchies developed by people in various human service and human resource fields. We have noticed that these mission hierarchies display a common logical thread. Almost invariably their central core contains (or implies) a sequence of objectives running from needs assessment through planning, implementation, and evaluation. This generic model, illustrated in Figure 2-3, seems to help our students in thinking about their own mission hierarchies.

FIGURE 2-3 • *A Generic Model of a Mission Hieararchy*

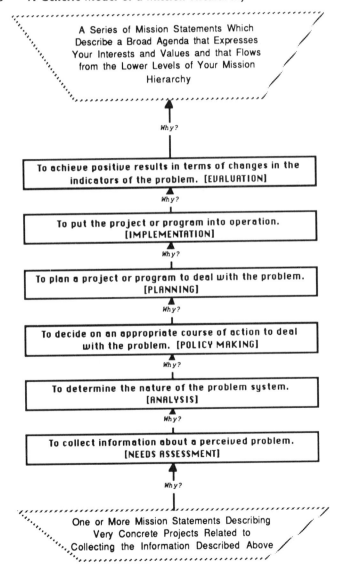

Using the Mission Hierarchy as a Political Tool in the Planning Process

The mission hierarchy was developed as a tool for clarifying the planning team's own agenda (within which the particular project is embedded). We have discovered that is is also very valuable as a tool for relating the project to the political agendas of other people and groups — an important facet because projects almost always require broad support for implementation. Thus, coalition building is a necessary and intrinsic part of effective planning processes. Just imagine, for the various people or groups whose cooperation you will need, what their agendas are and how your project fits into their agendas. The diagram in Figure 2-4 illustrates this idea schematically.

FIGURE 2-4 • *Using the Mission Hierarchy to Build Coalitions Around Your Project*

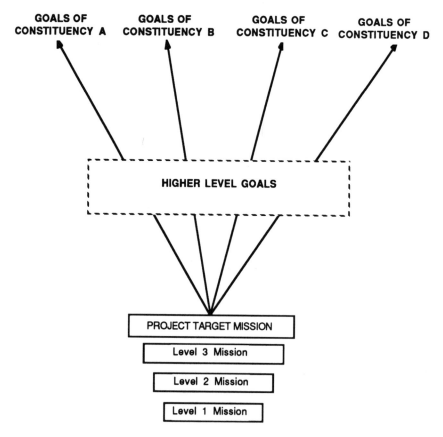

Facilitating various goals is the basis for political coalition building. People with different political agendas often find themselves supporting a project in common that each sees in terms of his or her own larger values and objectives. However, it is also important to recognize that larger agendas may affect the bottom-line operations of even relatively narrow projects. What may appear to be a simple project idea may actually represent very different undertakings within the context of larger purposes. For example, a community school project in a developing country can take on one character when it is framed by a vision of enhancing local autonomy, and it may look quite different when it is part of a centralized national economic and political agenda.

How to Develop a Mission Hierarchy

When you construct a mission hierarchy, there are two places you can start: at the top or the bottom. If you start at the top, you will identify a very broad goal and then define below it in the hierarchy other goals that are successively more narrow in scope. If you start at the bottom, the more common approach, you will begin with a mission statement that addresses a particular problem. Very likely, you will have defined and documented this problem through needs assessment and policy analysis. From this point you can build up the hierarchy by defining successively broader goals at each step.

An Example

Here is an example of how to develop a mission hierarchy. One workshop participant, Mardy Lower (rhymes with *flower*), was a nursing administrator. She felt that she had described what she wanted to do in the mission statement "To provide cancer patients with a comprehensive cancer treatment program."

Although this mission statement defines a project of significant scope, Lower felt that it was feasible and that it suggested a wide range of results. The way she developed her mission hierarchy is consistent with the examples given earlier.

1. She tentatively thought of her initial mission statement as Level 1 of her mission hierarchy.
2. She then asked herself why she wanted to pursue that project. She answered herself as follows: "In order to meet the physical, emotional, educational, and spiritual needs of cancer patients."

At this point, her emerging mission hierarchy looked as shown in Figure 2-5.

FIGURE 2-5 • *Lower's First Cut at a Mission Hierarchy*

Level 2: To meet the physical, emotional, educational and spiritual needs of cancer patients

Level 1: To provide cancer patients with a comprehensive treatment program

She then followed the same procedure in formulating the top statement in her short mission hierarchy. She asked herself why she wanted to meet the physical, emotional, educational, and spiritual needs of cancer patients. Her answer was that she wanted to enhance the quality of life for all patients suffering from cancer. She decided to treat this as her highest mission statement. It seemed very broad, beyond any goal she might hope to achieve in her lifetime. Her mission hierarchy then looked as shown in Figure 2-6.

FIGURE 2-6 • *Lower's Second Cut at a Mission Hierarchy*

Level 3: To enhance the quality of life for all patients suffering from cancer

Level 2: To meet the physical, emotional, educational, and spiritual needs of cancer patients

Level 1: To provide cancer patients with a comprehensive treatment program

Lower's mission hierarchy meets all the criteria discussed so far. It starts with a mission statement based on prior needs assessment and policy analysis. Each successive level of the hierarchy explains why the prior mission statement is desirable. What she was still missing, however, were narrower mission statements below the mission level she had tentatively identified as her project mission. Having at least two levels below the target mission is important, even if one or both have already been accomplished. You want to see the proposed project in relationship to a full range of options, of greater and lesser scope. You want to know for sure why you are proposing this project, not a larger or smaller one. Therefore, we asked Lower to write mission statements lower in the hierarchy. How she accomplished this illustrates two useful ideas: (1) how mission statements of lesser scope can be added at the lower end of a mission hierarchy and (2) the alternative method of constructing a mission hierarchy, that of beginning at the top of the hierarchy and working down instead of starting at the bottom and going up.

In her second draft (Fig. 2-6) the lowest level of Lower's hierarchy was "To provide cancer patients with a comprehensive treatment program." To write a lower-level mission statement, she asked, "What would have to be done first in order for that to happen?" Lower's answer to that question was "To gain approval for hiring more staff to provide care for cancer patients." At that point, then, her developing mission hierarchy looked as shown in Figure 2-7.

FIGURE 2-7 • *Lower's Third Draft of Her Mission Hierarchy*

Level 4: To enhance the quality of life for all patients suffering from cancer

Level 3: To meet the physical, emotional, educational, and spiritual needs of cancer patients

Level 2: To provide cancer patients with a comprehensive treatment program

Level 1: To gain approval for hiring more staff to provide care for cancer patients

You can see that the hierarchy has a new Level 1 and that each of the other levels is numbered one higher than it was before. Lower continued this downward process one more time. She looked at the tentative Level 1 and asked, "What would have to be done first in order for that to happen?" The answer to that question became the new Level 1 in the reconstructed mission hierarchy. Her final mission hierarchy is shown in Figure 2-8.

FIGURE 2-8 • *Lower's Final Mission Hierarchy*

Level 5: To enhance the quality of life for all patients suffering from cancer

Level 4: To meet the physical, emotional, educational, and spiritual needs of cancer patients

Level 3: To provide cancer patients with a comprehensive treatment program

Level 2: To gain approval for hiring more staff to provide care for cancer patients

Level 1: To increase administrative awareness of the need for a specific, designated cancer service

Mission Hierarchy Exercise I

Directions: Put the following scrambled mission hierarchy into its correct order. In their correct logical order, mission statements should proceed from the narrowest in scope at the bottom to the broadest in scope at the top. Place the narrowest mission statement at the bottom of the hierarchy and place progressively broader mission statements above it. Number the narrowest statement 1 and the broader statements successively to 5. Each succeeding mission statement should represent a reasonable answer to the question "Why?", directed to the preceding mission statement. [See the answer at the end of the chapter.]

- To access data on equipment sales and sales projections.
- To plan modifications in customer training programs.
- To project shifts in customer training needs.
- To deliver customer training programs that are consistent with customer needs.
- To gain authorization to access needed sales information.

5.

4.

3.

2.

1.

Another Example

This example from the work of George de George focuses on developing training programs for bilingual and English as a Second Language (ESL) program directors. In his background statement, an essential part of every planning document, de George wrote:

> *In comparison with instructional methods, the area of bilingual and ESL program management receives little focus in graduate programs funded to train bilingual and ESL personnel. On an in-service basis, whether through training programs organized in school districts or*

through statewide, regional or national conferences for bilingual and ESL educators, the real needs of bilingual and ESL program managers for training are dealt with only occasionally, often unsystematically, and with a focus on informing rather than on skill training. Part of the problem is that there are few individuals who are aware of the needs of such program managers and who, at the same time, have the expertise to organize the type of training that will address their needs

In the final paragraph of his background statement, de George added:

What is needed in the field at this time to assist educational administration faculty and coordinators of in-service training, therefore, is as complete and as detailed a syllabus as possible of all the critical content and skill areas which ought to be covered in the training of bilingual and ESL program directors.

De George's mission hierarchy is shown in Figure 2-9. You can see that the number of levels in mission hierarchies varies. Lower's contains five levels

FIGURE 2-9 • *de George's Mission Hierarchy*

9. To improve the quality of instruction, effectiveness, and morale of bilingual and ESL education programs
   8. To enhance the quality of management in bilingual and ESL programs
      7. To produce more and better trained managers of bilingual and ESL education programs
         6. To support the development of quality pre-service and in-service management training programs for directors of bilingual and ESL education programs
            5. To develop a comprehensive syllabus for pre-service and in-service management training programs for bilingual and ESL program directors
               4. To determine the training needs of directors of bilingual and ESL education programs in terms of content and skill areas
                  3. To ascertain from experts the key content and skill areas that comprise the domain of training for directors of bilingual and ESL programs
                     2. To extract from the literature the key content and skill areas that comprise the domain of training for directors of bilingual and ESL programs
                        1. To develop an organizational structure and resources related to the training of bilingual and ESL administrators

(Fig. 2-8), Moran's eight levels (Fig. 2-1), and de George's nine levels (Fig. 2-9). However, each describes a narrow task at Level 1 and a very broad goal at the highest level of the hierarchy. The number of levels between depends on how many logical steps there are without having either unclear logical leaps or tiny, trivial steps.

Some Common Errors in Mission Hierarchies

Students commonly make three types of errors in constructing their mission hierarchies:

1. The higher-level statement fails to answer the question "Why?" asked about the lower-level statement.
2. The "logical spaces" between the levels of the mission hierarchy are too big in places (i.e., there is a "leap" between two levels where important steps have been left out).
3. A mission statement is written in the form of a compound sentence and really contains two statements.

Failure to Answer the "Why" Question

A common kind of error related to the "Why" question is tht the higher-level statement is unrelated to the lower-level statement. Often in this case the two statements are both at the same logical level. This may occur when you need to do both activities but you don't need to do either of them in order to do the other. For example:

2. To collect information about students.
1. To collect information about teachers.

These mission statements may well be related to one another, but probably not hierarchically. One does not collect information about teachers in order to collect information about students. More likely, one collects information about teachers and students in order to do something else. For example, you may want to understand why some students learn better with some teachers than with others. Always check to be sure that you are doing the lower-level mission in order to do the higher-level one.

Large Logical Leaps Between Levels

You can sense that there is too much space between two levels of a mission hierarchy when the logical leap from the lower to the higher level is hard to follow. In this case, it helps to put in one or more explanatory steps in the middle. For example, in an earlier draft a part of Moran's mission hierarchy looked like this:

4. To improve the company's sales-training programs
3. To update product training books

In the final draft, Moran added an extra mission statement in order to make clear how updating product training books was going to help improve the company's sales-training programs:

5. To improve the company's sales-training programs
4. To improve instructional materials and methods for training sales people in the company
3. To update product training books

Compound Mission Statements

The question of the compound statement is also one that requires attention. Sometimes it will be necessary for you to use a compound mission statement. However, you must be careful to examine such a statement to see whether or not it implies a branch in the mission hierarchy.

A compound mission statement may indicate that you have two reasons for doing something that under some circumstances may not turn out to be compatible with one another. For example, as a school principal you may wish to involve parents in your school in order to "gain their political support for the school and to create home environments more conducive to students learning." However, these are really quite different mission statements. They imply different kinds of involvement, and, therefore, different kinds of projects. When this is the case, it is important for you to clarify your priorities. Not to do so is to leave open the possibility that later on, perhaps during the course of your project, a dilemma will surface. If you must choose later on, after you have committed substantial resources, between two goals that turn out to be incompatible, the issue may be costly to resolve.

Such a multiple mission hierarchy is what we call a *hydra-headed* hierarchy. In working with students we have identified four frequent sources of hydra-headed mission hierarchies. Often a person feels divided among goals. Typically some of these are personal in nature. Others relate to clients, organizations, or society. As illustrated in the diagram in Figure 2-10, it is not uncommon for people to hope to contribute to two or more agendas through any particular project they are working on.

Think of yourself in your own job. If you are like most of us, you want

FIGURE 2-10 • *A Generic Model of Hydra-Headed Hierarchies*

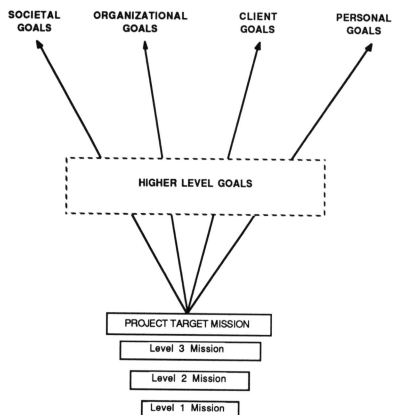

to further your own career. This is a personal goal. You also want to help your clients, patients, or students, etc. Thus you have client goals. You are also a loyal member of the company, firm, school, or hospital. You subscribe to organizational goals. Furthermore, you are a good citizen of your family, group, community, state, province, region, and nation. You share common societal goals.

It is not unusual to hope that any work you are involved in will be good for everybody. Sometimes it may be, but often there are tensions between what is good for you, your client, your company, or the world. Hydra-headed hierarchies can be useful in pointing out priority conflicts early in the planning process. Normally you should deal with them "up front," at the outset, and not cover them over. In this way you will avoid having them surprise you later. You will have worked through the tensions within yourself, and you will be ready later on to face difficult issues that may have to be negotiated with others. At least you will know your own priorities and the compromises you are and are not prepared to make.

Mission Hierarchy Exercise II

Directions: Break each of the following compound mission statements into two separate mission statements. Be sure to put them in the correct hierarchical order. If the given compound mission statement implies no hierarchical order, simply indicate the presence of a possible hydra-headed mission hierarchy. The key logical connectors are underlined. [See answer at the end of the chapter.]

1. To put together a planning proposal in order to develop political and financial support for the project within the organization
2. To develop political support for the school in the community and to improve parents' ability to help their children at home with their studies
3. To generate project support in the organization by presenting relevant needs assessment data

1.

2.

3.

Recapitulation

In summary, the following points will guide you in the development of a mission hierarchy:

There are two common starting points in constructing a mission hierarchy:

1. With the broadest purpose standing as the highest mission statement in the hierarchy
2. With the tentative mission statement that is located at a relatively low level in the mission hierarchy

In the first instance you must work downward, asking the question "What would have to be done first in order for that to happen?".

Using the second method (the more common method), you would work in an upward direction first, building toward the highest level in the mission hierarchy. Then you would work in a downward direction to be sure that there are at least two mission statements below the initial one. This requires asking the question "Why?" in the upward direction and the question "What would have to be done first in order for that to happen?" in the downward direction.

When the mission hierarchy is complete, make a final check and ask yourself:

1. As I move up from Level 1, does each succeeding mission statement explain why the preceding one should be done? Is it clear that you need to accomplish the lower-level mission in order to accomplish the higher-level mission?
2. Are there any obvious logical gaps in the sequence of mission statements that call for additional levels in between?
3. Are there compound mission statements that imply hydra-headed hierarchies and that suggest a lack of clarity about my higher-level priorities?

If this check reveals any hierarchy errors, you should resolve them early in the planning process.

You may still need to change this "final" mission hierarchy after you see how it fits logically with your output specifications, which are the subject of Chapter 4.

While it is meaningful to discuss the technical quality of a mission hierarchy, in terms of the logical criteria described, the content of a mission hierarchy is essentially subjective. Different people can construct different mission hierarchies from the same starting place because different people have different sets of larger goals. It is perfectly conceivable, for example, for a low-level project to contribute effectively to more than one set of broad goals.

Mission statements below the target-level mission can describe development objectives that you have already accomplished. Obviously, it would not be useful to build a mission hierarchy that mostly contains completed missions, but it is perfectly acceptable to show lower-level missions that have already been accomplished. Be certain, however, that the mission statement describing your project goes beyond any work that you have already completed. Many times the target mission is located precisely one level above the highest level of mission already accomplished, but this is not an inflexible rule. You may want to choose a mission more than one level higher, to allow yourself the flexibility of dropping back if necessary or because the timing is right to proceed more ambitiously.

Mission Hierarchy Exercise III

Directions: Put the following scrambled mission hierarchy into its correct logical order, with mission statements proceeding from the narrowest in scope at the bottom to the broadest in scope at the top. Number the narrowest statement 1 and the broader statements successively to 4. Each succeeding mission statement should represent a reasonable answer to the question "Why?" directed to the preceding mission statement. [See answer at the end of the chapter.]

- To optimize sales
- To facilitate effective customer utilization of purchased equipment
- To increase corporate profitability
- To enhance customer satisfaction with corporate products

4.

3.

2.

1.

Mission Hierarchy Exercise IV

Directions: Combine the four mission statements in Mission Hierarchy Exercise III with the five mission statements you encountered in Mission Hierarchy Exercise I (p. 16). Follow the same logical principles you used in doing Exercise III. Your task here is to create a single mission hierarchy with nine levels. [See answer at the end of the chapter.]

9.
  8.
    7.
      6.
        5.
          4.
            3.
              2.
                1.

Answers to Mission Hierarchy Exercises

Mission Hierarchy Exercise I
5. To deliver customer training programs that are consistent with customer needs
   4. To plan modifications in customer training programs
      3. To project shifts in customer training needs
         2. To access data on equipment sales and sales projections
            1. To gain authorization to access needed sales information

Mission Hierarchy Exercise II

1. *Higher-Level Mission Statement:* To develop political and financial support for the project within the organization

   Lower-Level Mission Statement: To put together a planning proposal
2. This statement contains two elements that do not appear to be hierarchically related. The two elements suggest different agendas, which would be represented in different upper mission hierarchies. Under some circumstances these agendas may not be operationally compatible with each other, that is, strategies that function to achieve one agenda may be in conflict with the other agenda.
3. *Higher-Level Mission Statement:* To generate project support in the organization

   Lower-Level Mission Statement: To present relevant needs assessment data

Mission Hierarchy Exercise III

4. To increase corporate profitability
   3. To optimize sales
      2. To enhance customer satisfaction with corporate products
         1. To facilitate effective customer utilization of purchased equipment

Mission Hierarchy Exercise IV

9. To increase corporate profitability
   8. To optimize sales
      7. To enhance customer satisfaction with corporte products
         6. To facilitate effective customer utilization of purchased equipment
            5. To deliver customer training programs that are consistent with customer needs

4. To plan modifications in customer training programs
3. To project shifts in customer training needs
2. To access data on equipment sales and sales projections
1. To gain authorization to access needed sales information.

Doing Your Own Project

As you study this book, you will find spaces for planning your own project. At this point you may want to try writing your mission hierarchy. You may not need to use all of the space provided, or your mission hierarchy may have more levels than are provided. You can easily make these adjustments on your own paper or computer. The important things to remember are:

1. Your mission hierarchy represents your vision and shows your project in relation to a longer-term agenda.
2. You should have at least two levels in your hierarchy that are below your target mission and usually four or five or more levels above your target mission.
3. The highest level in your mission hierarchy should be very broad, some version of "save the world."
4. The steps in your hierarchy should be even, like a ladder, without big logical leaps in between, and each mission statement should answer the "Why?" question with respect to the mission statement just below it ("In order to . . . ").
5. You should not have words in your mission statements like *by* or *in order to* or any of their synonyms that signal statements that should be divided into two levels.
6. You should not have *and* in a mission statement unless both sides of the *and* lead to the same next-higher-level mission statement.

My Mission Hierarchy

8. _____

_____

7. _____

_____

6. _____

_____

5. _____

_____

4. _____

_____

3. _____

_____

2. _____

_____

1. _____

_____

CHAPTER THREE

The Language of the Planning Process

Now that you have embarked on your project, it is time to consider the importance of language in planning. Research shows that using a noun, a verb, a gerund, an infinitive, or an imperative actually affects the way you think. The same is true about using the present, past, or future tense. We have found in working with students that giving them language guidelines and correcting their language usage helps them to clarify their planning concepts.

For example, using the infinitive to write mission statements in the mission hierarchy (see Chapter 1) emphasizes both the doing and the idea of "in order to." Writing output specifications in the future tense (see Chapter 4) makes clear that you are describing results hoped for at the project's end. In contrast to output specifications, input specifications (see Chapter 5) describe existing conditions, which are expressed most appropriately in the present tense. Project activities describe what you must do to accomplish the project mission. The imperative form of the verb carries this message well, whether in the PERT index (see Chapters 6 and 7) or in labeling activities in a decision flow diagram (see Chapter 9). Subsystems are sets of activities related to accomplishing a common function in a project (see Chapter 6). For example, if a community theater were putting on a play, "Choosing a Play" might be a common subsystem involving a number of individual activities. Although both activities and subsystems involve doing things, we recommend distinguishing them by using two distinctive verb forms. We use the imperative (e.g., "Determine a Set of Criteria for Choosing a Play") to define an individual activity. We use the gerund form of the verb (e.g., "Choosing a Play") for a subsystem. Finally, in labeling information flows in an information flow diagram (see Chapter 10), you should emphasize the particular pieces of information that are moving among people, offices, and files. Using nouns focuses attention on what is being moved in each information transaction.

The table in Figure 3-1 illustrates the language forms we recommend for different types of statements and labels. You may wish to refer back to it as you proceed through the book and as you practice using the planning formats discussed.

FIGURE 3-1 • *Language Guide for Planning Documents*

TYPE OF STATEMENT	MODELS
Mission Statement [Chapter 2]: Use the Infinitive	• *To update* product training books. • *To design* an alternative program.
Output Specification [Chapter 4]: in the Future Tense	• *There will be* a consistent look to the Write books, including covers, binding, page layout, format, type fonts, spacing, margins and indentations. • A detailed curriculum *will be developed* for the alternative program.
Input Specification [Chapter 5]: in the Present Tense	• The existing books *are inconsistent* in Write their level of detail and the type of information they contain; *however*, the instructors have a good idea of what should be in the books. • There *is no* detailed curriculum for the alternative program; *however*, the following conditions exist: a. the organization already *has* a 13 year history of contextualized curriculum design,; b. The program *offers* a one year urban training internship which can be taken as

FIGURE 3-1 *Continued*

part of all the master level degree

programs;

c. There *are* various models of

relevant curricula available from various

places;

d. The Vice President for Academic

Affairs and various members of

the faculty, *have* extensive experience in

curriculum design for theological

education.

Required Project Activities: [Chapter 5]:
Use the Imperative Form of the Verb

- *Write* a project design document
- *Meet* with members of the task force and
  the Vice President to discuss ideas for the
  new curriculum.specifying the project
  objective, the level of detail and the type
  of information to be contained in the books.

PERT Subsystem Label[: Chapters 6-7]:
Use the"ing" Form of the Verb

- *Establishing* Guidelines for the Books
- *Developing* an Urban M.Div. Curriculum

Continued

FIGURE 3-1 *Continued*

PERT Activity Label: [Chapters 6-7]:
Use theImperative Form of the Verb

- 110-120 *Collect* comments from instructors on which parts [Chapter of existing books are outdated or inappropriate.
- 400-415 *Obtain* information about urban M.Div. programs from other seminaries in major U.S. cities.

Decision Flow Diagram Activity Label [Chapter 9]: Use the Imperative Form of the Verb

- *Prepare* List of Experts
- *Telephone* Experts

Information Flow Diagram Note Column Information Label [Chapter 10]: Use Nouns

- Resource *Files* and *Lists*
- Survey of Literature *Report*

CHAPTER FOUR

Clarifying Project Objectives—Output Specifications

Output specifications are descriptions of what "will be" when you have successfully completed your project. Writing output specifications clarifies the meaning of your target mission and establishes a list of specifications for evaluating the project later. Let us look, for example, at the project mission statements of the three students whose mission hierarchies we presented in Chapter 1:

1. To update product training books (Moran)
2. To provide cancer patients with a comprehensive cancer treatment program (Lower)
3. To develop a comprehensive syllabus for pre-service and in-service management training programs for bilingual and ESL program directors (de George)

Each of these mission statements gives some sense of the nature of the proposed project; however, none makes clear exactly what results you can expect from the project. In this chapter we show you how to write output specifications that describe project results for your target mission, and we give examples that illustrate the methodology.

How Output Specifications Clarify Mission Statements

In writing your output specifications you describe in more detail than you did in your mission hierarchy the practical meaning of your target mission.

You do this by listing the major items that your project will deliver, together with their important qualities and characteristics.

You should always describe your anticipated results in the future tense. We recommend what we call *will be* statements. For example, Moran described nine anticipated outputs. His listing related to updating training books illustrates this format.

1. All training books will include the latest product information.
2. There will be:
    a. Consistency in the level of detail and type of information in the books
    b. A consistent look to the books
    c. Educationally sound behavioral objectives for each chapter
    d. Test questions, written in a consistent format, matching the objectives for each chapter
    e. An introduction and summary in each chapter
    f. Tables, graphs, charts, and illustrations in the books
    g. A consistent editorial style used throughout the books
    h. A table of contents, index, and glossary in each book

Output specifications play a central role not only in the planning process but also in management and evaluation. Output specifications describe the project targets. All your project activities should contribute to delivering the outputs specified; otherwise you don't need them. In the end, you will evaluate the success of your project by how well you achieved the results you promised to deliver in your output specifications.

In Lower's plan you can see another example of a set of output specifications. Where Moran's work was in the corporate world, Lower implemented her project in a hospital. You may remember that her goal was to provide cancer patients with a comprehensive cancer treatment program. She anticipated five important outcomes from her project:

There will be:

1. A clear policy statement with respect to providing a comprehensive cancer program at Providence Hospital
2. A clear definition of the scope of services for an inpatient cancer program
3. Specific educational programs for cancer patients
4. A multidisciplinary team approach to caring for cancer patients
5. A marketing strategy to provide information to the staff, community, state, and hospital corporation about the cancer program

De George's project gives you a third look at the writing of output specifications. His goal was to develop a comprehensive syllabus for pre-service and in-service management training programs for bilingual and ESL program directors. His measures of success included five deliverables. At the outset of the project, he identified the following expected results:

There will be:

1. A clear statement of purpose for the syllabus
2. A brief history of the development of bilingual and ESL education in the United States and of the role of the bilingual and ESL directors
3. Several typical scenarios illustrating the work of bilingual and ESL directors and a description of the qualities of an effective director
4. A summary of the relevant literature, resources, and sources of information and assistance for bilingual and ESL program management
5. A detailed, comprehensive breakdown of the content and skill areas that constitute the domain of bilingual and ESL management training

Output specifications do more than clarify your project objectives. They also define the scope of the project, setting clear end points for your work. From these you can begin to work backward to plan your project activities. Planning to achieve clear results is like trying to catch a train. You start by knowing what time you have to be at the train station and then you figure out what you have to do to get there on time. Similarly, when you describe a clear set of output indicators, you establish definite targets toward which to work.

Finally, output specifications allow you to analyze logically to what degree the target mission is, in fact, the right one. It is not unusual in our classes to find students whose output specifications suggest results that are different from what their project mission statements seem to imply. Rarely do a student's output specifications suggest an entirely different project. Often, however, the student's output specifications suggest results higher or lower in the mission hierarchy. Be sure to compare your project mission and your draft output specifications to see how they match.

What do you do if you find some discrepancies between them? It is not difficult to revise at this point. You may decide that the target mission you want is really higher or lower in the mission hierarchy, or you may decide to adjust your output specifications. Part of the benefit of systematic planning is in spotting inconsistencies early and making adjustments at the thinking stage rather than in the middle of implementing the project. The cost savings are obvious. Much of the planning process we teach involves frequently checking back for inconsistencies. Revision is a normal and expected part of planning.

How to Write Output Specifications

Your output specifications define the targets for your project mission. Your project mission is part of your mission hierarchy. Your mission hierarchy describes projects of lesser and greater scope. All the missions in this hierarchy describe potential projects related to a common long-term agenda.

Your output specifications must match the level of your mission in the hierarchy. Thus, it is incorrect to promise to deliver a plan when the target mission speaks only of collecting data for needs assessment. You should promise results consistent with your target mission. For example:

- Your output specifications should promise data and data analyses when your target mission describes what is commonly called needs assessment.
- Your output specifications should describe the expected contents and characteristics of a plan to be developed when your target mission uses words like *to plan* or *to design.*
- Your output specifications should delineate the components and qualities of a real operating system (i.e., staff, facilities, materials, equipment, clients, etc.) only when your target mission uses words like *implementing* or *developing* in the sense of establishing or putting an actual program in place.
- Sometimes your objectives go beyond collecting data, planning, and implementing programs. When you talk about the effects of the program on people, organizations, or society, then you must describe in your output specifications the evidence of those effects that would document the success of the project. In these cases merely showing that the program is in place is not enough. You must describe in your output specifications the kind of evaluation results you expect to obtain.

The general rule in planning is that you should promise to deliver results *only for the target mission and below,* never for any higher mission. Let us look at an example of an early draft of the output specifications written by one of our students, in which you will see examples of some typical problems in writing output specifications. This student was responsible for improving physical therapy services in the neurology and medical-surgical units of a hospital. Figure 4-1 shows her mission hierarchy. She highlighted the target mission (Level 3).

Let us look at three of her initial output specifications and critique them.

1. Follow-up studies of patients with physical disabilities will show them to be relatively active and well integrated in job and family.

What is wrong with this proposed output specification? Although it

FIGURE 4-1 · *A Hospital Staff Training and Development Project Mission Hierarchy*

6. To help create a world in which people with physical handicaps are integrated as full members of society
   5. To help people with physical disabilities resume happy, active lives within their homes and communities
      4. To help patients achieve an optimal level of functional independence and a minimal level of disability when discharged from the hospital
         3. To improve physical therapy services in the Neurology and Medical-Surgical units
            2. To increase staff skill in providing physical therapy to patients in Neurology and Medical-Surgical units
               1. To increase staff knowledge of physical therapy evaluation and basic therapeutic techniques

relates to the project and the larger family of objectives, it promises to deliver results at Levels 4 and 5 of the mission hierarchy. These goals have to do with achieving functional independence and integration in family and community. You can see that the proposed output specification goes beyond the target mission at Level 3.

2. General studies of physically handicapped people will show significant improvement over baseline levels in numbers employed and in levels of job placement.

This proposed output specification is inappropriate for a project at Level 3 in the hierarchy for the same reasons as the first example. It promises to deliver results broader than the targetr mission. The output specified is even broader than in the first example. You can see tht it focuses on one aspect of integrating people with physical handicaps fully into the society. This is consistent with Level 6 in the mission hierarchy, and it goes far beyond the scope of a project targeted at Level 3.

3. The technical knowledge and skill of physical therapists will show significant improvement over pretraining levels.

This proposed output specifiction is also a mismatch, but in a way that is different from the previous two examples. The promise here is for a particular result that is relatively narrow in scope and that is more consistent with a project targeted at Level 2 of the mission hierarchy than at Level 3. It is at Level 2 that the focus is on the knowledge and skill of physical therapists.

We recommend that you write output specifications for every level in your mission hierarchy up to and including the target mission. You will see in the next chapter that preparing output specifications at these levels helps you to know what activities to build into your project. It also gives you a sense of the sequential relationships among activities. However, you should keep the output specifications at the different levels separate from one another. You should not confuse expected results at different levels of the hierarchy.

Recapitulation

Writing output specifications helps you bring your whole project into focus. Careful output specifications give concrete meaning to the target mission and clarify the scope of the project. They define the targets you will need for planning project activities, and they set the criteria for final evaluation.

Specifying outputs above the target mission is not necessary. Such outputs are, by definition, beyond the scope of the mission. You should write lower-level output specifications along with those at the target level, but it is best to keep the two sets of output specifications separate.

By defining the desired outcomes, output specifications indicate where a project is going. They are an end point. Now we need to clarify the beginning point. Defining what we call the *input condition* of the project is the subject of Chapter 4.

An Exercise in Matching Output Specifications to the Correct Level of the Mission Hierarchy

Directions: Read the three sets of output specifications below, and suggest a reasonable target mission for each set. For each set identify whether the output specifications are at the level of needs assessment, design, implementation, or evaluation of the effects of implementation. [See the answers immediately following.]

Set One

1. Historical data going back five years will be available on:
   a. Types and quantities of equipment sold
   b. The nature and locations of customers:

- Size and location
- Equipment configurations purchased
- Functions specified for equipment purchased
- Training needs requested or suggested
- Problems encountered
- Typical modifications of functions and training needs over time

2. Projections and supporting rationales for future sales
3. Analysis of historical data and future projections
   a. Interpretations of the data
   b. Recommendations for modifying the existing customer training program

Set Two

1. A set of courses will be taught to corporate customers that train them to use equipment and configurations of equipment they have purchased to accomplish effectively their organizational functions.
2. Courses will be staffed by adequate numbers of properly trained instructional personnel.
3. Appropriate course materials keyed to customer training needs will be in place.
4. Instructional support equipment will be utilized consistent with course designs and customer training needs.
5. An effective system will be in place for scheduling and supporting customer training activities on site and in regional corporate training centers.
6. Appropriate accounting procedures will be in place and customer training will be cost-effective.
7. A system for monitoring and managing customer training will be in place.

Set Three

A planning document will be prepared. It will provide a set of courses to train corporate customers to use equipment and configurations of equipment they have purchased. There will be plans for the following system components:

1. Course designs, including objectives, activities, course materials, instructional support equipment, and bibliographies
2. Plans for recruiting, selecting, and scheduling training and support personnel
3. Plans for purchasing, producing, maintaining, and updating instructional materials and instructional support equipment

4. Schedules of courses, personnel, and equipment
5. Designs for financial accounting and management information systems
6. Descriptions of the management structure and of management responsibilities
7. Projected budgets for implementing and operating the customer training operation

Answers to the Output Specifications Exercise

The three sets of output specifications are related to one another. When put in the correct order (Set 1, Set 3, Set 2), they define target objectives at three successive levels of a mission hierarchy. People doing the exercise are likely to come out with different wordings; however, the sense of the answers should be the same. All three sets of output specifications have to do with the planning and implementation of a corporate training program for customers. High-tech firms commonly offer such programs, often as part of their sales departments.

The first set of output specifications deals with needs assessment. All the objectives described fall under this general heading. The target mission might be "To assess the need for and the useful characteristics of a program to train customers in future years."

The second set of output specifications skips a level in the mission hierarchy. It skips the planning level and describes objectives at the level of implementing the program. The term *implementation* implies putting into place actual operating systems. The target mission might be "To implement a program to train customers to use equipment they have purchased." This implies that courses will be properly scheduled. There will be qualified staff and appropriate course materials. A budget and an accounting system will be in place, along with management and evaluation systems.

The third set of output specifications in the exercise focuses on a target mission that lies hierarchically between needs assessment and implementation. This mission is at the level of design, or planning. The target mission at this level might be "To design a program to train customers to use the equipment they have purchased." It is common to find mission hierarchies that contain target missions that relate to needs assessment, planning, and implementation.

In general we assess needs in order to plan effectively. We plan in order to implement projects and programs to meet important needs. If we put the mission statements from the exercise in hierarchical order, they would look like this:

3. To implement a program to train customers to use the equipment they have purchased

2. To plan a program to train customers to use the equipment they have purchased
    1. To assess the need for, and the useful characteristics of, a program to train customers to use the equipment they have purchased

Doing Your Own Project

The next step in preparing your project plan is to specify desired outputs at each level of your mission hierarchy, from the target mission down. This is consistent with the results orientation of effective planning and management. Your output specifications will give meaning and clarity to your project. If your target mission is "To do X," your output specifications will make clear just what it means "to do X."

Take a look at your target mission. Ask yourself what kind of mission it is. Most projects fall along a hierarchy that runs from information gathering through planning, implementation, and evaluation of program effects. This is illustrated in our generic mission hierarchy (Figure 2-3, Chapter 2).

Diverse projects typically have much in common with one another with reference to this generic mission hierarchy. There are typical output specifications at each of these generic hierarchical levels. Figure 4-2 suggests some of these.

Sometimes a very simple output specification does the job quite well. For example, if you design a project to raise a certain amount of money, the output specification might appropriately read, "There will be $$$ raised." There really is nothing more to say. However, you usually need to describe output specifications in more detail.

For example, if your project is to implement a training program, you should describe both the elements of the program and any special qualities it should possess. You should describe such elements as the staffing, student or client population, facilities, materials and equipment, curriculum and curriculum materials, and so on. If any of those should be of a special character, you should indicate that. For example, if you want a school or preschool program to include participation of parents in the program and in decision making, you should make this clear in the output specifications. If you want relationships between parents and professional staff to have certain qualitative characteristics, you should describe these also in the output specifications.

Often in planning business, educational, and other human service projects and programs, output specifications are extensive. In these cases it is generally useful to organize your output specifications under headings and subheadings. For example, output specifications for implementing programs typically are organized under such subheadings as goals, staffing, facilities, participants, curriculum, evaluation, budget. Similarly, needs assessment projects often include such subcategories as information, analyses, and

FIGURE 4-2 • *Common Types of Output Specifications at Different Levels of a Generic Mission Hierarchy*

Type of Target Mission	Type of Output Specification
Evaluation	Descriptions of findings that will be available assessing the results of a project or program that has been established
Implementation	Descriptions of physical systems (people, procedures, facilities, equipment, etc.) that will be in place and functioning
Planning	Descriptions of documents to be prepared relating specific objectives and activities to goals and problem analyses
Policy Making	Descriptions of decisions to be made about projected courses of action
Analysis	Descriptions of reports that will be written suggesting factors and causes and recommendations about possible courses of action
Needs Assessment	Descriptions of reports to be prepared containing information relevant to the perceived problem

recommendations. Such organization adds clarity and helps in communicating the nature of the project to others.

My Output Specifications

At the Target Mission Level

_____

_____

_____

_____

_____

_____

At the First Level below the Target Level

At the Second Level below the Target Level

At the Third Level below the Target Level

_____

_____

_____

_____

_____

_____

_____

_____

_____

At the Fourth Level below the Target Level

_____

_____

_____

_____

_____

_____

_____

_____

_____

CHAPTER FIVE

Relating the Project to Existing Conditions— Input Specifications

In Chapter 4 you described the results you expect from your project — output specifications. Your output specifications give you a clear picture of where your project is headed, of what are often called the project's "deliverables." In aiming your project is is important to know what the targets are. However, it is also necessary to assess the nature of the conditions at the start of the project. These existing conditions provide the foundation for your project. Describing these conditions carefully will give you a basis for figuring out what kinds of activities you must include in the project in order to deal with potential problems and to take advantage of promising resources and sources of support.

In working through this chapter you will identify potential hindering and facilitating factors. We will ask you to think about project activities to deal with or circumvent the hindering factors and to make use of relevant prior work, sources of support, and various kinds of resources. Resources include sources of funds, technical assistance, and useful information, among other things. You will describe such factors as they relate to the project as a whole and as they relate to each and every one of your output specifications. All this is what we call *input specification* or *context evaluation*. Thus, in this chapter you will build on your knowledge of the project, the organization, and its environment to generate many ideas for project activities, engaging in what is commonly called *brainstorming*. This is a creative activity, a type of *divergent* thinking.

Later you will shape these ideas so as to determine what activities you will actually incorporate into your project. Beginning in Chapter 6 you will be asked to think in a more *convergent* mode to describe project subsystems and to place activities within these subsystems. You will plan what has to be done, in what order, how long it will take, what support systems it will require, and how much it will cost.

Planning Versus Doing

Now that you know where you want to go, you need to step back and look at where you are. Input specifications describe the point from which the project begins. They establish its baseline conditions.

Perhaps you are wondering why we haven't discussed this sooner. Why talk about inputs *after* examining the project's purposes and desired results? According to the classical systems model of production, the sequence of action flows logically from input through process to output (see Fig. 5-1). Why is the material in this book following a different order?

While the two are easy to confuse conceptually, the planning model is different from the production model. The logic of production goes from left to right. It goes from existing conditions through some action (process) to obtain the desired results. You are always planning a production system. This is true whether your product is hardware of some kind or something as "soft" as a change in the skills, beliefs, or attitudes of staff, client, or customer. What you actually do is a left-to-right process: You start with existing conditions and implement some activities to bring about change.

However, the design process works differently (see Fig. 5-2). Planning is mostly a method of *thinking backward*. We have organized this book according to the backward thinking logic of planning. According to this model you start with what you want—with your desired results, or outputs.

The idea of desired outputs begins with your values: profit, organizational or social reform, effective health care, etcetera. Planning begins with values, which are usually tacit. Doing a mission hierarchy helps you to clarify your purposes and values (see Chapter 2). Typically you think of problems in terms of differences between what you observe and what you would like to see in your organization, clients, or customers. Your values are implicit in the way you think things ought to be, in the results you are seeking to achieve (see Chapter 4).

Typical problems include, for example, a sense that greater profits could be made or that the salary gap between men and women or between blacks

FIGURE 5-1 • *Classical Production Model*

FIGURE 5-2 • *Planning Model*

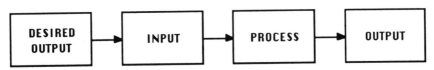

and whites could be narrowed. You may feel that crop yields could be higher or soil erosion diminished. Perhaps you would like to see lower infant mortality rates or a smaller "learning gap" between rich and poor children.

Each of these examples implies a desired output and an existing input condition. This is true of problems in general. There is a desired profit curve and a historical one. There is a desired salary or learning gap and an existing one. There are theoretical crop yields and infant mortality rates and those that have actually been experienced in the past. Implementation begins with existing conditions and moves through appropriate strategies, or processes, toward the kinds of goals that you have described in your work on output specifications (Chapter 4).

Planning starts with spelling out your desired outputs (see Fig. 5-2). Your next step is to define the existing conditions that you must deal with, if they are negative, or that you can take advantage of, if they are positive. These conditions establish the context for the project or program. Context information is crucial for designing appropriate activities to move from the input conditions to your desired output conditions.

Input Specifications

Remember that the input conditions are those that exist when your project begins, *before you have actually done anything.* You might think of them as the baseline conditions. To write what we call *input specifications* is to describe the relevant baseline conditions. Some writers refer to this kind of description as *context evaluation.* They refer to it in this way because it requires you to examine and describe the context of your project as it may influence what you do.

But why is it important to describe what exists before your project begins? Why bother doing it? It is important because it will make you aware of actions you must take to ensure the success of your project. It will remind you of activities that can help you guard against potential negative factors in the environment that can undermine your project. These can be political, cultural, legal, economic, or technical in nature. You will also want to note positive factors that you might be able to take advantage of. They can include potential sources of political or financial support, as well as human, intellectual, and material resources that you can tap if you go about your project in the right way. You can also take advantage of work that others have done related to various aspects of your project.

The most important part of doing an analysis of existing conditions is the part that comes after you have described them. This is when you describe the project activities that follow from the context evaluation. These are activities to protect against potential negative factors and to take advantage of available resources, prior work, and potential sources of support.

It is useful to think of describing the baseline conditions for your project in two stages. First, you describe the general conditions affecting the project. Then you look at your output specifications, one by one, and describe the existing conditions relevant to each of them. Your input specifications will include several components:

General Conditions
  1. Potential Hindering Factors
      a. General conditions in the project environment that could work against the project
      b. Project activities that will help guard against these potential negative factors
  2. Potential Facilitating Factors
      a. General conditions in the project environment that could help the project
      b. Project activities that can help take advantage of these potentially positive factors

Conditions Related to Specific Output Specifications
  3. Null, Moreover, and However Statements
      a. What has *not been done* with respect to each of the output specifications for your target mission *(null)* and *additional negative conditions* that might hinder you in achieving that particular deliverable *(Moreover)*
      b. Resources that are available to help you to achieve the desired output, including prior work that can be incorporated into your project, potential sources of support, and sources of information and technical assistance to help achieve the desired result *(however)*
      c. Project activities that you should include in order to take advantage of potential support, available resources, and prior work in seeking to achieve that particular output specification

How to Write Potential Hindering and Facilitating Factors

Potential hindering factors are those that may undermine or constrain the success of your project or program. It is important to include in your plan activities to mitigate potentially negative forces.

We define as potential facilitating factors those existing conditions that may make it easier for your project to be successful. Although some of them may help you regardless of what you do, you will probably have to act purposefully to take advantage of others. We believe that people often do not take advantage of potentially advantageous conditions in carrying out otherwise good projects. For example, funding may be realizable, but only if you generate contacts and write proposals. Similarly, political support may be accessible because of shared objectives with powerful interests, but only if you make connections and nourish relationships.

As suggested in the brief outline just given, you should identify possible hindering and facilitating conditions. You should include in your project activities to deal with the negatives and to take advantage of the positives. Here, too, we suggest some language guidelines.

One characteristic of these factors that should be reflected in the way you write about them is that they exist. They exist now. Therefore, you should describe them in the *present* tense. Furthermore, we suggest that you write required activities as commands to yourself. Do this! Do that! Write your activity statements using the *imperative* form of verbs. The following excerpt from de George's planning project illustrates these ideas. (Italics have been added to emphasize language choices.)

Potential Hindering Factors and Their Implications

1. *There* is *a potential difficulty in finding a single sponsor or in assembling a consortium with all of the needed resources.*

   Required Project Activity: Leave *ample time to seek out and coordinate sponsors and build resource needs into the project budget.*
2. *Offering this publication for sale* may hinder its marketability.

   Required Project Activity: Use *the market research results as a basis for deciding market issues.*
3. *A significant segment of the market* is spread *thinly over a vast geographical area.*

   Required Project Activity: Use *market research to plan strategies and* use *national conferences for marketing.*
4. *The project* is *potentially time-consuming and labor-intensive.*

Required Project Activities: Choose *a sponsor with the necessary resources to overcome these potentially negative factors.* Maintain *master lists of information and technical support services.* Construct *and* pilot *telephone scripts, interview protocols, and questionnaires.* Make use *of computers and computer software.* Delegate *tasks to support staff, allow slack time, and formulate a well-ordered system for storing and classifying information collected in the course of various substudies.*

5. *Some key works identified in the literature search* may be *unavailable or difficult to obtain.*

   Required Project Activity: Identify *information sources as early in the project as possible.*

Potential Facilitating Factors and Their Implications

1. There are *agencies and institutions likely to be willing to sponsor this project. These include colleges and universities, federally funded agencies, private contractors, and publishers.*

   Required Project Activity: Seek *an agency or institutional sponsor interested in the project.* Look *for one with sufficient resources and staff to do research, development, marketing, and distribution of print products.* Seek *an organization willing to integrate the project into its structure and ongoing activities.*

2. There are *potential funding sources, including federal and state funds and foundation grants.*

   Required Project Activity: Determine *the eligibility of the project for outside funds, including federal, state, and private foundation sources.*

3. *A small team of individuals* could do *the project on their own time and at their own expense.*

   Required Project Activity: Consider *this possibility in formulating alternative strategies.*

4. *Most sponsoring agencies and institutions* could build *the project into existing schedules and structures.*

   Required Project Activity: Draw up *alternative staffing patterns for the project and corresponding cost estimates.*

5. *In several agencies and institutions, some qualified personnel* may want *to participate in the project and lend it support.*

   Required Project Activity: *In seeking a sponsor,* choose *one in which several staff members are willing to participate or lend support to the project.*

6. *Flexible and cost-effective staffing arrangements* are *possible for this project, including the use of a small internal staff coupled with outside consultants and contractors.*

   Required Project Activity: Incorporate *this concept when drawing up alternative staffing patterns for the project and* use *it as a selling point when seeking a sponsor.*

7. *There* is *a definable national market for the syllabus.*

   Required Project Activity: Conduct *a brief, but well-focused market search in order to assess principal and secondary markets and to determine effective formatting, pricing, marketing, and distribution strategies.*

8. *Compendia* are *available that describe state administrative certification requirements.*

   Required Project Activity: Identify *these compendia and obtain information.*

9. *Several known organizations* can help *to identify colleges and universities having training programs in bilingual education.*

   Required Project Activity: Contact *these sources early in the project.*

How to Write One-To-One Output-Input Specifications and Their Implications for Project Activities

Students seem to have a natural tendency to talk about a project as if they were starting from scratch. In reality, no project begins from nothing. Support, expertise, prior work, and other resources are always available. It is especially important to identify sources of assistance in achieving particular output specifications. By accurately describing the positive elements in the environment that you can build on, you go a long way toward clarifying the activities you should include in your project.

In working on this part of your planning document, you should do several things for each output specification you have written:

1. Write an input specification custom tailored to each particular output specification.
2. Include in each input statement:
   a. A *null statement*—a description of what is lacking or has not been done in relation to the particular output specification, along with what might be called a *moreover* statement in which you add to the null statement further potential negative factors related to achieving that particular output specification.
   b. A *however statement* in which you describe, relevant to that

particular output specification, useful prior work, potential sources of support, and potential sources of information and assistance in achieving the desired output.

c. A list of activities required to: (1) deal with the potential negative factors described in the moreover statement; (2) take advantage of the prior work, sources of support, and sources of information and assistance described in the however statement; and (3) complete all the additional work necessary to achieve the specified output.

Examples of Input-Output Specifications

One of our students, Janet Buerklin, a teacher, was interested in establishing a special educational program to help minority students in her school. The program was based on research on how minority students learn and on a curriculum developed initially by an external researcher. In the following example, Buerklin represents one of her nine project output specifications. She describes in her corresponding input specification the current state of progress with respect to this output specification. She then suggests three project activities to move from the input condition to achieve the desired output. Her work illustrates the principles we have been discussing.

Output Specification
There will be information and activities provided for children. This information will primarily come in the form of lessons. It will present the concepts and vocabulary of the Student Efficacy Model and will focus on shaping student attitudes about themselves and their work.

Input Specification
There is no information about student efficacy being taught; however, the following conditions exist:

- There is an established knowledge base that has information on student efficacy. It is in the "Student Efficacy Manual."
- There is a curriculum guide with sample lessons, activities, and content.
- The school gives its teachers considerable responsibility to create and execute their own lessons.
- The school's staff has already received some training in the Student Efficacy Program.

Required Project Activities

- Teach student lessons about student efficacy principles, using the existing knowledge base, curriculum guide, prior teacher training, and lesson planning skills to develop lessons.
- Use efficacy vocabulary and concepts throughout the year in each classroom.
- Display visuals permanently in each classroom to emphasize key efficacy concepts.

Here are three further examples. These are excerpts from the work of Moran, Lower, and de George.

Moran

Output Specification   There will be consistency in the level of detail and type of information in the books. For example, the books will have a stated objective, aim at a defined audience, assume a prior knowledge of concepts but not of products, and will avoid marketing information.

Input Specification   The existing books are inconsistent in their level of detail and the type of information they contain; however, the instructors have a good idea of what should be in the books.

Required Project Activities

- Interview the instructors to get a profile of the target audience.
- Give existing books to the instructors, asking them to delete outdated or inappropriate information.
- Survey sales representatives in the field to determine positive and negative points of the existing books.
- Attend the training that precedes this course in the curriculum to better understand the incoming audience.
- Consolidate comments made by instructors about the existing books.
- Write a design document specifying the project objective, the levels of detail, and type of information in the books.
- Give the design document to the instructors for their comments.
- Consolidate the instructors' comments into the final copy of the design document.

Lower

Output Specification   There will be a clear policy statement with respect to providing a comprehensive cancer program at Providence Hospital.

Input Specification   No policy statement currently exists; however, there is a statement advocating for all members of the hospital community the caring and healing of patients in a compassionate way. A similar principle is set forth for the medical unit where cancer patients are treated.

Required Project Activities

- Develop a mission statement.
- Publish a pamphlet for cancer patients that includes the mission statement.

de George

Output Specification   There will be a summary of the relevant literature, resources, and sources of information and assistance in the area of bilingual and ESL program management.

Input Specification   There is no comprehensive summary of the relevant literature, resources, and sources of information and assistance for bilingual and ESL program management. However, there are searches of the literature, professional organizations, clearinghouses, federal and state agencies, bibliographies, and published hand-out materials that can supply information.

Required Project Activities

- Obtain existing bibliographies and literature searches.
- Do additional literature searches, as needed.
- Contact professional organizations in the field, clearinghouses, and federal and state agencies for fugitive materials and assistance.
- Prepare a summary of the relevant literature, resources, and sources of information and assistance in the area of bilingual and ESL program management.

Criteria for Writing One-to-One Output-Input Specifications

1. Is there a null statement? (There should be.)
2. Is there a moreover statement that indicates potential problems in addition to the null statement? (There may be.)
3. Is there a however statement? (There should be.) Does it seem to identify

a reasonable list that includes prior work and available resources related to accomplishing the specified output? (It should.)

4. Do the required activities listed:
   a. Relate to all problems listed in the moreover statement and all prior work and available resources listed in the however statement? (They should.)
   b. Refer to prior work and/or resources not mentioned in the however statement? (If this is so, then add those items to the however statement. The prior work and available resources listed in the however statement and those referred to in the required activities should match.)
   c. Include, in addition, a complete list of further activities needed to achieve the output specified? (They should.)

Recapitulation

At each step of the planning process, new understandings play back on prior planning work. Despite its cost and inevitable frustration, revision is a natural part of the planning process. A good planning process comprises multiple tasks. These include defining the mission, seeing it in a context of broader purposes, and clarifying the scope of your work. The task of describing desired outputs and related input conditions is a part of a process to avoid costly errors and omissions.

We have advised you that it is important to take the time to analyze the conditions surrounding your project before you start listing project activities. You have examined not only the conditions that you hope to change as a result of your project, but also the existing conditions that could affect the project positively or negatively. You have identified potential hindering and facilitating factors. You have matched existing conditions to your output specifications.

The process we have outlined for specifying input conditions also acknowledges the complexity and uncertainty of social change. Every project is in a multidimensional environment. Therefore, you have sought out and interpreted a great deal of information about the environment of your project. You have decided that the project is feasible. You have identified activities to prepare the environment for the project. You have been thinking all along about how to make the project compatible with the existing culture, politics, laws, economics, and technology.

You may notice that your planning process is now in a transition stage. Your idea of the mission and how to carry it out is probably quite different from what it was when the planning process began. In writing your input specifications you began by describing different relevant existing conditions.

Through a brainstorming process you ended up with many ideas for project activities.

You are now ready to describe and schedule project activities. Fortunately you have a flying start in determining the appropriate activities for your project. Just look at what you have already identified. You have a list of activities to deal with potential hindering and facilitating factors in the environment. You have identified many additional activities to take advantage of available resources and to achieve the output specifications you described earlier. You have the beginnings of your PERT diagram already. This is the subject of the next chapter.

Doing Your Own Project

My Input Specifications

At this point you will want to prepare two types of input specifications for your own project: (1) potential hindering and facilitating factors and (2) one-to-one output-input specifications. For each type of input specification you should describe project activities to:

- Deal with or work around the general potential hindering factors
- Take advantage of the general potential facilitating factors
- Deal with or work around the particular potential hindering factors described in your moreover statements
- Take advantage of the available resources identified in your however statements to help you achieve the results you want from the project
- Develop activities to move from the conditions described in your null statements to achieving all your desired outputs

Potential Hindering Factors

1. _____

_____

_____

Required Activities

a. _____

_____

b. _____

_____

     c. _____

     _____

2. _____

     _____

     _____

Required Activities

     a. _____

     _____

     b. _____

     _____

     c. _____

     _____

3. _____

     _____

     _____

Required Activities

     a. _____

     _____

     b. _____

     _____

     c. _____

     _____

4. _____

     _____

     _____

Required Activities

     a. _____

     _____

b. _____
_____

c. _____
_____

Potential Facilitating Factors

1. _____
_____
_____

Required Activities

a. _____
_____

b. _____
_____

c. _____
_____

2. _____
_____
_____

Required Activities

a. _____
_____

b. _____
_____

c. _____
_____

3. _____
_____
_____

Required Activities

a. _____

_____

b. _____

_____

c. _____

_____

4. _____

_____

_____

Required Activities

a. _____

_____

b. _____

_____

c. _____

_____

One-to-One Output-Input Specifications

1. *Output Specification:* _____

_____

   a. *Null Condition:* _____

_____

_____

   b. *However:*

_____

_____

_____

_____

Required Activities

a. _____

_____

b. _____

_____

c. _____

_____

2. *Output Specification:* _____

_____

a. *Null Condition:* _____

_____

_____

b. *However:*

_____

_____

_____

_____

Required Activities

a. _____

_____

b. _____

_____

c. _____

_____

3. *Output Specification:* _____

_____

a. *Null Condition:* _____

_____

_____

b. *However:*

_____

_____

_____

_____

Required Activities

a. _____

_____

b. _____

_____

c. _____

_____

CHAPTER SIX

Thinking Backward to Plan Activities and Subsystems

You must think backward in order to lay out a sensible schedule of activities for a project. You must think backward to figure out what activities you must do before other activities. You must think backward also in order to estimate the timing of the project. Imagine, for example, trying to catch a train on your way to a professional meeting. This is a simple, yet common example of backward thinking in planning. Usually we do this kind of planning intuitively; yet it contains all the elements of more formal efforts. For these reasons it seems like a good example to use, familiar but conceptually similar to larger, more complex projects.

You must set about three broad tasks in addressing this planning problem: (1) What tasks have to be done? (2) In what order should you do them? and (3) When will you have to start on the different tasks in order to get everything ready for the meeting and to get to the train on time? These tasks set the stage for thinking backward. You must establish the targets before you can plan your activities and the timing of those activities. You must first be clear about what time the train leaves and what you need to be ready for a successful meeting. Once you have established these "output specifications," you can calculate in reverse what to do and on what time schedule.

Presumably you would look at a railroad timetable to find out when the train leaves. You would also have to decide about appropriate dress and grooming for the meeting. Finally, you would determine what work materials you needed to have with you.

A second step would be to visualize the "subsystems" needed to achieve the specified outputs. Thinking backward, you might identify the following subsystems:

- Traveling to the Conference;
- Getting Ready in the Morning

There are also "prior" tasks that you must have completed earlier that suggest additional subsystems:

- Getting the Work Materials Ready for the Meeting
- Getting Clothes Ready for the Trip
- Taking Care of Personal Grooming
- Getting the Car Ready (if bus ride or walking to station is not feasible)

You could probably accomplish these four prior tasks simultaneously during the days, weeks, and months before the conference. Each would have its own time constraints. For example, you would probably have the car checked and gas put in a day or two before leaving. On the other hand, you might need weeks or months to get the work materials ready. Then, on the day of the trip, you would be engaged in (1) "Getting Ready in the Morning," and (2) "Traveling to the Conference."

You could draw a diagram to show the six subsystems (Fig. 6-1) and their logical sequence. It might look like the diagram in Figure 6-2. An arrow represents each of the subsystems. You draw arrows between numbered circles. In this diagram each arrow begins in a circle numbered to correspond to the number of the subsystem. There are six subsystems shown, the 100 subsystem, the 200 subsystem, and so on. The index preceding the diagram (Fig. 6-1) lists the subsystems by title and name. The 100 circle serves two purposes. It marks the start of the 100 subsystem; it is also the starting point of the entire project. Four subsystems flow from point 100, only one of which is the 100 subsystem. A solid arrow (100–500) represents the 100 subsystem. Dotted arrows connect the 100 starting point to the 200, 300, and 400 subsystems, respectively. Solid arrows (200–500, 300–500, and

FIGURE 6-1 · *Subsystem Index of the "Catch the Train" Example*

100 Subsystem	Preparing Work Materials
200 Subsystem	Getting Clothes Ready
300 Subsystem	Taking Care of Personal Grooming
400 Subsystem	Getting the Car Ready
500 Subsystem	Getting Ready in the Morning
600 Subsystem	Traveling to the Conference

FIGURE 6-2 • *An Initial Subsystem Diagram of the "Catch the Train" Example*

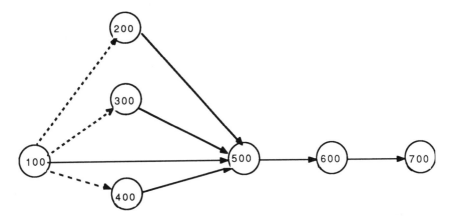

400–500) represent these subsystems. Thus, solid arrows represent subsystems; dotted arrows show other necessary logical connections.

Simple as it is, this diagram represents the entire project because it represents all the necessary subsystems. Since each subsystem is a set of more detailed project activities, the diagram contains (implicitly) all the project activities.

This is an example of modular thinking. If you visualize each subsystem as a module, the project is made up of these modules. Later you can look at each subsystem in greater detail. The modules are like boxes within boxes. The project consists of its subsystems. Each subsystem subsumes multiple activities. Each activity is a little project in itself.

Thus, once you have a sense of your subsystems, you can describe individual activities for each of them. Then you can order the activities and subsystems. You can figure out which you must do in sequence and which you can do simultaneously. All this requires thinking backward.

Figure 6-3 lists Moran's subsystems. The subsystem names suggest the outputs the subsystems are expected to produce. Moran indicated in his project notes that subsystem 100 had to be done first, along with subsystems 200 and 600, and that subsystems 300–500 could then be done simultaneously. But that all had to be completed before subsystem 700 could be begun. This was because "Preparing for the Project Kick-Off Meeting" (Subsystem 700) required information about all the guidelines and standards that were developed in the first subsystems. We can state this as a general rule, "An activity or subsystem must always follow another whenever it requires some condition or uses some product that is an expected result of the prior activity or subsystem." Moran also indicated that subsystems 700–1300 must follow each

FIGURE 6-3 • *Subsystem Index of Moran's Project*

100 Subsystem	Establishing Guidelines for Books
200 Subsystem	Establishing Publishing Standards
300 Subsystem	Setting Guidelines for Chapter Objectives
400 Subsystem	Setting Test Writing Guidelines
500 Subsystem	Setting Guidelines for Chapter Introduction, Summary, and Glossary
600 Subsystem	Establishing Guidelines for Tables, Graphs, Charts, and Illustrations
700 Subsystem	Preparing for the Project Kick-Off Meeting
800 Subsystem	Conducting the Kick-Off Meeting
900 Subsystem	Checking the Chapters
1000 Subsystem	Assembling of Individual Chapters into Preliminary Books
1100 Subsystem	Editing the Books
1200 Subsystem	Creating Table of Contents, Index, and Glossary
1300 Subsystem	Printing and Distributing the Books

other in sequence, one after the other. You will have an opportunity to see this in more detail when we discuss PERT diagramming in the next chapter.

We drew the diagram in Figure 6-4 of the project subsystems from the information in Figure 6-3 and the project notes. Notice, again, that the diagram shows the subsystems as arrows and that each arrow has a beginning and an end point. The beginning point is invariably a circle containing the subsystem number. The end point is a circle containing either the number of the next subsystem or the number of the end point of the project. In this case, as you can see, the project end point number is 1400.

Making a Subsystem Diagram from a Logic Table

A logic table is a useful tool for showing the logical sequence of activities or subsystems. This illustrative logic table in Figure 6-5 was developed by one of our students, Jim Hayes. It shows how his subsystems are logically related to one another.

The subsystems are shown in numerical order in the left-hand column of the logic table. The subsystem names are listed in the center. The right-hand column shows, for each of the subsystems, the subsystem or subsystems

FIGURE 6-4 • *Subsystem Diagram of Moran's Project*

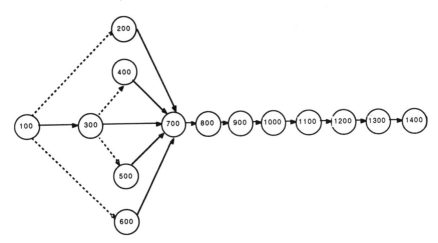

that must immediately precede it. This is called the *immediate predecessor subsystem,* or IPS. Each IPS produces one or more outputs required by the subsystems that are identified as depending upon it.

Some subsystems are shown in the logic table as having no immediate predecessor subsystem (i.e., the 100, 300, 400, 500, and 1500 subsystems). The implication is that these subsystems occur simultaneously at the beginning of the project (i.e., beginning at event 100). Subsystems occurring at the beginning of a project have available to them only those resources identified in the input specifications. Later subsystems may utilize these resources plus other resources developed up to their respective points in the project. Hayes's subsystem diagram in Figure 6-6 depicts the sequence of subsystems described in his logic table (Fig. 6-5).

Recapitulation

In this chapter we have asked you to think about your project in terms of activities and subsystems. We have pointed out that activities and subsystems are means to ends. The ends of your project are the outputs you specified in Chapter 4. Figuring out activities and time schedules requires knowing first where you are going and when you must get there. This is what we have called backward thinking.

This is the kind of thinking you did in Chapter 5 when you imagined activities to get from your input conditions (null, moreover, and however statements) to achieve your specified outputs. This involved envisioning

FIGURE 6-5 • *Hayes's Subsystem Logic Table*

Subsystems	Title	Immediate Predecessor Subsystem (IPS)
100	Revising Ability Level Designations	None
200	Defining Class Size	100
300	Creating a Textbook Inventory	None
400	Revising Program of Co-Curricular Activities	None
500	Defining Student Activity Fund Distributions	None
600	Identifying Double Period Courses	200
700	Identifying Alternate Year Courses	200
800	Planning for Innovative Programs	200
1000	Revising the School-Day Schedule	600; 700; 800
1100	Updating the Student-Parent Handbook	400; 1000
1200	Revising Course Outlines	600; 700; 800
1300	Re-Allocating Space	1200
1400	Defining Staffing Needs	1200
1500	Clarifying Reduction-in-Force Procedures	None
1600	Defining In-Service Needs	1400; 1500

activities to take advantage of prior work, available resources, and potential facilitating factors. Moreover, you had to figure out what you were going to do to deal with potential hindering factors.

Using your experience and imagination in these ways allowed you to generate ideas for project activities. These activity lists are the raw materials for planning exactly how you are going to do your project. This includes laying out your activities, eliminating repetitions, and combining activities when appropriate. It also involves grouping activities into subsystems and designing sequences of subsystems and activities. You also saw how logic tables could be used to show sequences of subsystems and how you could draw a subsystem diagram from a logic table.

In the next chapter you will learn more detailed procedures for laying out activity sequences, for laying out time schedules, and for keeping the project on time. Chapter 7 deals with PERT diagrams. Chapter 8 discusses Gantt diagrams and slack tables.

Doing Your Own Project

The next step in developing your plan is to collect and group all the activities you have identified so far. You defined these activities to deal with your

FIGURE 6-6 • *Hayes's Subsystem PERT Diagram*

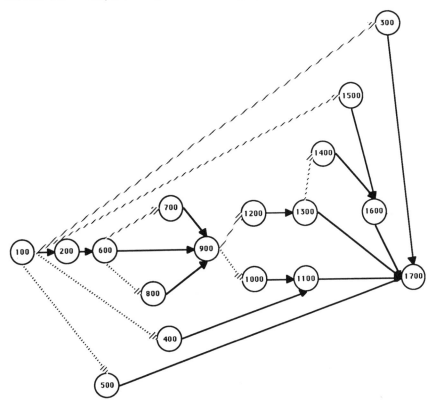

potential hindering and facilitating factors' to take advantage of prior work and available resources, and to achieve all your specified outputs. Your next tasks are to do the following:

1. Write each activity on a separate 3 × 5 index card.
2. Read through the index cards and group your activities into logical subsystems.
3. Check on the logic of your subsystems by assigning them names that reflect achieving specific results (e.g., "Setting Test Writing Guidelines").
4. Prepare a "Subsystems and Activities Index" along the lines of Moran's, shown in Figure 6-7. You will probably find that you will begin right away to list these pretty much in the order in which you expect to do them. Commonly, however, you will later change the order somewhat. Notice also how the language formats in Moran's index correspond to those described in Chapter 3. Subsystem headings use the gerund *(-ing)* form of verbs (e.g.,

FIGURE 6-7 • *Subsystem and Activity Index of Moran's Project*

100 Subsystem	**Establishing Guidelines for Books**
	Interview instructors to get a profile of target audience.
	Collect comments from instructors on which parts of existing books are outdated or inappropriate.
	Attend the training that precedes this course in the curriculum to better understand the incoming audience.
	Survey sales representatives in the field to determine positive and negative points of existing books.
	Consolidate comments made by instructors in activity 110-120.
	Write a design document specifying the project objective, the level of detail and type of information the books should contain.
	Collect comments on the design document from instructors.
	Consolidate the instructors' comments into the final copy of the design document.
200 Subsystem	**Establishing Publishing Standards**
	Identify potential sources of publishing standards.
	Meet with vendor who is providing the desktop publishing software.
	Meet with the publishing group within the company.
	Get sample cover designs from the in-house design group.
	Get samples of output produced by vendor's software.
	Get copies of corporate publishing standards that apply to this project.
	Decide on publishing standards.
	Write publishing standards.
300 Subsystem	**Setting Guidelines for Chapter Objectives**
	Give instructional designer a copy of the design document.
	Meet with instructional designer to explain project.
	Get a list of acceptable verbs and sample objectives from instructional designer.
400 Subsystem	**Setting Test Writing Guidelines**
	Give the testing consultant the design document.
	Meet with testing consultant to explain project.
	Obtain list of test writing guidelines.

Continued

FIGURE 6-7 *Continued*

500 Subsystem	Setting Guidelines for Chapter Introduction, Summary, and Glossary
	Meet with the instructional designer and agree upon guidelines for introductions, summaries, and glossaries.
	Draft guidelines for writing introductions, summaries, and glossaries.
	Review draft guidelines with instructional designer.
	Update guidelines as a result of review.
600 Subsystem	Establishing Guidelines for Tables, Graphs, Charts, and Illustrations
	Identify a person within the group capable of creating computer graphics.
	Send the computer graphics person for training on the project software.
	Ask the computer graphics person to create guidelines for the writers to use in creating their graphics.
700 Subsystem	Preparing for the Project Kick-Off Meeting
	Ask the instructors to provide lists of product experts.
	Get schedule of product update seminars conducted by engineering.
	Write guidelines for product experts stating objective of project and defining the kind of product information needed.
	Compile a list of electronic addresses of project participants to facilitate transfer of documents.
	Establish a design-freeze date for each chapter.
	Create schedule of meetings to update management on the project.
	Create schedule for weekly meetings with writers.
	Create project documents: PERT diagram, PERT index, PERT slack table, Gantt diagram, Decision Flow Diagrams, and Information Flow Diagrams.
800 Subsystem	Conducting the Kick-Off Meeting
	Conduct a kick-off meeting among writers, the operator of the desktop publishing system, the computer graphics person, the instructional designer, and the testing consultant.
	Explain the project in terms of its objectives, the level of detail and type of information in the books, as stated in the design document.
	Distribute the table of contents that was developed earlier.
	Distribute lists of product experts, developed earlier, to writers.
	Distribute publishing standards.
	Distribute list of verbs that are acceptable for use in writing chapter objectives, including samples of correctly written objectives, to writers.

FIGURE 6-7   *Continued*

	Distribute test writing guidelines to writers.
	Distribute guidelines for writing chapter introduction and summaries to writers.
	Distribute graphics guidelines to writers.
	Distribute information developed in Output Specification seven.
	Distribute design document.
900 Subsystem	**Checking the Chapters**
	Review each chapter for compliance with the design document and guidelines.
	Meet with writers to resolve potential conflicts in comments returned by product experts.
	Arrange meetings between testing consultant and any writers having difficulties with test construction.
	Meet with writers at least weekly to identify potential problems.
	Arrange meetings between instructional designer and any writers having difficulties with objectives, chapter introduction, or chapter summaries.
	Keep management informed with weekly status reports on chapters.
1000 Subsystem	**Assembling of Individual Chapters into Preliminary Books**
	Review chapters for repetition or contradiction of material appearing in other chapters.
	Merge graphics with texts.
	Write preface to book.
	Write title page.
	Merge chapter tests into Appendix A.
	Merge test answers into Appendix B.
	Merge chapter glossaries into a single glossary at the back of book.
	Consolidate electronic versions of chapters into one book-length document.
	Transmit book to editor.
1100 Subsystem	**Editing the Books**
	Receive edited, final copy from the editor.
	Check that editor has applied style standards consistently.
	Verify that trademarks page created by editor includes all trademarks mentioned in text of book.
	Run program that checks spelling.
	Transmit finished copy to operator of desktop publishing system.

FIGURE 6-7 *Continued*

1200 Subsystem	Creating Table of Contents, Index, and Glossary
	Assure that the operator of the desktop publishing system creates an automatic index.
	Assure that operator of desktop publishing system lays out pages properly.
	Assure that operator of desktop publishing system creates automatic table of contents.
1300 Subsystem	Printing and Distributing the Books
	Print the books using the desktop publishing system.
	Send books to the external organization that will reproduce, bind, box, warehouse, and distribute them.

1300 Subsystem, "Printing and Distributing the Books"). Activity labels use the imperative form of verbs (e.g., "Print the books using the desktop publishing system").

5. Make a logic table and draw a diagram of your project's subsystems. Do not try at this point in your work to diagram *all* your project activities. Just draw a diagram of your subsystems. The diagram should start with a circled 100. Like your logic table, it should show which subsystems you will do simultaneously and which must follow in sequence. (*Note:* There are some cases in which a subsystem can begin after you have finished only a part of a previous subsystem. In Chapter 7 we shall discuss this situation further. For now assume that your subsystems follow each other in whole units and draw your diagram accordingly.)

CHAPTER SEVEN

Using PERT Diagramming to Put Project Activities in Sequence

In the last chapter, which introduced the idea of backward thinking, one emphasis was on grouping activities from your context evaluation into project subsystems, and a second emphasis was on sequencing and diagramming these subsystems. We asked you to consider catching the train en route to a business meeting as an example of project planning and backward thinking. We identified six subsystems of this simple project and diagrammed them for you. We then asked you to carry these ideas over as you considered a corporate training project. We showed you a subsystem and activity index and asked to see the relationship between the index and a subsystem diagram of Moran's book project. Finally, we asked you to develop your own subsystem index and diagram. In doing this exercise you drew upon the activity lists you had formulated earlier.

Now we ask you to take the next step. In this chapter we present explanations and examples of what is commonly called PERT diagramming. PERT is an acronym for *P*rogram *E*valuation and *R*eview *T*echnique. Other terms you may have heard that deal with similar ideas are *network analysis, path analysis,* and *critical path method (CPM)*. Although these techniques have been distinguished historically, over time they have been blended in practice. We make no distinction among them in this book; we simply use the term *PERT diagramming*.

The format of this chapter is similar to that of Chapter 6. We focus first on the "Catch the Train" example to show how to draw PERT diagrams. Then we follow up with Moran's book project. The idea is to see how in his corporate project Moran follows the same basic principles of PERT diagramming that we do in the simpler example. Finally, we provide exercises for you to practice on and provide guidelines for you to proceed with your own project.

In essence, to construct your PERT diagram you would expand Figure 6-2 (p. 63). You would make a more detailed diagram. You would show each subsystem with all its component activities. Within each subsystem you would sequence the activities, some in series, others in parallel, according to the natural logic of how they must be done.

In the following section we take one subsystem at a time and explain how to diagram that subsystem's activities. Each diagram shows the sequence of activities in that subsystem. You already know that it is possible in constructing system diagrams to show that you can do some subsystems simultaneously and that you must schedule others to follow one another in sequence. The same is true of project activities. You will recall that a subsystem is a set of activities related to achieving a particular result or set of results. An *activity* is a more limited task. Activities are typically parts of subsystems. You have seen examples of activities, subsystems, and the relationships between them in Moran's index of subsystems and activities in Chapter 6.

The "Catch the Train" Example

Let's try diagramming activities for the "Catch the Train" example. We'd like you to prepare a more detailed PERT diagram of the "project." This means drawing a diagram that includes all the activities you feel need to be done in each of the subsystems. You should write the activities on index cards, one on each card. Then lay the cards out on the floor and rearrange them until you have them in a compelling logical order. Figure 7-1 shows our version of the subsystem and activity PERT index for the Catch the Train project. We identified twenty-eight activities to be accomplished. The index conforms to the format you saw earlier in Moran's index for his book project. However, we have added activity numbers that show how the activities are interconnected.

Compare this index with the subsystem index and diagram of the Catch the Train project (Fig. 6-1 and 6-2, pp. 62–63). You can see that the first activity in each subsystem begins with the subsystem number (100, 200, etc.). You can also see that the last activity in each subsystem ends with the number of the next subsystem in the subsystem diagram. Subsystems 100–400 end in 500; 500 ends in 600. The last (600) subsystem ends in 700, which is the end point of the project. Each activity number tells you exactly how to connect up that activity to all the others. Every one of the twenty-eight activities has a beginning number that is the same as the end number of the activity(ies) that directly precedes it. Every activity has an end number that corresponds to the beginning number of the activity(ies) that follow it.

Following this logic, you can draw a PERT diagram for each subsystem.

FIGURE 7-1 • *Subsystem and Activity Index of the "Catch the Train" Project*

100 Subsystem	Preparing Work Materials
100-110	Identify work objectives;
110-120	Design work procedures;
120-130	Do work-related research;
130-140	Do work-related writing;
140-150	Design work-related artwork;
150-160	Have work-related artwork prepared;
160-170	Review work materials and identify issues for the work conference;
170-500	Pack work materials for the trip.
200 Subsystem	**Getting Clothes Ready**
200-210	Have clothes cleaned and repaired;
210-220	Lay out clothes for trip;
220-500	Pack clothes for trip.
300 Subsystem	**Taking Care of Personal Grooming**
300-500	Get your hair cut;
400 Subsystem	**Getting the Car Ready**
400-500	Have car checked and gas put in.
500 Subsystem	**Getting Ready in the Morning**
500-510	Set alarm;
510-520	Get a good night's sleep;
520-530	Wake up on time;
530-540	Do wake-up exercises;
540-550	Brush teeth;
550-560	Take a shower;
560-570	Prepare breakfast;
570-580	Get dressed;
580-600	Eat breakfast.
600 Subsystem	**Traveling to the Conference**
600-610	Drive to the station;
610-620	Park the car;
620-630	Buy a newspaper;
630-640	Buy a ticket;
640-650	Board the train;
650-700	Travel to the work conference.

Each diagram will show the connections among all of that subsystem's activities (Fig. 7-2 through Fig. 7-7). Eventually you can connect all the subsystem diagrams together into a single PERT diagram for the whole project.

You can see that these subsystem PERT diagrams match the activities for the respective subsystems shown in the PERT index. Each arrow represents an activity, and the activity corresponds to the beginning and ending numbers shown in the index. So, for example, activity 610-620 in the PERT diagram corresponds to "Park the car" in the 600 subsystem. Activity 300–500 corresponds to "Get your hair cut" in the 300 subsystem.

Notice that the PERT diagram for each subsystem represents in detail what was represented on the subsystem diagram (Fig. 6-2, p. 63) by a single arrow. Each arrow in Figure 6-2 is now represented in Figures 7-2 through 7-7 by a sequence of activities. Notice, too, that the beginning and ending numbers in these subsystem PERT diagrams are the same as those in the subsystem diagram of the project shown in Figure 6-2. Therefore, if we simply substitute for each arrow in Figure 6-2 the corresponding PERT diagram (Figs. 7-2–7-7), we'll have a composite PERT diagram for the entire project. This is what we did to generate Figure 7-8.

General Principles of Activity Planning

In this simple PERT diagramming example, we have been able to identify and illustrate a number of basic planning concepts:

1. Task analysis is a process of working backward from the desired output condition, through a series of partial results, to get to the desired output condition. This requires going through sequences of tasks or *activities,* each of which is necessary to produce one or more partial results.

2. You can look at each activity as a "mini-project" in itself. Its outputs are among the partial results you need to achieve the desired outputs of the project. Each activity has its own set of input requirements. Input requirements all along the way are met either by initial input conditions (identified in the context evaluation) or by prior project activities. The results of early activities help to create the conditions and resources necessary to carry out later activities successfully.

3. Every activity is a small project in itself, and you can think of it as comprising even smaller activities. (For example, "Drive to the station" implies (a) opening the garage door, (b) opening the car door, (c) getting into the car, (d) starting the car, and so on. How large or small the activities are that you include in your PERT diagram is a matter of judgment. The questions that you typically address in this regard are "How much detail is helpful?" and "How much effort is it worth to me to put in a lot of detail?".

FIGURE 7-2 • *A PERT Diagram of the "Preparing Work Materials" Subsystem of the "Catch the Train" Example*

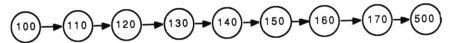

FIGURE 7-3 • *A PERT Diagram of the "Getting Clothes Ready" Subsystem of the "Catch the Train" Example*

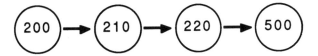

FIGURE 7-4 • *A PERT Diagram of the "Taking Care of Personal Grooming" Subsystem of the "Catch the Train" Example*

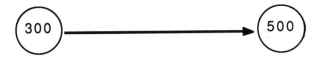

FIGURE 7-5 • *A PERT Diagram of the "Getting the Car Ready" Subsystem of the "Catch the Train" Example*

FIGURE 7-6 • *A PERT Diagram of the "Getting Ready in the Morning" Subsystem of the "Catch the Train" Example*

FIGURE 7-7 • *A PERT Diagram of the "Traveling to the Conference" Subsystem of the "Catch the Train" Example*

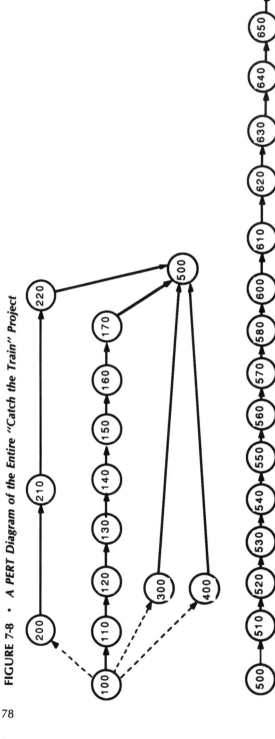

FIGURE 7-8 · A PERT Diagram of the Entire "Catch the Train" Project

4. You can also view each activity as part of a larger subsystem of the project. Each subsystem is made up of some set of sequenced activities, and the project is made up of some set of sequenced subsystems.

5. We view projects as sequences of planned activities to achieve higher values. The basis of a project is a perceived problem. The purpose of the project is to bring about some observable change in the problem situation. Implicitly, its starting point is always with the "way things are now." This is why a clearly specified description of the input conditions is important. The input specifications are the starting point; the desired outputs are the ending point. The project is a planned sequence of activities to get from one to the other.

6. In a PERT diagram the input conditions are assumed to include all of the relevant conditions and resources present at the start of the project. All activities emanate from this start event. The conditions present as signified by the start event are the input conditions (see Chapter 5). Project activities alter these input conditions sequentially, activity by activity, until you achieve the desired results. This is the logic of project planning, and this is the logic represented in a PERT diagram.

7. PERT diagramming is a way of showing in sequence what you must do to complete the project successfully. Remember that a project is complete only when you have achieved your specified outputs. In the course of a project you may come to believe either that the outputs you initially specified are too ambitious or not ambitious enough. In either case you may choose to change your output specifications. However, by definition, when you change your output specifications, you change your project.

General Rules of PERT Diagramming

There are certain rules that are normally followed in drawing PERT diagrams. Following these rules will help you draw diagrams that communicate clearly the logical sequence of activities and subsystems in any project.

1. Arrows represent activities.
2. Arrows start from and connect into small numbered circles.
3. The numbered circles represent the points in time when activities begin and end (these are referred to in some manuals as beginning and ending *events*).
4. The PERT diagram moves sequentially from left to right.
5. Every PERT diagram begins at a *start event,* which we arbitrarily tell our students always to label "100."
6. Consecutive arrows represent activities that logically must follow in sequence (i.e., in *series*).
7. Parallel arrows represent activities that may be done simultaneously (i.e., in *parallel,* even if those activities take different time periods to complete).

This implies that the completion time estimated for the completion of both of two simultaneous activities is the *longer* of the two completion times.

8. Parallel sequences of arrows (called parallel *paths*) represent sequences of activities that may be done simultaneously. Again, when you estimate the time necessary to complete both of two parallel paths, you must use the time estimated for completing the longer path.

9. There can be *one and only one arrow* drawn between any two numbered circles.

10. Each activity appears in the diagram as an arrow between two numbered circles. The index of a PERT diagram gives the titles or descriptors of the project's activities, listing them in numerical order by subsystem.

12. Each activity has a beginning number and an end number. You should list activities in the index in the order of their beginning numbers. Where two or more activities have the same beginning number, you should then sequence them further according to their end numbers. The beginning and end numbers of activities show how they link with other activities. You can construct a PERT diagram from a PERT index. Once you see a PERT index with all of its activity numbers, you can see the connections among the activities.

13. When more than one activity or sequence of activities can take place at the same time, the PERT diagram shows these as parallel activities flowing from a common point. For example, the PERT index (Fig. 7-1) and the PERT diagram (Fig. 7-8) show that you can do activities 300–500, 400–500, and the entire 100 and 200 subsystems simultaneously. Some of these activities and subsystems may take longer to do than others; however, they can all be worked on during the same time period. They all have 100 as their beginning point.

The index and diagram also show that you cannot do the 500 subsystem until you have done everything you need to do in the 100, 200, 300, and 400 subsystems. They all have 500 as their end point.

Finally, the figures show that you cannot do the 600 subsystem until you have completed the 500 subsystem. Thus, point 600 represents the end of the 500 subsystem (580–600) and the beginning of the 600 subsystem (600–610).

Dummy Activities

When logic suggests that two activities might have the same beginning and ending numbers, add a dotted arrow to eliminate confusion. We call these dotted arrows *dummy* activities. Unlike the solid arrows in a PERT diagram, the dotted arrows are only graphic place holders. They do not represent real project activities See, for example, the dotted arrows in Figure 6-4 (p. 65).

Those are dummy activities. Figure 7-9 illustrates the most common situation in which you need to use a dummy activity. Instead of showing two project activities numbered 120–130, show one as 120–130 and the other as 120–140. Use a dummy arrow to make the necessary connection back to the common end point (140).

So far we have presented two situations in which it is necessary to use dotted arrows in PERT diagrams. Dotted arrows were used in both the "Catch the Train" example and in Moran's book project. They were used so that the first activity in each subsystem would begin with the same number as the subsystem (see Fig. 6-2, p. 63, and Fig. 6-4, p. 65). Dummy activities were also used so that no two activities in the diagram woud have the same beginning and ending numbers (Fig. 7-9).

A third situation in which you would use dummy activities in a PERT diagram is when one activity requires outputs from a *pair* of prior activities but another activity requires output from *only one* of that pair of activities. Take, for example, the following situation. The table lists a set of project activities in the first column and, in the second column, the prior activities on which they directly depend for certain resource conditions. The task is to

FIGURE 7-9 • *Using a Dummy Activity to Avoid Having Two Parallel Activities with the Same Pair of Index Numbers*

Don't do this!

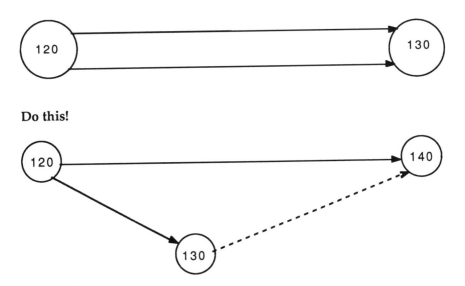

Do this!

draw a PERT diagram that represents the sequence of activities described by the information contained in the table.

Activity	Directly Dependent on Outputs from What Prior Project Activity(ies)
A _____	None
B _____	A
C _____	None
D _____	B and C
E _____	C

When we try to draw the diagram (see Figure 7-10), we encounter a logical problem different from any that we have encountered before. The problem is to show simultaneously that activity D requires, as input, outputs from activities B and C and that activity E requires as input one or more outputs from activity C but not from activity B.

You must draw a dummy activity in order to solve the problem. Furthermore, you must draw it in the correct direction, from the end of activity C (300) to the end of activity B (400). In such a case the dotted arrow serves as a kind of an extension cord carrying the current in the direction the arrow is pointed, not in the other direction. As you can see in Figure 7-10, the dummy activity "carries" the outputs from activity C to a point (400) at the end of activity B. It represents the availability of these joint outputs as inputs to activity D. In contrast, activity E is drawn as an arrow emanating only from the end point of activity C. Thus, the diagram shows, as the table

FIGURE 7-10 • Using a Dummy Activity to Handle a Logical Problem in "Wiring" a PERT Diagram

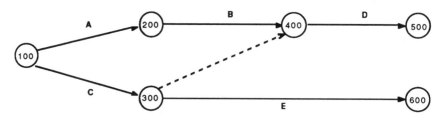

indicates, that activity D is dependent on outputs from two activities (B and C), whereas activity E is dependent on outputs from activity C alone.

Numbering and Indexing Your PERT Diagram by Subsystem

The examples given so far have illustrated how you can number subsystems in a PERT diagram. There are alternatives, however, to the scheme used in the examples given. In this section we discuss alternative approaches to numbering PERT diagrams.

The Basic Numbering Pattern

PERT subsystem numbering and indexing are simplest when activities proceed sequentially in a single line. See Figures 7-11 and 7-12.

FIGURE 7-11 • *Basic PERT Subsystem Numbering*

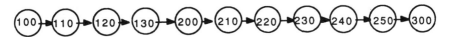

FIGURE 7-12 • *PERT Index for Figure 7-11*

Doing "X" ("100" Subsystem)

100-110	Do X_1
110-120	Do X_2
120-130	Do X_3
130-200	Do X_4

Doing "Y" ("200" Subsystem)

200-210	Do Y_1
210-220	Do Y_2
220-230	Do Y_3
230-240	Do Y_4
240-250	Do Y_5
250-300	Do Y_6

Basic PERT Numbering with Network Subsystems

The same numbering and indexing system works without any problem even when one of the subsystems has multiple parallel paths. See Figures 7-13 and 7-14.

FIGURE 7-13 • *Basic PERT Numbering with Network Subsystems*

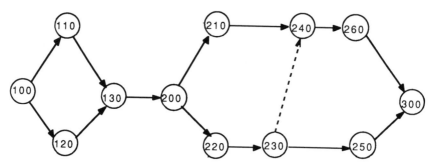

FIGURE 7-14 • *PERT Index for Figure 7-13*

Doing "X" ("100" Subsystem)

100-110	Do X_1
100-120	Do X_2
110-130	Do X_3
120-130	Do X_4
130-200	Do X_5

Doing "Y" ("200" Subsystem)

200-210	Do Y_1
200-220	Do Y_2
210-240	Do Y_3
220-230	Do Y_4
230-240	Dummy Activity
230-250	Do Y_5
240-260	Do Y_6
250-300	Do Y_7
260-300	Do Y_8

However, whenever two subsystems branch off the same event, a numbering issue is raised that must be resolved in one of two ways. Either way is all right as long as you use it consistently throughout the PERT diagram. It is poor practice, however, to mix numbering schemes in the same PERT diagram.

Alternative Numbering Method I

The first alternative numbering method is a direct extension of the basic numbering method. See Figures 7-15 and 7-16.

FIGURE 7-15 • *PERT Alternative Numbering Method I with Branching Subsystems*

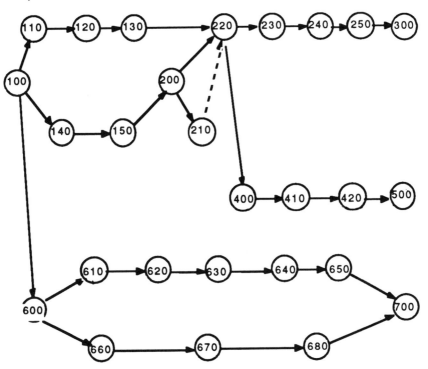

FIGURE 7-16 • *PERT Index for Figure 7-15*

Doing "A" ("100" Subsystem)

100-110	Do A_1
100-140	Do A_2
110-120	Do A_3
120-130	Do A_4
130-220	Do A_5
140-150	Do A_6
150-200	Do A_7

Doing "B" ("200" Subsystem)

200-210	Do B_1
200-220	Do B_2
210-220	Dummy Activity
220-230	Do B_3
230-240	Do B_4
240-250	Do B_5
250-300	Do B_6

Doing "C" ("400" Subsystem)

220-400	Do C_1 [Note that although the beginning index number of this activity is a "200" number, the activity is actually the first activity of the "400" subsystem.]
400-410	Do C_2
410-420	Do C_3
420-500	Do C_4

Doing "D" ("600" Subsystem)

100-600	Do D_1 [Note here, too, that although the beginning number is connected to another subsystem (the "100" subsystem), the activity is actually the first activity of a different subsystem (the "600" subsystem).]
600-610	Do D_2
600-660	Do D_3
610-620	Do D_4
620-630	Do D_5
630-640	Do D_6
640-650	Do D_7
650-700	Do D_8
660-670	Do D_9
670-680	Do D_{10}
680-700	Do D_{11}

Alternative Numbering Method II

Some PERT users dislike having the first activity of a new subsystem start with an index number belonging to a previous subsystem. We saw this in the 400 subsystem (220-400) and in the 600 subsystem (100-600) in Figures 7-15 and 7-16. Alternative Numbering Method II avoids this by placing a dummy activity between the new subsystem and the previous one in each case where it is needed to avoid the problem. This has the effect of starting the new subsystem with its own index numbers and of pushing all subsequent numbers up one interval in value. See Figures 7-17 and 7-18.

The number of real activities indexed in the 400 and 600 subsystems under PERT Alternative Method II (Fig. 7-17) is the same as under PERT Alternative Method I (Fig. 7-15). Under Method II, however, you use dummy activities to set up real 400 and 600 numbers for real 400 and 600 subsystem activities. This results in (1) two extra dummy activities (one in each of the two subsystems) and (2) pushing up the numbers in each of those subsystems by an interval of ten.

FIGURE 7-17 • PERT Alternative Numbering Method II with Branching Subsystems

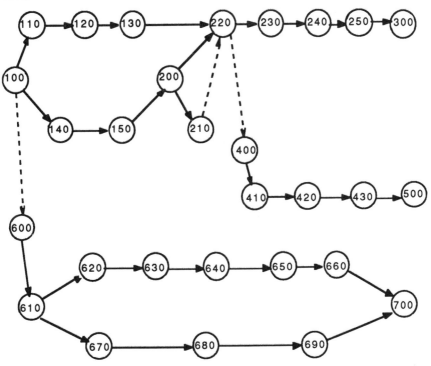

FIGURE 7-18 • *PERT Index for Figure 7-17*

Doing "A" ("100" Subsystem)

100-110	Do A_1
100-140	Do A_2
110-120	Do A_3
120-130	Do A_4
130-220	Do A_5
140-150	Do A_6
150-200	Do A_7

Doing "B" ("200" Subsystem)

200-210	Do B_1
200-220	Do B_2
210-220	Dummy Activity
220-230	Do B_3
230-240	Do B_4
240-250	Do B_5
250-300	Do B_6

Doing "C" ("400" Subsystem)

220-400	Dummy Activity [Note that the dummy activity is used to make sure that the first real activity of the subsystem begins with a "400" number instead of with a "200" number.]
400-410	Do C_1
410-420	Do C_2
420-430	Do C_3
430-500	Do C_4

Doing "D" ("600" Subsystem)

100-600	Dummy Activity [Note that the dummy activity is used to make sure that the first real activity of the subsystem begins with a "600" number instead of with a "100" number.]
600-610	Do D_1
610-620	Do D_2
610-670	Do D_3
620-630	Do D_4
630-640	Do D_5
640-650	Do D_6
650-660	Do D_7
660-700	Do D_8
670-680	Do D_9
680-690	Do D_{10}
690-700	Do D_{11}

Another Small Numbering Problem

When you use intervals of ten within subsystems, as in the examples given, you have space for ten activities in a single hundred series. What if you have more than ten activities in a particular subsystem?

There are two common ways of handling this problem. One is to reduce the intervals in that subsystem (not necessarily in all subsystems) to fives, or even to ones (see Fig. 7-19).

FIGURE 7-19 • *Numbering a Subsystem by Fives*

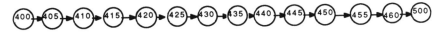

Another solution is to use more than one hundred series for a subsystem containing more than ten activities. Thus, you might call the subsystem the 400-500 subsystem (see Fig. 7-20).

FIGURE 7-20 • *Using More than One Hundred to Number a Subsystem*

Moran's PERT Diagram

We have looked once before at Moran's index of subsystems and activities. In Chapter 6 we used it as a basis for understanding the principles of subsystem diagramming (Fig. 6-7, p. 68). At that time the index showed sets of activities grouped into subsystems. However, the index did not yet display the PERT activity numbers. Therefore, it was not possible to know from the information given in that version of his index precisely how he thought his project activities should be sequenced. Now, in Figure 7-21, you see his index fully numbered. Look at the relationship between the numbered index and his PERT diagram (Fig. 7-22).

By examining the numbers assigned to the first activities in the 200, 400, 500, and 600 subsystems, you can see that Moran chose to employ Alternative Numbering Method I. That is, he chose not to use extra dummy activities. Initial activities in some subsystems begin with a number from a prior subsystem. You can see, for example, that the first activities listed in subsystems 200, 400, 500, and 600 are, respectively, 100-200, 300-400, 300-500, and 100-600. Thus, the initial activity in the 200 subsystem begins with 100, not 200; the initial activity in the 400 subsystem begins with 300, not 400; and so on. The PERT diagram for his project is presented in Figure 7-22a, 7-22b, and 7-23c. We present the diagram in three parts because it is long. The parts overlap at points 700 and 1010 to form a complete diagram.

FIGURE 7-21 · *PERT Index of Moran's Book Project*

100 Subsystem	**Establishing Guidelines for Books**
100-110	Interview instructors to get a profile of target audience.
110-120	Collect comments from instructors on which parts of existing books are outdated or inappropriate.
110-130	Attend the training that precedes this course in the curriculum to better understand the incoming audience.
110-140	Survey sales representatives in the field to determine positive and negative points of existing books.
120-140	Consolidate comments made by instructors in activity 110-120.
130-140	Dummy Activity.
140-150	Write a design document specifying the project objective, the levels of detail and type of information to be contained in the books.
150-160	Collect comments on the design document from instructors.
160-300	Consolidate the instructors' comments into the final copy of the design document.
200 Subsystem	**Establishing Publishing Standards**
100-200	Identify potential sources of publishing standards.
200-210	Meet with vendor who is providing the desktop publishing software.
200-220	Meet with the publishing group within the company.
200-230	Get sample cover designs from the in-house design group.
210-230	Get samples of output produced by vendor's software.
220-230	Get copies of corporate publishing standards that apply to this project.
230-240	Decide on publishing standards.
240-700	Write publishing standards.
300 Subsystem	**Setting Guidelines for Chapter Objectives**
300-310	Give instructional designer a copy of the design document.
310-320	Meet with instructional designer to explain project.
320-700	Get a list of acceptable verbs and sample objectives from instructional designer.
400 Subsystem	**Setting Test Writing Guidelines**
300-400	Give the testing consultant the design document.
400-410	Meet with testing consultant to explain project.
410-700	Obtain list of test writing guidelines.
500 Subsystem	**Setting Guidelines for Chapter Introduction, Summary, and Glossary**
300-500	Meet with the instructional designer and agree upon guidelines for introductions, summaries, and glossaries.
500-510	Draft guidelines for writing introductions, summaries, and glossaries.
510-520	Review draft guidelines with instructional designer.
520-700	Update guidelines as a result of review.

FIGURE 7-21 *Continued*

600 Subsystem	Establishing Guidelines for Tables, Graphs, Charts, and Illustrations
100-600	Identify a person within the group capable of creating computer graphics.
600-610	Send the computer graphics person for training on the software to be used for this project.
610-700	Ask the computer graphics person to create guidelines to be used by the writers in the creation of their graphics.
700 Subsystem	Preparing for Project Kick-Off Meeting
700-710	Ask the instructors to provide lists of product experts.
700-720	Get schedules of product update seminars conducted by engineering.
700-730	Write guidelines for product experts stating objective of project and defining the kind of product information needed.
700-740	Compile a list of electronic addresses of project participants to facilitate transfer of documents.
700-750	Establish a design-freeze date for each chapter.
700-760	Create schedule of meetings to keep management updated on project status.
700-770	Create schedule for weekly meetings with writers.
710-770	Dummy Activity
720-770	Dummy Activity
730-770	Dummy Activity
740-770	Dummy Activity
770-800	Create project documents: PERT diagram, PERT index, PERT slack table, Gantt diagram, Decision Flow Diagrams, and Information Flow Diagrams.
750-770	Dummy Activity
760-770	Dummy Activity
800 Subsystem	Conducting the Kick-Off Meeting
800-805	Conduct a kick-off meeting among writers, the operator of the desktop publishing system, the computer graphics person, the instructional designer, and the testing consultant.
805-810	Explain the project in terms of its objectives, the levels of detail and type of information to be contained in books, as stated in the design document.
810-815	Distribute table of contents, which were developed at a lower mission level.
810-820	Distribute lists of product experts, which were developed at a lower mission level, to writers.
810-825	Distribute publishing standards.
810-830	Distribute list of verbs that are acceptable for use in writing chapter objectives, including samples of correctly written objectives, to writers.
810-835	Distribute test writing guidelines to writers.
810-840	Distribute guidelines for writing chapter introduction and summaries to writers.
810-845	Distribute graphics guidelines to writers.

FIGURE 7-21 *Continued*

810-850	Distribute information developed in Output Specification seven.
810-900	Distribute design document.
815-900	Dummy Activity
820-900	Dummy Activity
825-900	Dummy Activity
830-900	Dummy Activity
835-900	Dummy Activity
840-900	Dummy Activity
845-900	Dummy Activity
850-900	Dummy Activity
900 Subsystem	**Checking the Chapters**
900-910	Review each chapter for compliance with the design document and guidelines.
910-920	Meet with writers to resolve potential conflicts in comments returned by product experts.
920-930	Arrange meetings between testing consultant and any writers having difficulties with test construction.
920-940	Meet with writers at least weekly to identify potential problems.
920-1000	Arrange meetings between instructional designer and any writers having difficulties with objectives, chapter introduction, or chapter summaries.
930-1000	Dummy Activity
940-1000	Keep management informed with weekly status reports on chapters.
1000 Subsystem	**Assembling of Individual Chapters into** Preliminary Books
1000-1010	Review chapters for repetition or contradiction of material appearing in other chapters.
1010-1020	Merge graphics with texts.
1010-1030	Write preface to book.
1010-1040	Write title page.
1010-1050	Merge chapter tests into Appendix A.
1010-1060	Merge test answers into Appendix B.
1010-1070	Merge chapter glossaries into a single glossary at back of book.
1010-1080	Consolidate electronic versions of chapters into one book-length document.
1080-1100	Transmit book to editor.
1100 Subsystem	**Editing the Books**
1100-1110	Receive edited, final copy from the editor.
1110-1120	Check that editor has applied style standards consistently.
1110-1130	Verify that trademarks page created by editor includes all trademarks mentioned in text of book.
1130-1140	Run program that check spelling.
1140-1200	Transmit finished copy to operator of desktop publishing system.

FIGURE 7-21 *Continued*

1200 Subsystem	Creating Table of Contents, Index, and Glossary
1200-1210	Assure that the operator of the desktop publishing system creates an automatic index.
1200-1220	Assure that operator of desktop publishing system lays out pages properly.
1220-1300	Assure that operator of desktop publishing system creates automatic table of contents.
1300 Subsystem	Printing and Distributing the Books
1300-1310	Print the books using the desktop publishing system.
1310-1320	Send books to the external organization that will reproduce, bind, box, warehouse, and distribute them.

FIGURE 7-22a • *Part I of Moran's PERT Diagram*

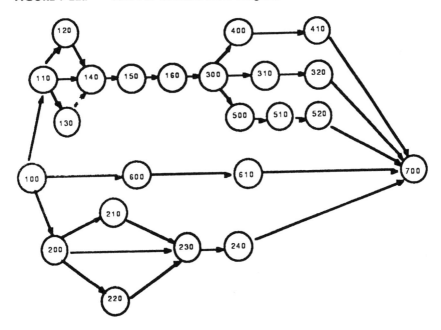

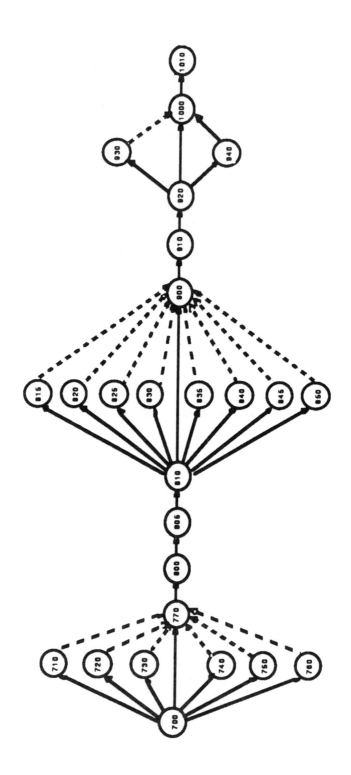

FIGURE 7-22b · Part II of Moran's PERT Diagram

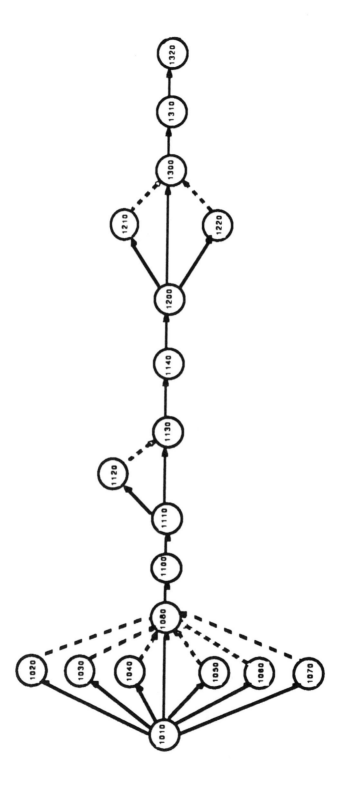

FIGURE 7-22c · *Part III of Moran's PERT Diagram*

95

Compare Moran's PERT diagram with his PERT index (Fig. 7-21). Look at the last activity in each subsystem and then look for it on the PERT diagram. you can see how the diagram represents the subsystems listed in the index.

PERT Diagramming Exercises

Directions: Construct a PERT diagram from the information given in each of the following tables. Number the start event "100." Number subsequent events in multiples of ten (i.e., "110," "120," etc.) Label each activity arrow with its correct letter designation (i.e., "A," "B," etc.). All arrows should be straight lines. All arrows should flow from left to right. All numbers should flow up from left to right (i.e., no activity should be numbered such that its end event has a lower number than its beginning event). (See answers following.)

Exercise 1

Activity	Directly Dependent on Outputs from What Prior Project Activitiy(ies)
A	None
B	None
C	None
D	A
E	B
F	C
G	D
H	E
I	F
J	G
K	H
L	I
M	J

Exercise 2

Activity	Directly Dependent on Outputs From What Prior Project Activity(ies)
A_____	None
B_____	A
C_____	A
D_____	B and C
E_____	None
F_____	E
G_____	F
H_____	E
I _____	F and H

Exercise 3

Activity	Directly Dependent on Outputs from What Prior Project Activity(ies)
A_____	None
B_____	A and D
C_____	B and E
D_____	None
E_____	D
F_____	E
G_____	F

Exercise 4

Activity	Directly Dependent on Outputs From What Prior Project Activity(ies)
A_____	None
B_____	None

C _____	A
D _____	B and C
E _____	A
F _____	D
G _____	C
H _____	G
I _____	F and G

Answers to the PERT Diagramming Exercises

You will see a diagram for each of the exercises, followed by an explanation. Please note that every diagram has several elements:

1. Numbered circles.
2. Arrows going from left to right from one circle to another.
   - Most of the arrows are solid (showing real activities).
   - Some of the arrows—in exercises 2, 3, and 4—are dotted (showing dummy activities).
3. In some cases, there is more than one arrow coming out of the same circle; these are called *branches.*
4. *Sequences of activities (called paths) emerging from the branches.*

Some elements in the PERT diagram are fixed. Certain activities must follow other activities, as given in the tables. Branches must be in the right places. Dummy activities must also be in the right places, and in the right direction.

Other elements can vary a bit. Wherever there is a branch, it is up to you which branch you decide to put above or below the other. Either choice is correct. You must number the first circle "100" as given in the directions. We call this the *start event.* However, the numbering of the rest of the diagram is flexible. The only rule is that *no number at the head of the arrow can be lower than the number at the tail of the same arrow.* That is, all numbers mut go up in numerical value from left to right. It is not necessary to use subsystem numbering for these exercises since there is no information given about what the subsystems are.

The diagrams may be different in certain ways and still be correct. However, there are limits on how they may be different. Typical differences are in numbering and graphics. Different people may put different numbers in different circles. The only rules are that the first circle should be 100 and that you should always draw arrows from a lower to a higher number. Secondly, different people may draw arrows of different lengths. *The length* of an arrow has no meaning. Thirdly, wherever you have parallel sequences of activities, you may put them in different orders from top to bottom. For example, we give two examples of correct answers to Exercise 1, switching the order of the parallel paths from top to bottom. Actually there are six different top-to-bottom combinations possible for Exercise 1, although we show only two of them.

Exercise 1

As just indicated, there are six possible correct answers to Exercise 1 because there are three, and only three, branches. You can put them in different orders from top to bottom. Within each branch, however, there is only one correct sequence of activities. See Figure 7-23a and 7-23b.

FIGURE 7-23a • *First Answer to PERT Exercise 1*

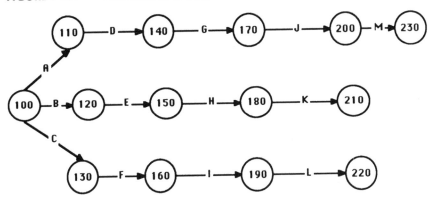

FIGURE 7-23b • *Second Answer to PERT Exercise 1*

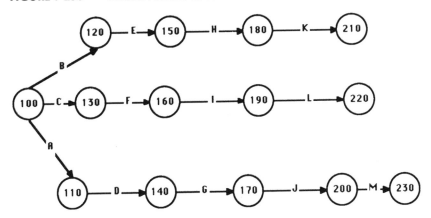

Exercise 2

In exercises 2 through 4 you have to include some dummy activities in order to draw the diagram correctly. Compare the following diagram in Figure 7-24 to yours. Remember that you may have put the "E" branch above the "A" branch, or the "C" branch above the "B" branch, or the "H" branch above the "F" branch. Thus, your diagram could look a little different from the one shown and still be correct. It is important that the dummy activities be drawn in the correct places and in the correct directions. Also, all left–right paths must show the same sequences of letters as the diagram in Figure 7-24.

Why the dummy activities? In this exercise, part of the reason is the same in both instances: A third activity (e.g., "D") is dependent upon the successful completion of two prior activities (i.e., "B" and "C"). This means that you must draw the ends of the arrows representing activities "B" and "C" to the same circle. Why? Because they must have a common end event to show that "D" can begin only after you complete "B" and "C." Let's take a simple example. Suppose that "D" is "Stuffing and mailing envelopes." You can't do that unless you have the addressed envelopes and the letters or flyers

FIGURE 7-24 • Answer to PERT Exercise 2

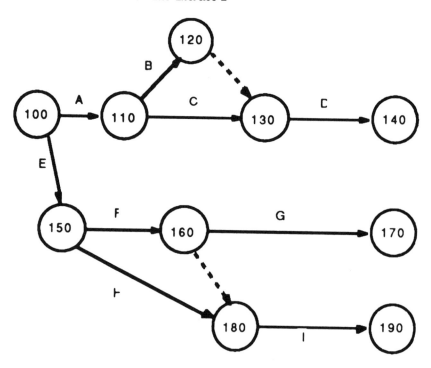

that you are going to put in them. So, "B" might be "Putting address labels on the envelopes," and "C" might be "Running off copies of the material that you are going to stuff in the envelopes." You can't do "D" until "B" and "C" are done.

However, according to the rules of PERT diagramming, you may not draw parallel lines between the same two circles, as in the diagram in Figure 7-25 (see also Fig. 7-9). Therefore, you have to draw one of the two activities ("B" or "C") to a separate end point. Then you must draw a dummy from that end point to the end point of the other activity, as shown in Figure 7-26.

This is relatively simple. However, in the "E" branch (including events 100, 150, 160, 170, 180, and 190) you have to think about a second issue in drawing your dummy activity arrow. This is an issue you didn't have to think about in the "A" branch. In the "A" branch you could have drawn the dummy arrow in either direction, as shown in Figure 7-27.

You can choose to divide either Activity B or Activity C into a real activity (110-120) and a dummy activity (120-130). Whichever you decide, the logic does not change. The diagram still says that you have to complete activies B and C no matter where you draw the dummy arrow. In branch

FIGURE 7-25 • *No Two Activities with the Same Pair of Numbers in a PERT Diagram*

FIGURE 7-26 • *Using a Dummy Activity to Avoid Having the Same Pair of Numbers in a PERT Diagram*

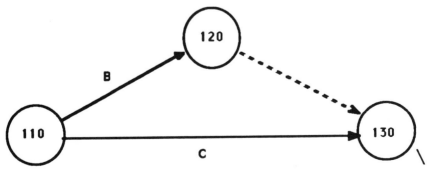

FIGURE 7-27 • *Sometimes There Is a Choice about Where to Draw the Dummy*

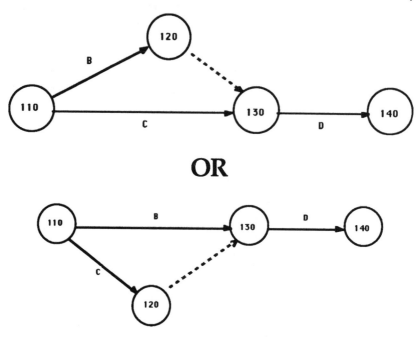

OR

"E," however, the situation is different. This is because of Activity G. Why is this?

Activity I (Fig. 7-23) is like the last activity (Activity D) in branch "A." You can't begin it until you have completed both Activity F and Activity H. However, this is not true of Activity G. It is true that you have to finish Activity F before you can begin Activity G, but you don't have to do Activity H before you do Activity G. If you draw the dummy from 180 to 160 (i.e., from the end of Activity H to the end of Activity F, instead of the other way around), you change the logic of the diagram, unless you also reverse the locations of activities G and I. The point is that the direction of the dummy arrow is important (see also Fig. 7-10 and the discussion on p. 00).

Exercises 3 and 4

The diagrams for Exercise 3 and Exercise 4 are shown in Figure 7-28 and Figure 7-29.

FIGURE 7-28 • *Answer to PERT Exercise 3*

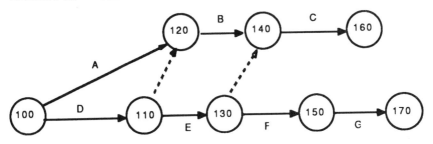

FIGURE 7-29 • *Answer to PERT Exercise 4*

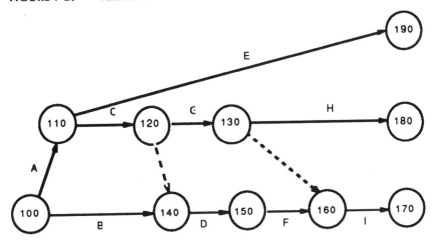

Recapitulation

In this chapter you learned how to draw PERT diagrams. The "Catch the Train" example was used to illustrate basic techniques. Through this example you saw how you can group activities in subsystems. You saw how you can draw PERT diagrams showing the sequencing of activities in subsystems. You also saw how you can combine subsystem PERT diagrams to show sequences of activities for the whole project. We provided a set of general guidelines for you and illustrated the use of dummy activities. We illustrated using dummy activities to help with numbering and to present more clearly the logical flow of activities. Moran's work illustrated how in a corporate project you could group activities into subsystems and how you could combine subsystem diagrams to form PERT diagrams for a whole project. The PERT exercises tested your growing knowledge of PERT concepts and afforded you the chance to solidify your technical skills.

Doing Your Own Project

At the end of Chapter 6 your project task was to go through your activity index cards and group your project activities into subsystems. You then formulated an index in which you listed all your activities under their respective subsystem headings.

The next step is to work with your activity index cards on a table or on the floor. Work with each subsystem separately. Lay out your index cards to show which activities in that subsystem must be done in what order. Very likely, some activities and sequences of activities can be done at the same time as others. When you are satisfied that you have your activities in an order that will work, draw a PERT diagram for each subsystem.

Remember that each subsystem will have its own number series (i.e., 100, 200, etc.) and that each card on the floor or table will be represented by an arrow in the PERT diagram. You will have to draw circles between the arrows and number them. In doing this, follow the guidelines and examples we have given you.

You should show in your numbering where activities in one subsystem connect to later subsystems. Choose either of the two alternative subsystem numbering systems and stick with it throughout your PERT diagram. Be consistent.

Finally, combine all your subsystem diagrams into a single PERT diagram for your project. See Moran's PERT index (Fig. 7-21) and diagram (Fig. 7-22) as illustrations of how to do this.

CHAPTER EIGHT

Project Time Management

It is widely agreed that time is money. Often you must complete your project on time for financial reasons. Sometimes there are other reasons, which commonly have to do with politics, pride, or being seen as a competent manager. Concern for time is prevalent in modern industrial cultures. It is often important to be able to estimate in advance how long a project is likely to take. Once you know your deadlines, you can monitor your project to be as certain as possible that you complete it on schedule.

You are already familiar with the idea of a PERT diagram, having worked with diagramming in the last two chapters. However, up until now we have focused on it as a tool for figuring out and displaying the sequence of activities in your project. Now we would like to introduce you to PERT diagramming as a tool for time management.

PERT diagramming is a basic tool for structuring time estimates. Together with slack tables and Gantt diagrams,[1] PERT diagrams are commonly used to develop and update project timetables, to display them to different audiences, and to monitor projects over time. The length of a project depends on how long it takes to do each of the project's individual activities. You must make a judgment about every activity in your PERT diagram. This lengthy work is strictly empirical. You base your time estimates upon past experience with different project activities or with similar activities. You also use information gathered from contractors and others with relevant experience.

The time estimates for your project can be no better than your artistry in collecting information and making time estimates for individual project activities. We cannot overemphasize the importance of these activity time estimates and the care required to make them. However, specific procedures for estimating how long individual activities are likely to take are beyond the scope of this book. They vary among projects and industries. You must consider detailed situational conditions. These include all reasonable sources of delay, such as scheduling problems, labor unrest, and necessary rework.

The Slack Table

A basic tool for managing a project in relation to time deadlines is the slack table. A slack table is a project timetable that includes four elements:

1. The event numbers taken from the PERT diagram. Each event is represented on the diagram by a numbered circle. You build a time schedule for the project around these events.
2. Your estimated time of arrival at each event (T_E). These are based on your time estimates for your project activities (t_e's). Be sure that your t_e's are in whole numbers (i.e., no fractions) and that the time unit for all your t_e's is the same (i.e., don't mix weeks and days). If you find that you are doing your time estimates in weeks and that you have some fractional t_e's, do the estimates in days instead. Remember, too, that time estimates have to allow for all kinds of delays. The analogy that comes to mind is a football game. The actual playing time is exactly one hour. However, as anyone knows who has watched a football game, or waited for one to be over, it usually takes about 3 hours to play the game. Following the analogy, the t_e for the typical football game would be 3 hours, not 1 hour. Similarly, if you are planning to call several people to set up a meeting, you could probably do it in a half hour. In reality, though, it might take several days to find people in and to get them to call you back. Thus, the t_e for that activity would likely be 3 days, not 30 minutes. Also, if you're making your time estimates in days, it's usually a good idea to use 1 day as your minimum time estimate for any activity.
3. The latest "on-time" date for reaching each of those points in the project (T_L).
4. The amount of extra time, (or "slack" time), you have at each point in the project. Slack time is the difference at each event between the latest on-time time (T_L) and your estimated time of arrival (T_E).

To construct a slack-time table, you need the following:

1. A PERT diagram for the project.
2. Time estimates [t_e's] for the individual project activities represented in the PERT diagram.
3. The specified time for the entire project (T_S). The specified time is a number of days or weeks. This is the amount of time, given your project deadline, that you have to complete the project.

With these in hand, it is possible to calculate for every event in the PERT diagram three pieces of information:

1. The estimated time of arrival at each event (T_E)
2. The latest required time of arrival at each event (T_L)
3. The slack time at each event ($T_L - T_E$).

Calculating Estimated Time of Arrival (T_E) at Each Event

Calculation Rules
The rules for calculating the estimated time of arrival at each successive point in the project are as follows:

1. T_E's are calculated successively moving forward from the start event.
2. Initially, the start event is called the "old event." The T_E at the start event always equals zero.
3. The next event whose T_E is being calculated is called the "new event."
4. When there is only one activity leading into the new event, its T_E equals the T_E of the old event plus the time estimate [t_e] of the activity. The new event is then relabeled "old event," once its T_E has been calculated.
5. When there is more than one activity leading into the new event, calculate the T_E of the new event in all possible ways and then use the highest value as the T_E of the new event.
6. Proceed in this fashion until you have calculated the T_E of the end event. When you have completed this task, you will have a T_E for every event in the PERT diagram.

Figure 8-1 shows a PERT diagram developed by one of our workshop participants, George Watson. We will present the entire diagram and then take small parts of it to explain how to calculate T_E's (estimated times of completion), T_L's (latest required times of completion), and slack times. The PERT diagram for Watson's entire project (Fig. 8-1) represents all the project activities as arrows between numbered circles, and it shows the estimated times required for the individual activities as numbers on the arrows. You may also want to look at his subsystem index (Fig. 8-2), which will give you a sense of the substance of Watson's project.

An Example of Calculating T_E's
Now let us take one portion of Watson's activity network, as diagrammed in Figure 8-3. What is the T_E of event 180? This is an interesting problem because there are two paths leading into event 150, which precedes event 180. We must calculate the time estimates along both these paths and then use as the T_E of event 150 the highest value calculated. There are three subsequent paths between events 150 and 180. We must calculate the time estimates along these paths, again taking the highest as the T_E of event 180.

FIGURE 8-1 · *Watson's PERT Diagram*

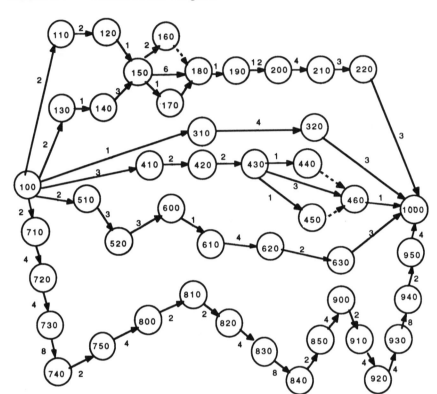

Proceeding from top to bottom along the two possible paths leading into event 150, you can calculate the T_E's for the various events as follows.

First, the T_E at event 100 (the start event) is given as 0. We now have to track two paths to event 150, each of which is made up of activities with different time estimates. One of the paths is 100-110-120-150. The other is 100-130-140-150.

There are three activities on the first path to 150: 100-110, 110-120, and 120-150. The time estimates for these activities are 2 weeks, 2 weeks, and 1 week, respectively. Adding these times together produces one possible value of the T_E at event 150: 5 weeks.

There are also three activities on the second path to 150: 100-130, 130-140, and 140-150. The time estimates for these activities are 2 weeks, 1 week, and 3 weeks, respectively. Adding these times together produces a second possible value for the T_E at event 150: 6 weeks. Which of these two values is the correct one? The logic is as follows:

FIGURE 8-2 · *Watson's Subsystem Index*

100 Subsystem:	Developing and Implementing the Applications Analyst's Toolbox
200 Subsystem:	Obtaining Computer Based Training for All Vendor Supplied Software
300 Subsystem:	Planning and Implementing Bi-Monthly Staff Meetings for Application Analysts
400 Subsystem:	Establishing an Approved Plan for the Attendance at Vendor-User Conferences
500 Subsystem:	Developing and Implementing Procedures for the Generation of Preliminary Studies
600 Subsystem:	Developing and Implementing Procedures for the Generation of Technical Reviews
700 Subsystem:	Evaluating Alternatives and Acquiring File Maintenance Software
800 Subsystem:	Evaluating Alternatives and Acquiring Report Generating Software
900 Subsystem:	Evaluating Alternatives and Acquiring Application Generating Software

Activities along the two paths, which are parallel paths, can be worked on at the same time. However, the time estimate (T_E) at event 150 must be high enough to allow for all the activities to be completed up to that point, along both paths. Therefore, the correct value of the T_E at event 150 must be 6 weeks, since this will allow enough time to complete the 6-week path (100-130-140-150), as well as the 5-week path (100-110-120-150).

We now know that the T_E at event 150 is 6 weeks. Knowing the T_E at event 150, what is the T_E at event 180? To figure the T_E at event 180, we must add the estimated activity times along each of three further parallel paths: (1) 150-160-180, (2) 150-180, and (3) 150-170-180. The correct value of the T_E at event 180 will then be 6 weeks (the T_E at 150) plus the estimated time along the longest of the three activity paths between 150 and 180. The time estimates aslong the first path from 150 to 180 are 2 weeks for activity 150-160 and zero for the dummy activity (160-180).

Consistent with our earlier explanation of dummy activities, the dummy activity 160-180 is used only to avoid having two activities labeled with the same beginning and ending numbers, 150-180. Thus, a "make-believe" activity is created in the diagram to avoid this ambiguity. Since "activity" 160-180 is not a real activity, it has neither real work nor real time associated with it. Therefore, the t_e (activity time estimate) for 160-180 is zero.

Adding the time estimates along this path: 6 weeks (at 150), 2 weeks, plus 0 weeks (for the dummy) gives us a possible T_E at event 180 of 8 weeks. Adding the time estimates aslong the second path (150-180) gives 6 weeks

FIGURE 8-3 • Watson's 100 Subsystem

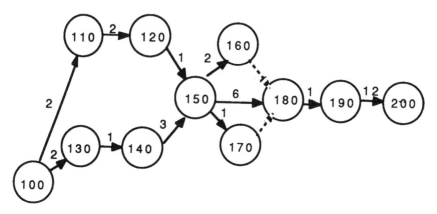

(at 150) plus 6 more weeks (150-180), for a total of 12 weeks as a possible T_E at event 180. The third path produces values of 6 weeks (at 150) plus 1 week (150-170) plus 0 weeks (another dummy activity, 170-180), for a total of 7 weeks as the third possible value of the T_E at event 180.

As already discussed, the time estimate must allow enough time to complete all the activities along all the paths to any point in the diagram. Therefore, we must take the highest of the three possible values as the correct value for the T_E at event 180. Thus, the correct value is 12 weeks. This is the T_E along the longest path to event 180: 100-130-140-150-180. Actually, this path is the longest of six possible paths to event 180 in the PERT diagram:

1. 100-110-120-150-160-180
2. 100-110-120-150-180
3. 100-110-120-150-170-180
4. 100-130-140-150-160-180
5. 100-130-140-150-180
6. 100-130-140-150-170-180

Calculating the Latest Required Time of Arrival (T_L) at Each Event

Calculation Rules

Here, again, the procedure is clear. However, instead of working forward to calculate the T_L's, we must begin with the specified time for the project (T_S) and work backward.

1. T_L's are calculated successively moving backward from the end event (if there is only one, or from each of the end events, if there are more than one).
2. Initially, the end event is called the "old event." The T_L at the end event always equals the specified time for the project (T_S).
3. The next event whose T_L is being calculated is called the "new event."
4. Where there is only one activity leading back into the new event, its T_L equals the T_L of the old event minus the time estimate [t_e] of the activity. The new event is then relabeled "old event," once its T_L has been calculated.
5. When there is more than one activity leading back into the new event, calculate the T_L of the new event all possible ways and then use the lowest value as the T_L of the new event.
6. Proceed in this fashion until you have calculated the T_L of the start event. At this point you will have a T_L for every event in the PERT diagram.

An Example of Calculating T_L's

What is the T_L of event 430 in the portion of Watson's PERT diagram shown in Figure 8-4?

This is a problem because there are three paths leading back into event 430. We must calculate the T_L's of all events from the end event (1000) back to event 430 and then use as the T_L of event 430 the lowest value calculated. Take as given (from Watson) that the specified time for the project T_S is 82 weeks.

Following the rules, we take this value for T_L of event 1000 (the end event). Thus, the T_L of 1000 = 82. The T_L of 460 = 82 − 1 = 81. Now there are three paths leading back from event 460 to event 430: 460-440-430, 460-430, and 460-450-430.[2] When we add up the time estimates for the activities along these three paths, we obtain the following results as possible values of the T_L at event 430:

FIGURE 8-4 • *Another Portion of Watson's PERT Diagram*

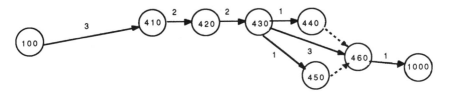

1. 460-440-430: 81 − 0 − 1 = 80 weeks
2. 460-430: 81 − 3 = 78 weeks
3. 460-450-430: 81 − 0 − 1 = 80 weeks

Which is the correct value of the T_L at event 430? The lowest value, of course. Thus, the correct value for the latest allowable time for the project to be finished up to event 430 in the PERT diagram is 78 weeks.

This may seem strange to you if you look carefully at the rest of the diagram, especially if you look at the activity path from the start event (100) to event 430. You will see that the T_E for event 430 — that is, the time it is expected to take to do activities 100-410-420-430, which is the longest path to event 430 — is only 7 weeks. How can the PERT diagram suggest that you have up to 78 weeks to do what you estimate will take only 7 weeks to do?

It may seem strange, but it is true. What you are seeing is an example of a lot of *slack time*. Watson has 71 weeks of slack time at event 430. What this means is that there could be up to 71 weeks of delays in doing the activities in the 400 subsystem without taking the project beyond the 82 weeks specified for it. This is partly because the specified time (T_S) for the project is generous. It allows 12 weeks beyond the 70 weeks Watson estimated that it will actually take to complete the project. However, most of the slack time exists because there is little work to do in the 400 subsystem compared to other parts of the total project. Only 11 weeks are needed to complete the 400 subsystem, many fewer than are required to complete the path that includes the 700, 800, and 900 subsystems (see Fig. 8-1). This parallel path requires 70 weeks to complete. Extra slack time always occurs on parallel paths that require less time to complete than alternate parallel paths.

Calculating Slack Time at Each Event

Remember that the two major purposes of network analysis are:

- To make clear exactly what activities form the project and how they are sequenced over time to achieve the desired results
- To establish a clear relationship between the estimated time needed for the various activities and the established project deadlines

Explicit descriptions of individual project activities and their sequences help in performing several key management functions. These include:

- Assigning managerial responsibilities for activities
- Formulating a project budget
- Developing an effective information system to support decisions made during the project

With a clear picture of the time requirements and time relationships across all project activities, planners have a basis for monitoring project progress over time. They can also set and review important milestones. Finally, they can evaluate their options whenever a reallocation of resources seems necessary. Of course, there is always the possibility that unanticipated events will force a change, even in the best of plans. It is important to monitor actual progress systematically and review time estimates. Sometimes managers must shift priorities as slowdowns create critical time problems where they did not exist before.

The concept of slack time is useful in planning, monitoring, and reviewing project progress along the multiple paths of the project network described by the PERT diagram. Monitoring slack time is an important dimension of network analysis. Indeed, it is a concept associated more with the network itself than with specific project activities. We speak of slack time along one of the networks of paths that make up a project. The more slack time along a path, the more "extra time" there is as a cushion to cover any unexpected delays along that particular path. Although it is often the case that two paths may have some or even many activities in common, no two paths through the project network are exactly alike.

You have seen that some paths have much less slack time (in relation to the specified date for completing the project) than others. Sometimes, in fact, slack time may be negative (i.e., less than zero). Negative slack times indicate that the estimated time of completing the project is greater than the time specified for it. For example, in Watson's project, slack time along the critical path is 12 weeks. As noted earlier, this is because he has 82 weeks to complete a project he estimates will require only 70 weeks. Imagine, however, that he had been given only 65 weeks to do the same project. Then he would be 5 weeks late from the start. Slack time along the critical path would be -5 weeks (i.e., negative 5 weeks) to show this lateness. This is not unusual. Frequently in our experience we have been part of projects that "started late" in the sense that from the very beginning few people thought they could be finished on time. In general, the less slack time available along a path, the more critical it becomes to manage time effectively for activities along that path. There are two basic reasons for this:

- Any delays that occur along the critical path can be expected to extend the time it takes to complete the project. Delays where there is more slack time are less critical. Since there are often costs associated with failing to bring a project to completion on time — financial costs, political costs, or costs to one's career — managers usually want to avoid being late. Typically an exception to this is when they think that the costs of additional resources needed to bring the project in on time are greater than the perceived costs of being late. This is almost always a judgment call.

- Any time that can be saved along the critical path will reduce the total time it will take to complete the project.

Therefore, you should periodically monitor the slack time at each point in the project network. Furthermore, you should consider the managerial implications of changes in slack time based on current project data. Should you, for example, reallocate resources from activities and subsystems where there is more slack time to those that have the least slack time? Of course, moving staff members from one part of a project to another is easier and less costly when they have been cross-trained and are able to perform a wide range of organizational functions. When staff members possess highly specialized knowledge and skills, it is harder to reallocate their time from one task to another.

In the previous section of this chapter, we explained a method for calculating T_E's and T_L's and discussed the concepts involved. T_L's are useful to the manager in and of themselves in that they provide a project timetable for activities, similar to a train schedule. The railroad engineer knows at each intermediate station whether the train is on time and can consider ways to make up time if necessary. In a similar way the project manager can monitor the completion of project activities against the list of latest times for completing those activities [T_L's]. Each checkpoint becomes a place to consider whether you need to make adjustments to speed up the project.

Of course, good management practice does not necessarily dictate that you must make adjustments to keep a project on time. You will have to assess the nature and wisdom of specific adjustments, or of any adjustments at all. You can evaluate the comparative costs of the options for keeping the project on time against the financial or political costs of being late.

Putting the Numbers into a Slack Table

Slack tables constitute a specific tool for monitoring project progress. They allow you to estimate initial slack times along various paths in the project network. They also provide a format for tracking the project against updated information over time.

Note in Watson's slack table (shown in Figure 8-5) that for each event in the project network, the table shows three figures:

1. The latest allowable time (T_L)
2. The estimated time (T_E)
3. The slack time

FIGURE 8-5 · *Watson's Slack Table*

EVENTS	T_L	T_E	SLACK TIME.
100	12	0	12*
110	50	2	48
120	52	4	48
130	49	2	47
140	50	3	47
150	53	6	47
160	59	8	51
170	59	7	52
180	59	12	47
190	60	13	47
200	72	25	47
210	76	29	47
220	79	32	47
310	75	1	74
320	79	5	74
410	74	3	71
420	76	5	71
430	78	7	71
440	81	8	73
450	81	8	73
460	81	10	71
510	66	2	64

Continued

FIGURE 8-5 *Continued*

520	69	5	64
610	73	9	64
620	77	13	64
630	79	15	64
710	14	2	12*
720	18	6	12*
730	22	10	12*
740	30	18	12*
750	32	20	12*
800	36	24	12*
810	38	26	12*
820	40	28	12*
830	44	32	12*
840	52	40	12*
850	54	42	12*
900	58	46	12*
910	60	48	12*
920	64	52	12*
930	68	56	12*
940	76	64	12*
950	78	66	12*
1000	82	70	12*

The asterisks in the column designating slack time mark the events along the critical path. Note that slack time $= T_L - T_E$ in each case and that events along the critical path are consistently those with the least slack time (in this instance, 12 weeks).

You have already seen how to calculate the T_L and the T_E. Once you perform these calculations, you can determine the slack time by subtracting, in each case, the T_E from the T_L (i.e., slack time = $T_L - T_E$). Examine the table to see how simple this operation is. The path most critical to the project manager is that with the least slack time. Thus, this path is called the *critical path*. Asterisks mark this path in the slack table. Sometimes a project will have more than one critical path.

An Example of a Slack Table

Watson's slack table (Fig. 8-5) corresponds to his PERT diagram (Fig. 8-1). For each of the events indicated, from the start event (100) to the end event (1000), it shows the T_L, the T_E, and the slack time at that event. In each case the slack time equals the T_L minus the T_E. Calculations are based on the activity time estimates (t_e's) shown in the PERT diagram. The times shown are in weeks. Asterisks mark the critical path.

Slack Table Exercise

Directions: Use the information shown on the PERT diagram in Figure 8-6. The numbers on the arrows indicate the time estimates (t_e's), in weeks, for the project activities. The specified time (T_S) for the project is 40 weeks. Construct a slack table showing, for each event, the latest allowable time (T_L), the estimated time of arrival (T_E), and the slack time at each event. Note that the dotted arrows show dummy activities. Assume that the start time

FIGURE 8-6 • *Slack Table Exercise*

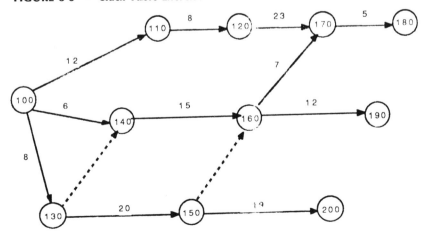

for the project equals 0. Mark with asterisks the slack times in your slack table that lie along the critical path (See the answer at the end of the chapter.)

Gantt Diagramming

Network analysis is one approach to program evaluation and review, and PERT diagramming can give you a good understanding of how it works, which is why we have given a thorough explanation and included some exercises. However, with today's computer software to perform the calculations, make the updates, do the record keeping, and format the reports, hand calculations are no longer necessary. With computer support systems readily available to simplify the use of PERT diagramming, network analysis remains a basic tool for project design and control. Still, PERT diagrams are not always the best way to display project information, particularly to top policy makers, prospective funders, and lay audiences.

The PERT diagrams give a precise picture of the configuration and timing of project activities. In this regard they are unsurpassed as management tools. However, because of the detail they provide, PERT diagrams are complex in form and can appear dense and difficult to many audiences. Even sophisticated observers often cannot devote the time to absorb in detail the information contained in a complex PERT diagram.

An Alternative Way to Communicate Time Factors

One useful alternative, simpler in form, for displaying information to certain audiences about project subsystems or activities and time schedules is the Gantt diagram. The basic purpose of Gantt diagrams is to locate project activities in relation to project calendars. In such diagrams each activity is shown as a horizontal bar against a project calendar specified below.

The simple diagram in Figure 8-7 shows a single activity against a project timeline displayed in months. Note that the activity shown begins at one point in time, ends at another, and takes the indicated time interval to complete. Designation of the month is by first initial only. This activity is scheduled to begin in July and is expected to take until April to complete. The total

FIGURE 8-7 · *A Simple Gantt Diagram*

M   A   M   J   J   A   S   O   N   D   J   F   M   A   M   J   J   A.

project time is shown as 18 months, from March of one year through August of the next. The particular activity shown occupies some portion of the total project time.

How to Draw Gantt Diagrams

In Figure 8-7 the activity is unidentified. In practice the activity bar would be coded in some way — in words, color, or graphic design — to show classes of activities as distinct from one another. For example, the 400 subsystem in Watson's project deals with establishing an approved plan for attendance at what he calls vendor/user conferences. The 300 subsystem deals with planning and implementing bi-monthly staff meetings for application analysts. The two subsystems, like others in Watson's project, can be implemented simultaneously; neither subsystem is dependent on the other. On a Gantt diagram, activities in these sequences could be coded to show at a glance which had to do with the attendance plan and which with the bi-monthly staff meetings.

Figure 8-8 illustrates such a diagram. The rules for sequencing activities in a Gantt diagram are simple:

1. Those activities that begin earliest are located at the top of the chart.
2. Later activities are located further down in the diagram.
3. Whenever two activities start at the same time, put the shorter activity first. Compare activities 100-310, 100-420, and 100-410 in Figure 8-8. Also, compare activities 420-430 and 320-1000 in the same figure. Placing the activities in the diagram according to these rules provides an easy visual flow to follow. This flow takes the form of a broad sweep from the upper left to the lower right.
4. Label each bar with the activity title. Sometimes it is also helpful to show the PERT number of the activity along with its title.
5. Include a project calendar above and below the activity bars. The calendar should show that part of the project time line covered by the activities shown in the diagram. Depending on your purposes, you may show all or only a portion of the entire project timeline. The only rule in this regard is that the time interval you show on the calendar must be continuous (without gaps).
6. Also include a key with the diagram (shown in Fig. 8-8 below the calendar) if you have coded your activities by color, shading, or graphic design. As indicated in the accompanying key, the activities in Figure 8-8 that are part of Watson's 300 subsystem are shown in black, while those from the 400 subsystem are represented in white.

FIGURE 8-8 · *An Illustrative Gantt Diagram of Two Subsystems of Watson's High-Tech Development Project*

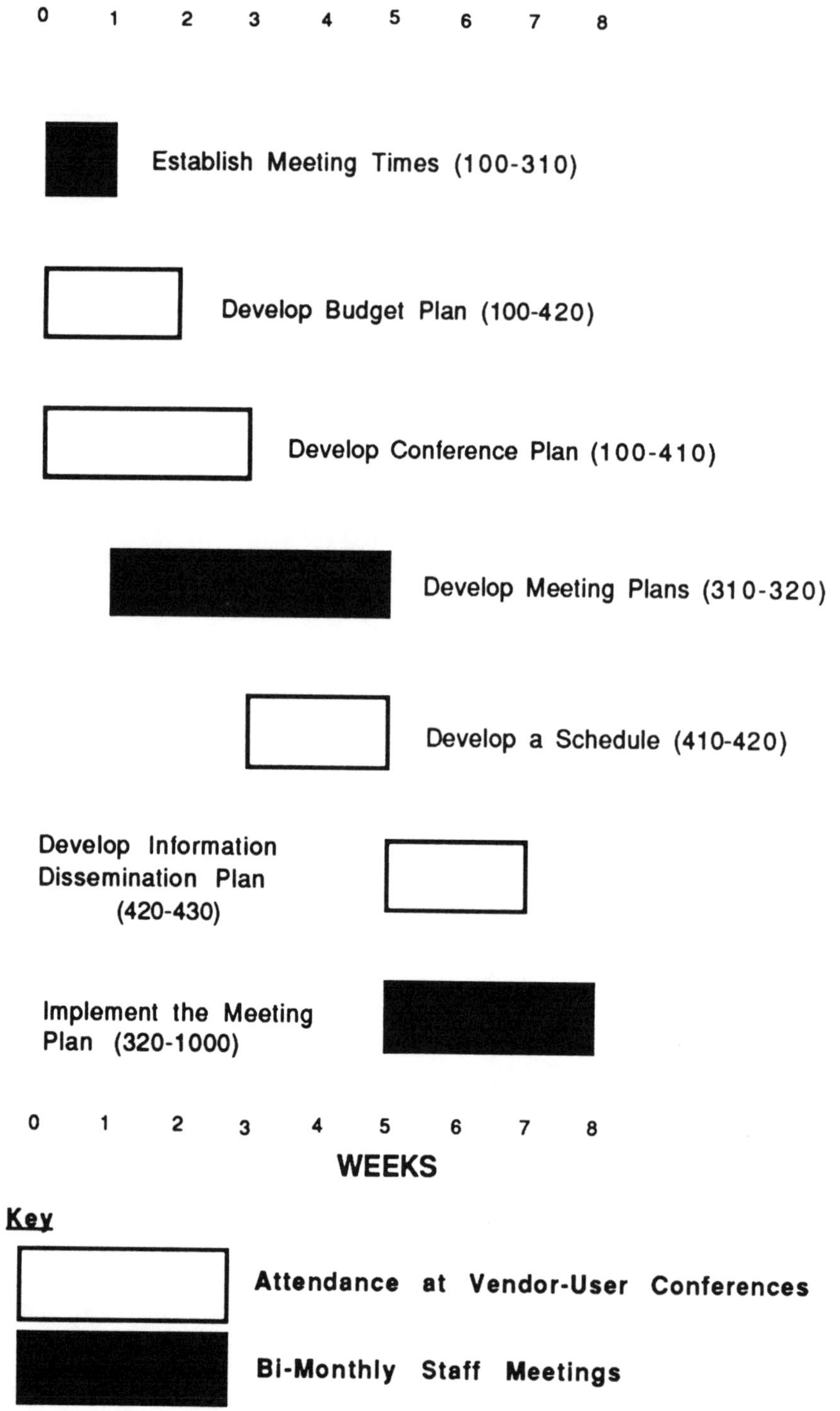

A sample worksheet (Fig. 8-9) accompanies our example Gantt diagram. This worksheet summarizes the relevant information about activities related to the attendance plan and about activities related to the bi-monthly staff meetings. It includes information about the time periods during which the activities will be carried out and about the nature of the activities. The Gantt diagram displays this information in visual form. For different audiences and for different purposes, a Gantt diagram may show project subsystems, all project activities, or only selected subsets of project activities. Figure 8-8 displays selected activities from each of two project subsystems.

Recapitulation

In this chapter you have learned how to make slack tables and Gantt diagrams. Learning how to make PERT diagrams gave you a way to organizing your project activities and subsystems sequentially. Now you also have the tools for planning, managing, and communicating about time schedules for the project. The next step is to get inside of subsystems and activities. You need tools for thinking about and displaying information about detailed processes within subsystems. The next chapter will teach you about flow diagramming ideas and techniques. These will help you focus your attention on the micro-processes that are at the heart of accomplishing your goals.

FIGURE 8-9 • *Illustrative Worksheet for a Gantt Diagram*

Activities to Establish an Approved Plan for Attendance at Vendor/User Conferences		
Activity Number	Weeks Scheduled	Activity
100-420	1-2	Develop Budget Plan
100-410	1-3	Develop Conference Plan
410-430	4-5	Develop a Schedule
420-430	6-7	Develop an Information Dissemination Plan
Planning and Implementing Bi-Monthly Staff Meetings for Application Analysts		
Activity Number	Weeks Scheduled	Activity
100-310	1	Establish Meeting Times
310-320	2-5	Develop Meeting Plans
320-1000	6-8	Implement the Meeting Plan

Answer to the Slack Table Exercise

The calculations from which the slack table in Figure 8-10 was constructed are shown on the original PERT diagram (Fig. 8-11). Note that the slack time along the critical path (100-110-120-170-180) is negative. This indicates that the project is estimated to be running 8 days late. The slack times along the critical path are designated in the slack table by asterisks (*). The slack table shows also that other parts of the subsystem are expected to run 7 days late (− 7 days slack time). Still other segments are on time (zero slack time) or ahead of schedule (5 days slack time).

Doing Your Own Project

Now you are ready to use your project PERT diagram not only to represent the sequencing of project activities but also to make a project timetable. The slack table is such a timetable. You will base your calculations on how much time you think it will take to do each of your project activities (t_e's). Your slack table will show at what point in time (project days or weeks) you should have completed what activities (T_E's). It will give you an idea of whether the project is on time or not (slack time) and at what points in the project time is most critical (critical path). Thus, your slack table helps you to estimate how

FIGURE 8-10 • The Slack Table for the Slack Table Exercise

EVENTS	T_L	T_E	SLACK TIME
100	-8	0	-8*
110	4	12	-8*
120	12	20	-8*
130	1	8	-7
140	13	8	5
150	21	28	-7
160	28	28	0
170	35	43	-8*
180	40	48	-8*
190	40	40	0
200	40	47	-7

FIGURE 8-11 • *The Calculations of the T_L's and T_E's on the Slack Table Exercise PERT Diagram*

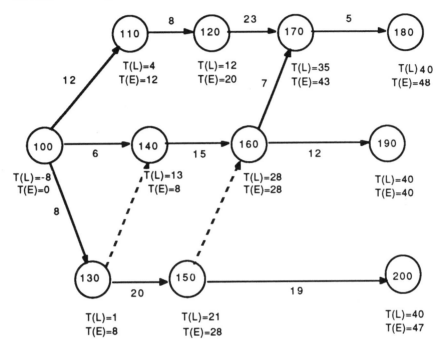

likely it is that you can complete a proposed project within given time limits. It provides a basis for thinking about the possibilities of redesigning critical project activities and staffing the project more efficiently. It will also help you to monitor whether the project is on schedule and to make the management decisions needed to keep it on time. You also know how to make a Gantt diagram. Gantt diagrams are simple tools for showing various audiences when you have scheduled different subsystems and activities.

Project Activities

1. Prepare a slack table for your entire project based on your PERT diagram.
2. Construct a Gantt diagram showing the major subsystems of your project. Show all the subsystems as bars on the diagram. Be sure that the starting and ending dates of each subsystem are consistent with the T_E's shown on your slack table and with the activity time estimates (t_e's) shown on your PERT chart.

Notes

1. Henry Gantt developed the concept of representing project activities and subsystems as bar graphs displayed in relation to a timeline. Such displays have come to be known as Gantt diagrams.

2. An extended note discussing the similarities and differences between what we do to calculate T_E's and what we do to calculate T_L's is in order.

The path configuration here is similar to that in the previous example, the one in which we were figuring T_E's. However, in the T_E example we looked at the paths going from left to right in the diagram; here in the T_L example we are looking at the paths going from right to left.

When we were going from left to right, we were *adding time estimates* to calculate the T_E's. Since we had to allow enough time for doing all the activities along the *longest path,* we always chose the *highest possible value* among several paths to an event.

In figuring T_L's, the exact opposite is true. When we look at paths from right to left, backward from the end point of the PERT diagram, we *subtract* time estimates in calculating T_L's, instead of adding them.

In figuring the latest allowable time for the project to reach any particular point in the PERT diagram (T_L) — and still be on time — we are really thinking about how much time *we will need to have left* in order to finish the rest of the project from that point on. Therefore, when there are multiple activity paths between a particular event and the end of the project, we must allow enough time to do all the activities along *the longest path remaining.*

This implies that, when there are different possible values for the T_L, we should take *the lowest value* as the correct one. This, then, is the rule we shall follow: Where there are multiple activity paths between an event and the end of the project, subtract from right to left from the end point of the diagram. Take the lowest of the possible values as the correct value for the T_L at that event.

A PERT diagram can be drawn with a single end point, or sometimes with multiple end points. Just remember that the value of the T_L *at every end point* in the diagram is equal to the specified time for the project (T_S).

In calculating the T_L for a particular event in the PERT diagram, you may work from only one end point, or you may have to work from more than one. This depends on whether the activity paths from the particular event lead to one or more than one end point. In either case you will subtract activity time estimates along all possible paths and take *the lowest value* as the correct T_L for the particular event.

CHAPTER NINE

Describing Micro-Processes— Decision Flow Diagrams

While PERT diagrams and Gantt diagrams are extremely helpful in planning, they imply a simplifying assumption that can limit their usefulness in management. PERT and Gantt diagrams focus planners and managers on the sequence and timing of activities in a project. They allow them to anticipate variations around time estimates and to make calculations that take those variations into account. But they do not represent any of the contingencies that might cause variations in activity times.

You may be familiar with the concept of the inset map, which shows in more detail a particular place of interest. For example, a map of an entire country or region may show a blow-up of a particular city in the form of an inset map. Similarly, a city map may include an inset of the central zone that shows particular streets and intersections. Analogously, *decision flow diagrams* show in greater detail than PERT diagrams the course of subactivities, of contingencies and decision points, and of branch activities associated with these decision points. They represent visually the logical flow of activities to accomplish project objectives. They display critical decision points relative to action sequences.

The focus of the decision flow diagram is on the detailed workings that are deliberately left out of PERT and Gantt diagrams. PERT and Gantt diagrams focus on the overall activity flow and timing of the project. Decision flow diagrams direct attention to the specific choices that managers must make. They provide bases for (1) planning and monitoring alternative courses of action and (2) clarifying information needs to support decision making.

For example, a training program may provide different types of training to different students. Students may have different entry characteristics. Some may find certain skills or concepts difficult to learn. Decision flow diagrams can highlight alternative training sequences. They can emphasize the criteria for assigning students to different subprograms. They also highlight the need to have information for making decisions. In this chapter you will learn how to construct decision flow diagrams. Managing information to support activities and decisions is the subject of the next chapter.

Format

As you have learned, PERT and Gantt diagrams have particular formats and graphical symbols. Decision flow diagrams have different formats and graphics. As in PERT diagrams, there is a start point and an end point between which there is a flow of activities. However, in decision flow diagrams, the start and end points are identified by ovals labeled "Start" and "End" (see Fig. 9-1). Each activity is shown as a rectangle (see Fig. 9-2). Arrows are used to indicate sequence (see Fig. 9-3).

We define an activity as doing something, or engaging in a process. Activity "A" (Fig. 9-2 and 9-3) is unspecified. In actual planning situations your activities will have substantive labels, such as "Contact All Prospective Donors." You should use verbs to label activities because verbs describe action, which is what activities are all about. Notice the verb *contact* in the example given. Notice, too, that we use the imperative (or "command") form of the verb in formulating activity labels. Using only the symbols given so far, a sequence of activities could be represented as a sequence of boxes and arrows (see Fig. 9-4).

Notice that this graphic is entitled "A Simple Flow Diagram." It is not yet a decision flow diagram because, like a PERT diagram, it simply shows a sequence of activities (i.e., activity "A" followed by activity "B"). However, it makes no explicit representation of the choices that commonly characterize action plans. This representation requires another symbol, one that can represent decision points and allow for the indication of alternative courses of action (branches).

FIGURE 9-1 • *Start and End Symbols*

FIGURE 9-2 • *The Activity Symbol*

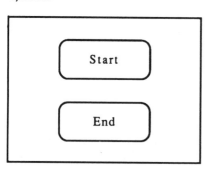

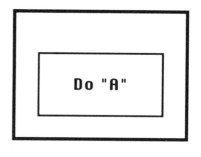

FIGURE 9-3 • *Arrows Showing Activity Flow*

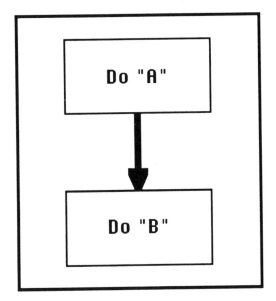

In decision flow diagramming the graphic symbol used to represent a decision point is a diamond with a question inside it (Fig. 9-5). When such a symbol is placed in the flow of activities, it constitutes a *branch point*. The symbol indicates that the process diagrammed will follow one course of action or another depending on the criterion implicit in the decisional question. In order for the process you are diagramming to work effectively, you must be clear about the criteria determining which branches to follow under what conditions.

The questions you put into the diamond-shaped decision symbols identify these criteria. They also suggest what information you will need to implement the decisions in practice.

Decision points in decision flow diagrams are like traffic lights. They describe junctures in your process where it may take different paths. For example, a decision point may describe the conditions under which you will continue to process an employment or admissions application or not. It may describe the conditions under which you will implement intensive supervision with a problem employee or finally dismiss the person. It may flag situations in which rocket-launching procedures may be halted, checks implemented, and the process continued or the mission scrubbed.

In a sense, decision flow diagrams are tools for describing standard operating procedures (SOPs). Representing SOPs in the form of these diagrams can help you to clarify exactly what your or your organization's

FIGURE 9-4 · *A Simple Flow Diagram*

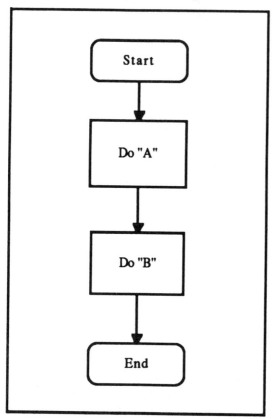

policies are and to communicate how they are supposed to work. As one of our students remarked, "I think this is one of the greatest things about decision flow diagrams, being able to take a real close look at how things are supposed to look." Diagramming processes while planning projects can help you to think them through and work out possible bugs.

The simple example in Figure 9-6 illustrates the function of a decision point in a decision flow diagram. Compare figures 9-6 and 9-4. Figure 9-6 differs conceptually in an important respect from Figure 9-4. Despite its simplicity, Figure 9-6 is a true decision flow diagram. In contrast to Figure 9-4, the flow of activities is no longer "automatic" and undifferentiated. In Figure 9-6 the answer to the question "Mastered Activity A?" determines whether or not the participant proceeds directly from activity A to activity B. If yes, proceed directly from A to B; if no, do C before doing B. The presence of the decision point also implies that information is needed in order to answer the question. In this case it is information about the participant's performance of activity A.

FIGURE 9-5 · *The Decision Point Symbol in a Decision Flow Diagram*

Figure 9-6 represents in microcosm the essentials of any decision flow diagram. It focuses planners and managers on the decisions to be made, the information required to make those decisions, and the consequences that follow. Thus, this simple diagram contains the essence of the logic of branching.

The initial part of Lower's decision flow diagram (Fig. 9-7) serves as a realistic example of the concepts explained so far. It includes a start point, several preliminary activities, and a decision point leading to two different courses of action (i.e., branches).

This partial decision flow diagram shows some of the initial elements of Lower's 300 subsystem, "Planning for a Comprehensive Cancer Program." In this part of her project she is trying to locate cost-effective models of diagnosing and treating cancer. She analyzes relevant data to assess the cost-effectiveness of models for treating different types of cancers. Based on this assessment, she makes a decision either to drop the program ("Go to End") or to continue planning. This diagram shows only that she prepares and submits a report to a planning task force if she has, in fact, located any cost-effective models.

Further Basic Concepts

A full discussion of the technical details in decision flow diagramming is beyond our purposes here. Nevertheless, five additional concepts are common and can be useful in planning and managing a project:

- Repeat loops
- "Escape" mechanisms

FIGURE 9-6 • *A True Decision Flow Diagram*

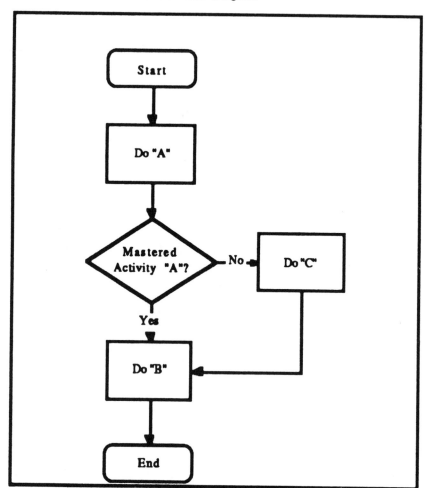

- Information "input" or "output" symbols
- "Go to" symbols
- Connector points

Repeat Loops

In describing a sequence of activities for a program, you will often find that you want to repeat certain actions until you have met some criterion. The partial decision flow diagram in Figure 9-8 illustrates a process for

FIGURE 9-7 • *A Partial Decision Flow Diagram of Lower's 300 Subsystem*

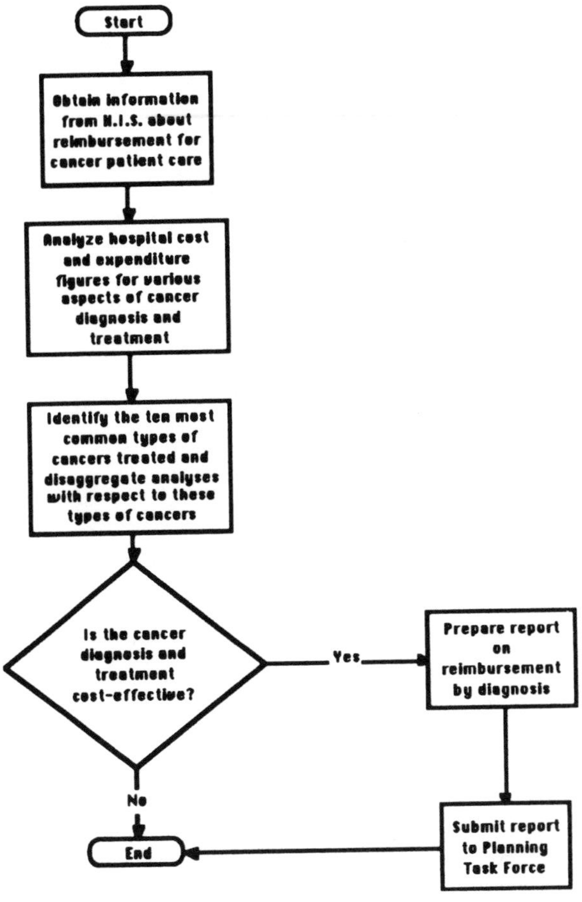

collecting information from a panel of experts. It represents a small part of de George's project. The process involves telephoning a number of experts to verify fifteen who are willing to be interviewed. De George puts together the initial list of experts before the diagrammed process begins.

The Escape Mechanism

In the previous example, de George telephones sequentially a group of experts from a list he has previously compiled. He telephones the next expert on the list when (1) the expert just called has declined an interview or (2) he has gotten an interview appointment with one of the experts but he is still short of fifteen on his interview list.

FIGURE 9-8 • *Using a Repeat Loop to Show a Process of Telephoning a Group of Experts*

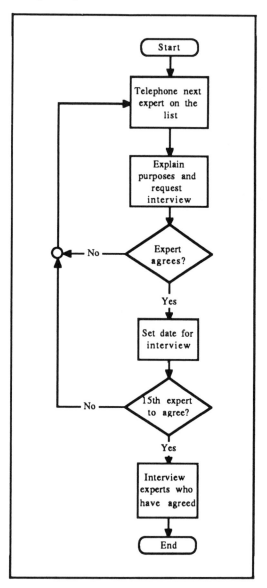

But how many calls should be made? The diagram indicates that de George will stop calling only after fifteen experts have agreed to interviews. Theoretically the telephoning could go on forever. However, de George felt confident that he would be able to get fifteen experts to agree to talk to him.

Otherwise, he might have needed to specify a second criterion for ending the telephoning process. The use of a second criterion for ending a repeat process in case the first criterion cannot be met is called an *escape mechanism*.

For example, de George might have decided that he would devote no more than a certain period of time to calling people on his list of experts. He might have said that he would continue calling only until he had gotten fifteen interview appointments or, failing that, until 1 month had passed. Or he might have decided to continue calling, if need be, until he had called all the experts on his list. If he had set this latter guideline as an escape criterion, he could have diagrammed the process as shown in Figure 9-9. Following the arrows in the diagram, you can see that after he has called the last expert on his list, de George goes on to interview those experts who have agreed even if they are fewer than fifteen.

Connector Points

Sometimes you will need to connect one arrow into the middle of another arrow. In the example shown in Figure 9-10, there is a performance check that follows two activities. If the performance is satisfactory, the process is over. However, if the performance is not satisfactory, another activity is added to the process and the performance is checked again. Since the process does not repeat doing "B," the diagramming must connect the arrow from doing "C" back into the arrow between doing "B" and the decision point that asks whether the performance is satisfactory. Using the connector point symbol makes the flow clear. You can see other examples of using connector points in later figures in this chapter.

Sequencing

Even though decision flow diagrams usually cover only part of a project, they can easily take up several pages. Visually, open space is important. People who view the diagram will find it easier to follow if it does not look cramped. here are some basic rules that have proved effective in sequencing the elements of a decision flow diagram.

Think first of a whole page as the "field" on which you will draw the diagram. Should it be necessary to put more information on a single page, think of the paper as divided into two or three subfields (see Fig. 9-11). Typically the choice of the number of fields per page depends on issues of cost, the need for clarity, and the psychological effects of crowding on a page. Determining factors may also include the relative complexity of the material presented and the relative sophistication and interest of the audience.

FIGURE 9-9 • *An Example of Using the Escape Mechanism*

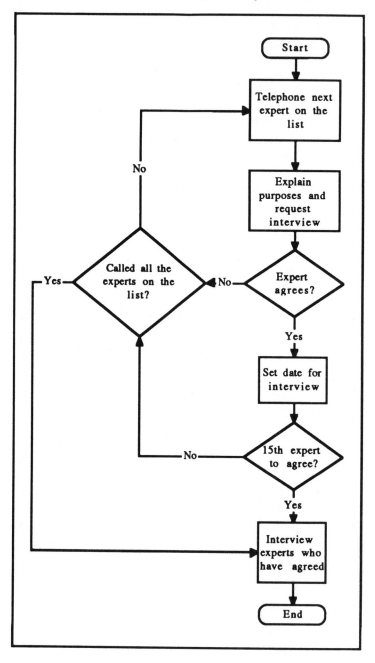

FIGURE 9-10 · *Using a Connector Point to Flow One Arrow into Another*

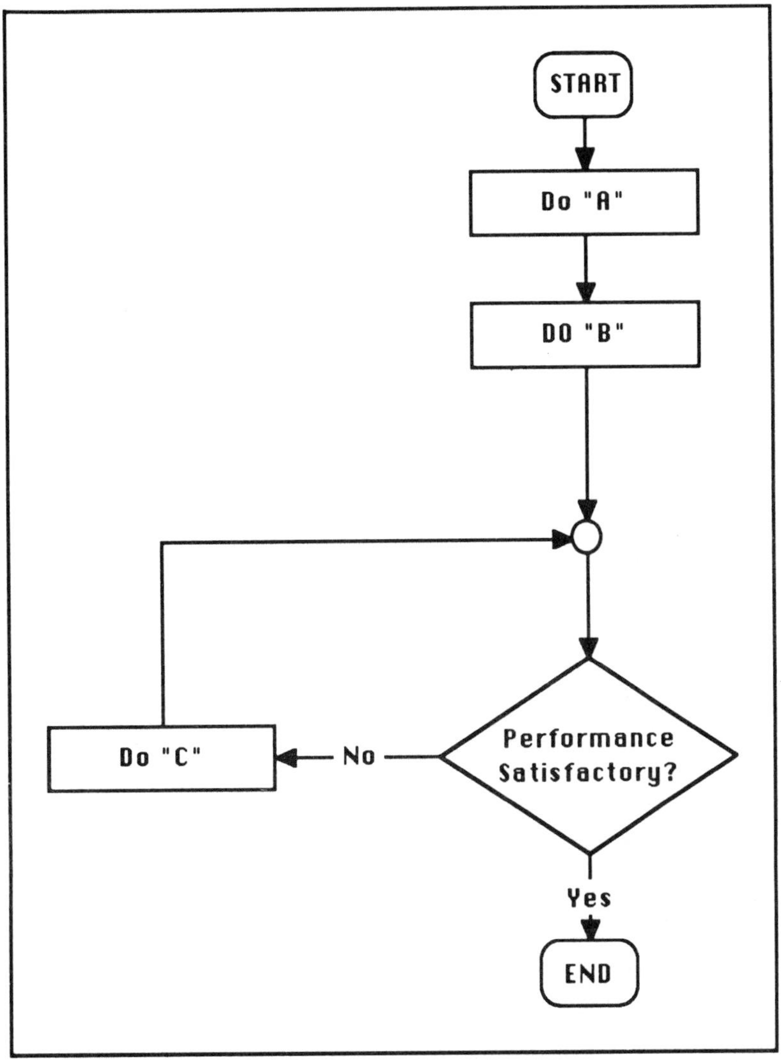

In general, the more branching you have in the process you are describing, the more complex the diagram will be. The more complex the diagram, the greater the importance of graphical clarity. If your audience is technically sophisticated and interested in the project, it will likely have more tolerance for complexity. In any case, we show our examples in a one-field-per-page

FIGURE 9-11 • *Different Numbers of Fields per Page*

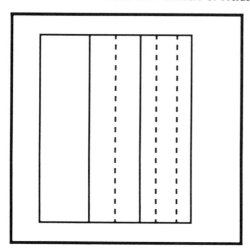

format. You can readily adapt your own work to a multiple-field format if you want to.

In preparing a decision flow diagram, there are three types of flow that must be considered graphically. The first is the main flow downward from one activity or decision point to another (e.g., see the left side of the diagram in Fig. 9-7). A second type of flow incorporates repeat loops that flow back and upward from a decision point to an earlier activity in the main flow of activities (e.g., see the left side of the diagram in Fig. 9-8). Finally, there are branches tht flow down and forward from a decision point to a later activity or decision point in the main flow of activities (e.g., see the right side of the diagrams in Fig. 9-6 and 9-7).

In general, there are clear rules for handling the graphics associated with these three types of flow within a field:

1. The main flow of activities and decision points is down the center of the field.
2. Repeat loops (i.e., branches that flow back and upward) are placed to the left of center.
3. Branches that flow down and forward from a decision point are placed to the right of center.

Graphics

Graphics do not always exactly fit the general rules. For example, one branch from a decision point could lead to a second decision point. A typical case in point is when you include an escape mechanism (e.g., see Fig. 9-9). An escape mechanism is always part of a repeat loop. Until either the original or the escape criterion is met (i.e., until either fifteen experts have agreed to be interviewed or 1 month has elapsed), the repeat loop is continued. This suggests that the piece of the diagram should go to the left.

However, after the escape criterion is met, the flow is shifted. This shift is usually forward in the flow, either to a later activity (e.g., see Fig. 9-9, "Interview Experts Who Have Agreed") or to "End" (if the project must be aborted). Thus, the general rules serve as useful guidelines; however, there will be occasions when adjustments must be made to fit the particular logic being diagrammed. As in Figure 9-9, we prefer to place a repeat loop to the left even where the branch also includes a down and forward component. Sometimes, however, some other graphics problem interferes. When this happens, you may end up putting a repeat loop to the right instead of to the left.

The "Go to" Symbol

So far the discussion of the three general rules has assumed that the flow of activities and decision points in all three subfields — main activities, repeat loops, and down-and-forward branches — is represented by directional arrows connecting one location to another without interruption. A person could literally move a finger directly along the arrows from one activity or decision point to another, forward or backward from one page to another. This is the ideal graphic presentation.

There are times, however, when it becomes cumbersome or messy to draw long arrows across several pages of a diagram and other times when, because of the complexity of a diagram, arrows begin to cross each other. Figure 9-12 shows a symbol for crossing lines. However, such crossings can make a diagram difficult to follow and for some audiences can present an unnecessary psychological barrier. An alternative to long and/or crossing lines in a decision flow diagram is the "Go to" symbol. As its name suggests, this symbol directs the eye from one location in the diagram to another. Go-to symbols can use letters, numbers, or other designations. Figure 9-13 shows some examples that are commonly used. Notice that the "Go to" symbol directs the reader to a location marker with the same letter or number as the "Go to" symbol.

A "Go to" symbol can be used anywhere in your diagram in place of

FIGURE 9-12 • *A Method of Showing Lines That Cross*

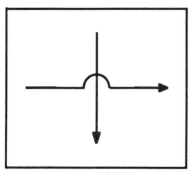

an arrow. In general, however, "Go to" symbols should be used only when the arrow it replaces would be long and continue from one page to another. The location markers themselves should be placed in numerical or alphabetical order from the beginning to the end of the diagram (see, for example, the last figure in this chapter). Doing this makes it easier for the reader to locate the markers.

Some people use "Go to" symbols to move the diagram from page to page. Others reserve the symbol for moving a branch of a diagram from one location to another location on a later page. In this case the "Go to" symbol typically indicates a choice emanating from a decision point and directing the reader to a distant location in the diagram. "Go to A" and "Go to 100" in Figure 9-13 are examples of this. We use the letter symbol to mark transitions from the end of one page to the beginning of the next. We use numerical labels (e.g., "Go to 100") to replace long arrows between distant locations in a flow diagram. Since arrows are easier to follow than "Go to" symbols, we recommend using arrows to represent all flows on a single page unless doing so forces you to cross lines.

Logic Versus Graphics

By now you have probably realized that there are two aspects of decision flow diagramming that require thoughtful consideration. The first, and more important, is the substantive logic of the processes being described. These processes flow from the purposes of the project, from careful output-input analyses, and from an understanding of the cultural-political context of the project. These processes represent your best judgment about how to accomplish your desired results. Therefore, the following cardinal rule applies to all PERT and flow diagrams: "Never change the process you are

FIGURE 9-13a • *Using an Alphabetical "Go to" Symbol*

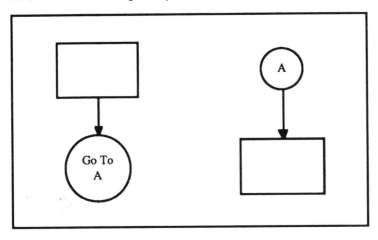

FIGURE 9-13b • *Using a Numerical "Go to" Symbol*

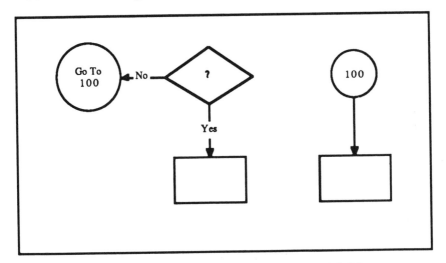

diagramming in order to make the graphics look good." Diagrams must always serve the project—never the other way round. Our experience is that however you have decided the process must go, you can always diagram it that way.

However, graphics are important. Good graphics serve two critical purposes:

1. They communicate information about projects clearly to diverse audiences.
2. They help planners and managers think better.

Moreover, compelling graphics suggest to various audiences that the planners and managers are people of competence.

Recapitulation

Decision flow diagramming is a tool for describing standard operating procedures for manufacturing, making personnel decisions, and providing instruction. Key elements of decision flow diagrams include start and end points, activities, decision points, branching, repeat loops, escape mechanisms, and "Go to" symbols. Arrows in decision flow diagrams show how the process moves from one step to the next. Graphics are important in drawing clear and communicative diagrams; never, however, should graphic considerations lead to changes in substantive processes. A good decision flow diagram can be drawn to illustrate any understandable organizational process.

By making choices explicit (through decision points and branching), decision flow diagrams emphasize the need for information to facilitate organizational processes. Information is required to support project activities and to make branching decisions. Also, activities and decision making typically generate new information. Thus, drawing decision flow diagrams and reflecting on the processes they represent lead us to consider what we call *information co-flows*. This is an important idea for designing management information systems. Managing information is the subject of the next chapter.

Decision Flow Diagramming Exercises

There are six exercises presented here for you to practice on. The first four constitute a set; the remaining two are unrelated. The set of four builds developmentally on the same basic process, teaching decision flow diagramming to a group of students. The first exercise takes students as a group through a teaching, testing, review, and retesting process until 90 percent of the students score at least 90 percent on the test. For the second exercise the process is the same except that an escape mechanism is built into it. The review and retesting components of the process will not continue past the third test. In the first two exercises, all the students are taken through the review and retesting process until one of the criteria is met to bring the process to a close. In the third exercise, only the students who don't do well on the test are taken through the subsequent review and retesting components. Finally, in the fourth exercise, students who don't do well on the test are taken individually through the review and retesting components instead of being treated as a group.

We recommend that you compare and contrast these four exercises to see how the diagrams reflect the subtle changes in process. Exercises 5 and 6 provide opportunities to practice diagramming different and somewhat more complex processes.

Answers immediately follow Exercise 6.

Flow Diagramming Exercise 1

This exercise provides practice in drawing a flow diagram made of activities, decision points, and repeat loops. Don't forget to put in your start and end points. There are no escape mechanisms. Keep in mind that the process described has been kept simple to provide practice for you. It is not presented as the best possible instructional procedure. Draw a flow diagram for the following:

1. Have students read the text material on decision flow diagramming.
2. Present the main ideas and discuss examples of decision flow diagramming in class.
3. Have students do practice exercises on decision flow diagramming.
4. Test the students' ability to draw a decision flow diagram from exercise instructions.
5. If 90 percent of the students do well on the test (e.g., score 90 percent or better), go on to the unit on information management.
6. If less than 90 percent of the students do well on the test, review the problems that showed up on the test, have the students do more practice exercises, and retest them. Continue this review, practice, and retest cycle until 90 percent of the students do well on the test.

Flow Diagramming Exercise 2

This exercise provides practice in drawing a flow diagram made of activities, decision points, and repeat loops. It differs from Exercise 1 in that it also includes an escape mechanism. Again, keep in mind tht the process described has been kept simple to provide practice for you. Draw a flow diagram for the following:

1. Have students read the text material on decision flow diagramming.
2. Present the main ideas and discuss examples of decision flow diagramming in class.
3. Have students do practice exercises on decision flow diagramming.
4. Test the students' ability to draw a decision flow diagram from exercise instructions.

5. If 90 percent of the students do well on the test (e.g., score 90 percent or better), go on to the unit on information management.
6. If less than 90 percent of the students do well on the test, review the problems that showed up on the test, have the students do more practice exercises, and retest them. Continue this review, practice, and retest cycle until 90 percent of the students do well on the test or until you have tested the students for the third time. Then go on to the unit on information management.

Flow Diagramming Exercise 3

This exercise provides practice in drawing a flow diagram made of activities, decision points, and repeat loops. It differs from Exercise 2 in that it treats the students who don't do well on the test separately from the other students. Drawn a flow diagram for the following:

1. Have students read the text material on decision flow diagramming.
2. Present the main ideas and discuss examples of decision flow diagramming in class.
3. Have students do practice exercises on decision flow diagramming.
4. Test the students' ability to draw a decision flow diagram from exercise instructions.
5. If 90 percent of the students do well on the test (e.g., score 90 percent or better), go on to the unit on information management.
6. If less than 90 percent of the students do well on the test, review the problems that showed up on the test with only those students who got less than 90 percent, have these students do more practice exercises, and retest them. Continue this review, practice, and retest cycle until 90 percent of all the students do well on the test or until the unsuccessful students have taken the test for the third time. Then go on to the unit on information management.

Flow Diagramming Exercise 4

This exercise provides practice in drawing a flow diagram made of activities, decision points, and repeat loops. It differs from Exercise 3 in that it treats the students who don't do well on the test individually. Draw a flow diagram for the following:

1. Have students read the text material on decision flow diagramming.
2. Present the main ideas and discuss examples of decision flow diagramming in class.

3. Have students do practice exercises on decision flow diagramming.
4. Test the students' ability to draw a decision flow diagram from exercise instructions.
5. If 90 percent of the students do well on the test (e.g., score 90 percent or better), go on to the unit on information management.
6. If less than 90 percent of the students do well on the test:
    a. Identify the students who didn't do well.
    b. In working with each of the students who didn't do well, first review the problems that showed up on his or her test, then provide more practice exercises, and, finally, give the student a retest. Work individually in succession with each of these students until he or she has scored 90 percent on the test or taken the test three times.
    c. When each student has scored 90 percent on the test or taken the test for the third time, work with the next student, until you have completed the cycle with all the students who didn't do well on the test.
    d. After all the students who didn't do well on the test have either scored 90 percent on a retest or taken the test three times, go on to the unit on information management.

Flow Diagramming Exercise 5

Diagram the process described below by which a theater group designates a play reading committee (PRC). Diagram the process as given, even if you would prefer a different set of procedures.

1. From the general membership list of the theater group, call members and ask them to serve on the PRC. Continue this procedure until either:
    a. Five (5) members have accepted the invitation or
    b. You have run out of names on the general membership list.
    Your process should guarantee that no member who answers the telephone is called more than once. However, if needed, members who don't answer the first call may be called one and only one more time after all other members have been called once.
2. After the list of five is complete or there are no more members to call— even if less than five members have agreed to serve—the PRC convenes with the director. If no members have agreed to serve, the director will constitute a PRC of one.

Note
Your process will have to include activities to keep track of who has

been called, whether or not they answered the phone, and whether or not they agree to serve.

Flow Diagramming Exercise 6

Again, diagram the process as given, even if you think that a different set of procedures makes better sense. You may wish to read the note that follows the exercise before drawing your diagram. The information in the note is designed to help you think through the structure of the diagram before you draw it.

Directions
Read the following problem all the way through, think carefully about it, and construct a flow diagram to represent its logical sequence of activities. Make the diagram as simple as possible.

1. Recruits are asked as a group to fill out a personal information sheet. They are then run one at a time through an examination process to determine their future status. The process continues until all recruits have been examined and assigned a status.
2. The personal information sheet is examined for "unusual responses." Any recruit giving any unusual response is examined personally by a special examining officer. Recruits who, on the basis of this special examination, are deemed unfit are dropped out at this point.
3. Any recruit whose personal information sheet is all right initially or who passes the special examination is given a routine medical examination. Recruits with perceived medical problems are sent to a specialist for further examination. Recruits who fail the specialist's examination are dropped from the program.
4. Recruits passing either the routine or special medical exams are given a psychological examination. Recruits failing the psychological examination are dropped from the program.
5. Recruits passing the psychological examination are given a Vocational Aptitude Test. This aptitude test is scored and is followed by a personal interview. If the recruit's scores on the Vocational Aptitude Test match his or her personal vocation choice (identified in the Personal Information Sheet and clarified in the personal interview), the recruit is assigned that vocational status.
6. If there is a mismatch, the recruit is given the option of changing his or her personal vocational choice to match the results of the Vocational Aptitude Test.
7. If the recruit does not wish to make a change in vocational choice (and

has not had a second interview already), he or she may enroll in a two-week Intensive Vocational Preparation Program (IVPP) in the vocation of his or her choice. Otherwise he or she is dropped from the program.

8. If the recruit so opts, he or she takes the IVPP and then retakes the Vocational Aptitude Test and the personal interview. If a match then exists between the recruit's scores and his or her personal vocational choice (or if the recruit chooses to change his or her choice of vocation in order to make a match), he or she is assigned that vocational status.

9. However, if after the second interview (and after the recruit has been given an opportunity to reconsider his or her vocational choice) there is still a mismatch, the recruit is dropped from the program.

Note

Ask yourself, "What is this process that I am diagramming intended to do?" The answer is that it takes a group of recruits through a multiple test procedure, each of which involves some branching. That is, for each test, depending on whether the recruit passes or not, different things can happen.

In some cases if the recruit does not pass a test the first time, he or she gets a second chance. In other cases there is no second chance. In every test situation the recruit may fail out and be dropped. Recruits who pass one test go on to the next until all tests have been passed and the recruit has been assigned a vocational status. In the end, one way or another, every recruit is either dropped or assigned a vocational status.

However, it is important to recognize that, although the testing of a particular recruit ends when that person has either been dropped or assigned a vocational status, the larger testing process does not end until every recruit has been tested and either dropped or assigned a vocational status.

You can see that there are two processes going on, one embedded in the other. The process of testing each recruit is embedded in the larger process of testing all recruits. To draw a diagram that says that the process ends after one recruit is tested is wrong. Whenever a recruit is dropped or assigned a vocational status, your diagram must include a mechanism for (1) checking to see if there is another recruit left in the group and (2) going on to the next until the last recruit is tested and either dropped or assigned a vocational status. The project cannot be shown to go to "End" until all members of the group of recruits have been dealt with. This is represented in the diagram by the overarching repeat loop that takes every individual through the entire process until all individuals in the original groups have either been dropped or assigned vocational statuses.

Furthermore, there is another repeat loop particular individuals may go through. Note the language in the description that you have been given of the process that deals with the Vocational Aptitude Test and the match or mismatch between the results of this test and the recruit's personal vocational choice:

> *If there is a mismatch, the recruit is given the option of changing his or her personal vocational choice to match the results of the Vocational Aptitude Test. If the recruit does not wish to make a change in vocational choice (and has not had a second interview already), he or she may enroll in a two-week Intensive Vocational Preparation Program (IVPP) in the vocation of his or her choice. . . . If the recruit so opts, he or she takes the IVPP and then retakes the Vocational Aptitude Test and the personal interview.*

This process has to be shown as a repeat loop within the vocational matching part of the decision flow diagram. Thus, it is possible to have one process embedded within a second, larger process and one repeat loop embedded within a second, larger repeat loop. In the computer world, looking at a process this way, in terms of its overall logical structure, is called *top-down, structured programming*. Sometimes processes within processes are called *subroutines*. It's an interesting way to think.

Answers to the Exercises

Exercise 1
See Figure 9-14.

Exercise 2
See Figure 9-15.

Exercise 3
See Figure 9-16.

Exercise 4
See Figure 9-17.

Exercise 5
See Figure 9-18.

Exercise 6
See Figure 9-19a and 9-19b.

FIGURE 9-14 • *Diagram for Decision Flow Diagramming Exercise 1*

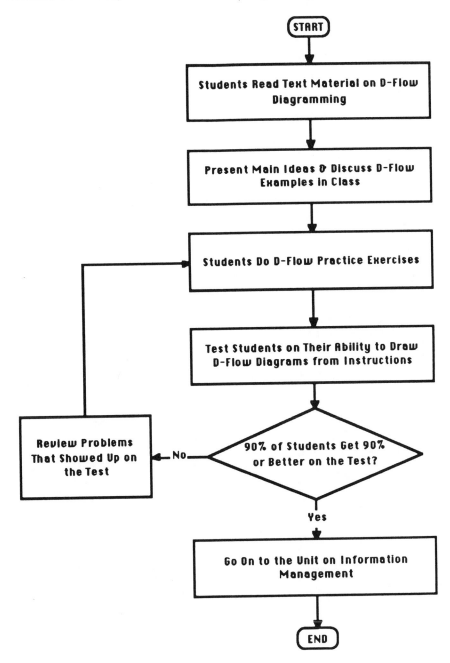

FIGURE 9-15 • *Diagram for Decision Flow Diagramming Exercise 2*

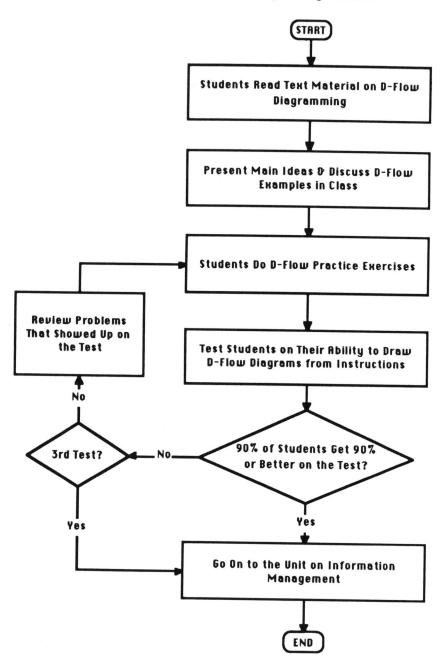

FIGURE 9-16 · *Diagram for Decision Flow Diagramming Exercise 3*

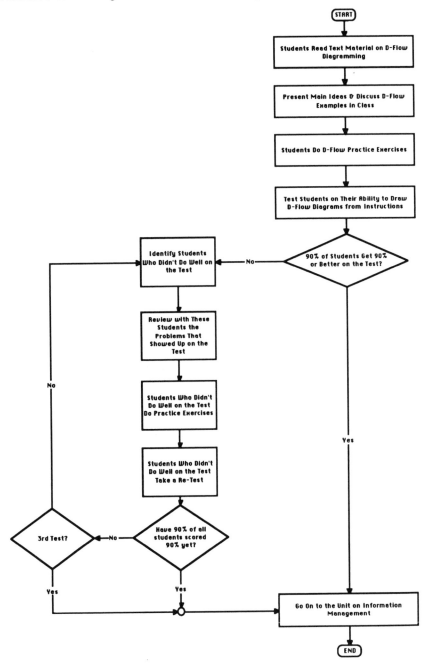

FIGURE 9-17 • *Diagram for Decision Flow Diagramming Exercise 4*

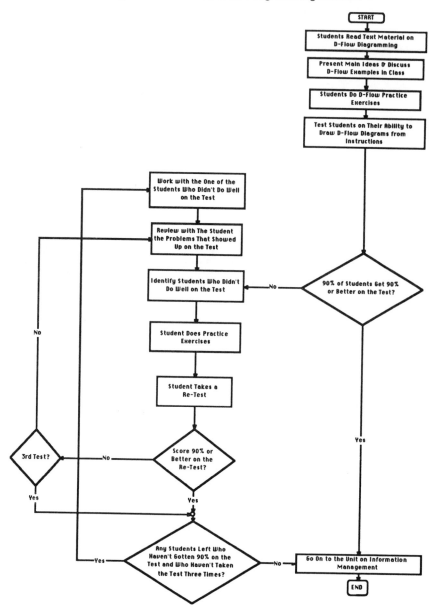

FIGURE 9-18 • *Diagram for Decision Flow Diagramming Exercise 5*

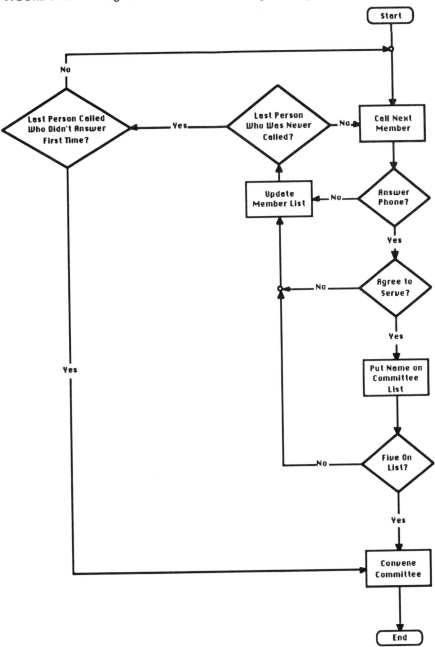

FIGURE 9-19a • *Part I of Diagram for Decision Flow Diagramming Exercise 6*

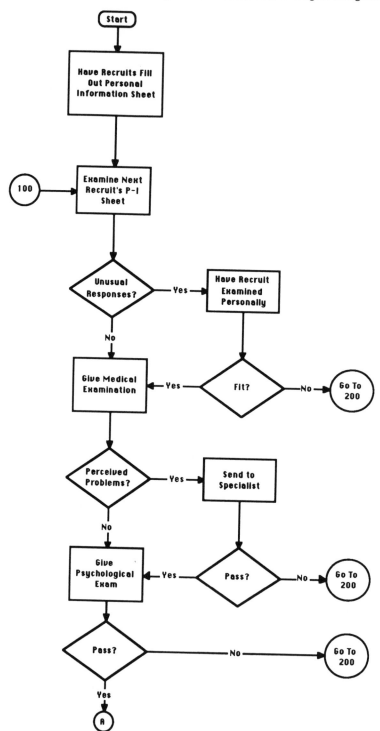

FIGURE 9-19b • *Part II of Diagram for Decision Flow Diagramming Exercise 6*

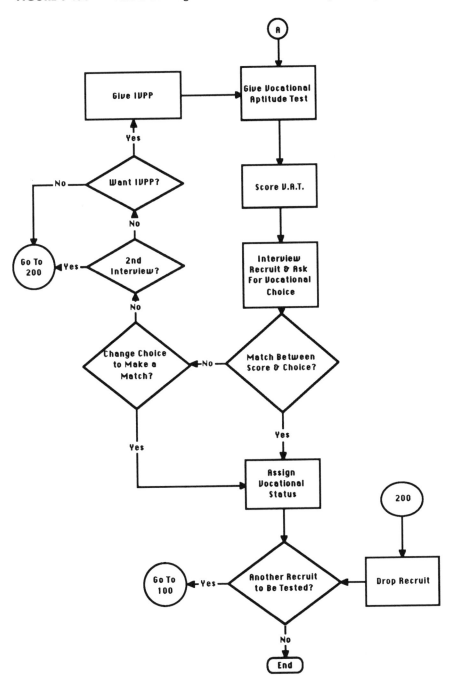

Doing Your Own Project

Choose an activity from your project and draw a decision flow diagram to describe how that activity will be carried out. The activity could be to produce a product, such as Moran putting together the components of his training book toward the end of his project (see subsystems 1000, 1100, and 1200 in Moran's PERT index, pp. 196–200). Alternatively it could be a personnel activity, such as hiring administrators or staff. Perhaps you will choose an activity to raise money or obtain authorization for your project or a part of it. The activity you choose could be any component of your project that has a clear purpose. Remember, it is achieving the desired results from an activity that establishes its end point.

Drawing a decision flow diagram is like simulating the process being diagrammed. The preparation of the diagram helps you and your colleagues to be surer that the process is right.

Be sure to include in your diagram examples of all the elements of decision flow diagramming discussed in this chapter. This will give you good practice applying for these techniques to your own work. In addition, you may wish to develop decision flow diagrams for other parts of your project.

CHAPTER TEN

Management Information Systems—Information Flow Diagrams

In this book we have asked you to organize your planning in a variety of succinct formats, many of them diagrams. These language formats and diagrams may appear casual to the unreflective observer. However, in the course of working with this book, you have experienced many times how developing the next step in this integrated process has led you to reassess and revise prior work.

We believe that linking these formats in an integrated planning method is crucial. These formats and diagrams are not simply technical tools. Each of them is a representation of a theory of organization and work. In concert they trigger you to organize in your mind a complex view of what makes organizations work effectively. Planning and management are about alignment. They are about getting all of the pieces to work together, even when no one can imagine all of the pieces.

It is our hope that this organic view of organizations comes through in this book. Even at the level of individual projects, we all want a vision that holds us together. We need to understand this vision in terms of goals and objectives that go beyond any particular project, that relate to larger agendas focusing on valued ends. Relating projects to larger values puts our heads in the sky. But we also need to feel our feet on the ground. We need to understand our projects in terms of the results we expect them to deliver. We need to organize our actions around these desired results, and we need to coordinate our efforts so that different groups and individuals among us can contribute semi-independently and yet have everything come together in the end, on time. Because information is the life blood of organizations, planning for information systems is not a job left to computer programmers or data processing specialists; concern for information flow is a central task of management.

Information is crucial for decision making. Rational decision making has no meaning without criteria for choosing among alternatives, without information about the choices available, and without knowledge of the conditions under which the choices must be made. Although the criteria are often relative and the information partial, there must be some information upon which to base decisions if those decisions are to be viewed as rational.

The effective manager anticipates what information will be needed for making decisions and plans its flow accordingly. Good information can be characterized as

- Relevant
- Accurate
- Well formulated
- Cost-effective.

Furthermore, information needs to be presented to the right people, at the right time, and in the right form to allow for the making of choices that are consistent with the appropriate criteria. While no information is ever perfect, the idea is to have the best information possible that conditions allow and costs permit.

The material in this chapter builds on what you have already learned about using decision flow diagrams to analyze the procedures by which you accomplish results. Think for a minute about the significance of the decision flow diagram as a management idea. Such a diagram appears abstract, just lines and boxes on a piece of paper or in a computer. Of course it is abstract. At the same time, however, it is a powerful abstraction, one that gives you the ability to simulate in your mind exactly how things work in your business and how you want them to work. It is precisely our ability to manipulate the world in our minds, ethically and operationally, that gives us vision and power.

Decision flow diagrams enable us to think about organizational processes in terms of sequences of activities, often repetitive, controlled by decision making. Both the activities and the decisions that guide them require pieces of information in order to be effective. This is true whether they are large or small.

For example, when you are writing to a colleague, client, or customer, you cannot do so without a great deal of background information. When, as in Moran's case, you are developing new training materials, you must elicit and manage information from product experts, writers, and documents. All projects and myriad routine standard organizational procedures require constant flows of information in order to be implemented successfully.

Also, making decisions always requires information. Decision implies choice; no one can make choices without information, about the choices and about the conditions surrounding the choices. Information streams must be coordinated to match the flows of activities and decisions that characterize organizational processes. Activity and decision flows are represented in decision flow diagrams. These same diagrams can be extended to include what we call information co-flows.

In this chapter you will learn two approaches for managing information systems. You will learn first how to specify where information is needed to catalyze activities and decision making. Related to this, you will also be asked to identify times and places in your project where new information is generated in the course of doing work and making decisions. You will learn how to add information input and output symbols to decision flow diagrams as ways of tying information to work flow. These information symbols make it easy to build on work you have already done in order to provide a foundation for designing management information systems.

You will also learn a technique for describing the sequential flow of information (i.e., the information co-flow) represented by the information symbols you have added to your decision flow diagrams. The information flow diagram is the last of the planning formats we will present in this book. This diagramming technique helps you to show pieces of information moving over time among people, offices, and files in (and outside of) your organization.

Information Input and Output Symbols on Decision Flow Diagrams

As suggested earlier, information in the form of books, reports, documents, visual displays, and oral presentations is essential for making decisions and carrying out all sorts of project activities. These are what we call *information inputs.* Also, in almost every project, there are activities that produce *information outputs,* particularly reports of one kind or another. Such information outputs stand in contrast to material outputs or activities, such as changes in skills, attitudes, and levels of political or financial support. Often information outputs are for use outside of the project. Other times they are for use within the project, for decision making or as a resource for later activities. In either case it is useful to represent information elements in relationship to decisions and activities in decision flow diagrams.

The transactional relationships among information, program activities, and decision making are critical to effective planning and management. Information is essential to control certain activities—for example, to maintain effective relationships in business firms among sales, production, and inventory. Information is important to catalyze activities such as teaching or training, where information is used to stimulate and engage participants in the learning process. Certain activities use information as a raw material, reformatting and repackaging it. Finally, information is central to all decision-making processes, to processes that determine subsequent courses of action by relating factual information to criteria for judgment. For all these reasons, information is essential for maintaining effective organizations.

Both the needs for and the sources of information in organizations are rooted in the processes described in decision flow diagrams. Later in this chapter you will learn about information flow diagrams. Information flow diagrams describe the movement of information among people, departments, files, and organizations to support organizational processes. An important way to use decision flow diagrams, one that is sometimes overlooked, is to highlight the connections between information and activities and decisions.

Often the design of "management information systems" focuses on linking "users" up to large data bases that are prepared and updated independent of the users. Such stand-alone data bases are important. However, one should also note that the users are often also creators of information that is used later by themselves and others. Information is necessary to make decisions, but decisions also are information. News of a decision is important. Management information systems must store facts about decisions and make them available as needed. Similarly, other information products are generated regularly and must be managed for later activities and decision making.

The following symbol shown in Figure 10-1 is the one that we employ to designate a piece of information that is used for or generated by activities and decisions.

FIGURE 10-1   •   *The Information Input or Output Symbol*

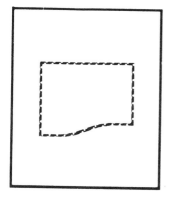

Since solid arrows and figures are used in flow diagrams to represent the sequential flow of activities and decisions in a decision flow diagram, dotted figures and arrows are used to show that particular pieces of information are used in or generated by activities and decision making (see Fig. 10-2). The dotted arrow and information output symbol indicate that a piece of information is coming into or going out of the process that is described by the decision flow diagram, while the process itself goes on to the next activity or decision, as shown by the solid arrows and figures in the diagram. The direction of the dotted arrow, to or from the information symbol, indicates whether information is going (1) into the process from the outside, (2) out of the process to the outside, or (3) from one part of the process to another, later part. The piece of a decision flow diagram in Figure 10-3, developed by de George, illustrates how information is used to prepare a list of experts and how the list of experts, once prepared, is used to support the activity of telephoning experts to set up interviews.

Information Flow Diagrams

Information flow diagrams show the movement of information among the various elements that constitute the working structure of the project, such as key personnel, offices, files, committees, and task forces. Information flow diagrams focus planners and managers on the important decisions to be made and on how information becomes available to support project activities and decisions.

FIGURE 10-2 • *An Example of an Information Output*

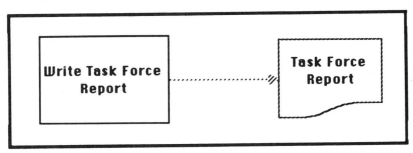

FIGURE 10-3 • A Partial Decision Flow Diagram Using Information Input and Output Symbols

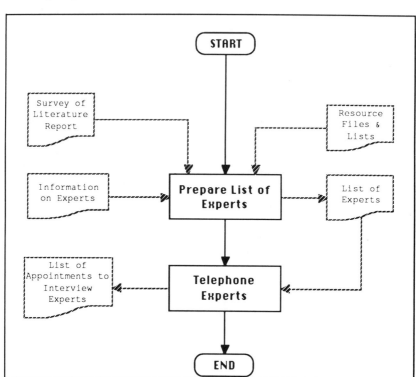

Theoretical Background

Our concept of information flow diagramming is rooted in the theoretical work of Anatole Holt.[1] A key element in Holt's thinking is that useful information systems represent networks of elements that include both users and creators of information, a concept that stands in contrast to the more traditional view of users as separate from data bases that are externally generated and updated.

Earlier in this chapter we called your attention to the relationship among activities, decisions, and information flows. We pointed out that information is used as an ingredient in making decisions and as a resource to support activities. We also pointed out that information is often generated in the course of activities and that news of a decision is, itself, a useful piece of information. We also noted that information generated at one point in time may be used later on. Figure 10-3 illustrates how information input and output symbols are used in decision flow diagramming to show these connections.

Decision flow diagrams show where information is required in the course of a project or program to facilitate activities and decisions and where information is generated by certain activities and decisions. In contrast, information flow diagrams describe where information comes from and where it goes.

Constructing Information Flow Diagrams

An information flow diagram shows the flow over time of particular pieces of information among identifiable elements of a project or program. These elements include mainly people and often manual or electronic files that are used for storage and retrieval purposes. The graphics employed in these diagrams are straightforward and are illustrated in Figure 10-4.

The essential material in the note column (see Fig. 10-4) is a description of the nature of the information being transacted. You should key your notes by number to the transactions shown in the diagram. You may also add additional notes that help to document the transaction. In terms of language formatting, you should describe the information as a noun with appropriate modifiers. Sometimes the gerund form of the noun (i.e., the *ing* form) is useful; however, no verbs should be used in the note column.

The action involved in the exchange of information is implied in the arrows. It is clear from the arrows that information is being transferred, from whom, and to whom. Although you can sense from the information transfers that people are carrying out other activities "behind the scenes," you should not show them on the information flow diagram. You should show *activities* on PERT and decision flow diagrams. Use information flow diagrams only to show the information transactions themselves, not the activities that produce and transform the information in between transfers.

The diagram is essentially a matrix. You place along the top of the diagram the *organizational components* that will be involved in one or more information transactions. An *information transaction* is defined simply as the transfer of any piece of information from one organizational element to another. You represent each organizational component over time by a vertical line under its heading at the top. You show transfers of information by drawing arrows perpendicular to the vertical lines.

Each transaction shows the movement of a specific piece or package of information (e.g., a report) from one organizational element to another. Each transaction involves two, and only two, organizational elements (e.g.,

FIGURE 10-4 • *The Basic Information Flow Diagram*

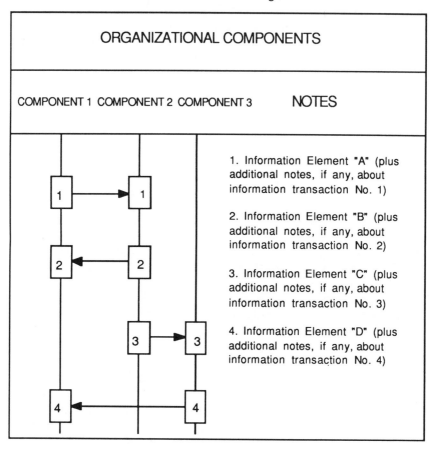

a set of recommendations from a task force to a decision-making group or person). Transactions occur in sequence (although you cannot tell from the diagram how much time passes between transactions). Transactions farther down the diagram occur later in time than those earlier in the diagram. The space between transactions is not proportionate to the time intervals, and simultaneous transactions must be shown as sequential. One way of showing that certain transactions are simultaneous is to give them all the same number or to number them with alphabetic subscripts (e.g., 4_a, 4_b, 4_c). You can also make references to time in the note column.

Always draw transactional arrows between two boxes. Locate the boxes on the lines associated with the particular persons, offices, or files involved in the information transfer. The direction of the arrow shows the direction of the information transfer, from the organizational unit at the tail of the arrow to the one at the head of the arrow. The small boxes simply represent markers on the vertical lines that are used for numbering the transactions.

Notice that the transfer activity itself is represented graphically in the diagram by the arrow between the two boxes. No words are needed to describe this action. Neither are words needed to describe the participants in the information transfer. These are also shown graphically by the boxes under the column headings. The only words needed in the note column are those that describe the information being transferred. Thus, you should use no verbs in the note column, only nouns.

The information flow diagram displayed in Figure 10-5 describes the flow of information represented by the information input and output symbols in Figure 10-3, which, although it relates to only a small portion of one

FIGURE 10-5 • *An Information Flow Diagram Keyed to Information Inputs and Outputs on a Decision Flow Diagram*

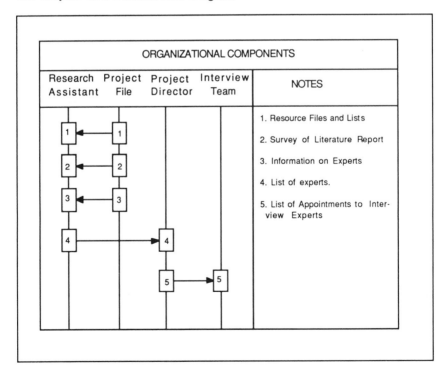

of de George's project subsystems, illustrates the central features of all information flow diagrams. Following are some of the rules you should keep in mind in making information flow diagrams:

1. Information flow diagrams identify the organizational components involved in the movements of information that support your project or some part of it. These components typically include people, organizational units, and various files, manual and electronic. These are the elements involved in the generation, storage, retrieval, transfer, and use of project information. Information transfers may involve elements within and outside of the project.

2. Information flow diagrams include "time lines" for the various organizational components. These are vertical lines drawn for each element involved, once or many times, in moving project information.

3. Information flow diagrams show each information transfer separately as a numbered transaction whose direction is indicated by an arrow. Transaction numbers are written in the boxes. Numbered transactions are shown in chronological order, although the time intervals between transactions are not indicated, except as dates may be displayed in the note column.

Even transactions that are essentially simultaneous are shown sequentially on the diagram. A common convention is to bracket simultaneous transactions in the note column to identify them as such. An alternative is to use the same number, with alphabetical subscripts for simultaneous information transfers.

Occasionally *double-headed arrows* are used to represent situations such as face-to-face meetings and telephone conversations where ideas are exchanged. (See Information Flow Diagramming Exercise 1 and its answer for examples of using double-headed arrows in information flow diagrams.)

4. The numbered transactions are keyed to correspondingly numbered notes written in the note column.

Recapitulation

This chapter has emphasized the essential relationship between process and information. Decision flow diagrams are process diagrams. By adding information symbols you can highlight the places in your processes where information is required to support activities and decisions and where new information is generated by activities and decisions.

Information flow diagrams enable you to analyze and describe the movement of information among people, departments, and files to support activities and decisions. Information flow diagrams show these organizational elements along the top of a matrix. Arrows and boxes represent the sequential and numbered transfers of pieces of packages of information between pairs of elements. Numbered notes describe the information involved in the transactions and provide further information about the transactions if desired.

Information Flow Diagramming Exercises

(The answers to the exercises are in the section immediately following.)

Information Flow Diagramming Exercise 1

Directions: Described below is a sequence of information flows among people and files in a school system. Included also are vendors, who are outside of the school system, per se. Read through the transactions to identify where information is coming from and where it is going. Then construct an information flow diagram showing, in sequence, the information flows described.

1. The School Superintendent sends budget allocation figures to the Principal.
2. The Principal sends appropriate budget allocation figures to the Department Heads.
3. The Department Heads send requests for prioritized lists of budget items and allocation figures to Teachers.
4. Teachers send prioritized lists of budget items to Department Heads.
5. Department Heads send draft order request lists to the Teachers.
6. Department Heads and Teachers share ideas and suggestions for revisions in the order request list.
7. Department Heads send order forms to the School Secretary.
8. The School Secretary gives a summary of orders by department to the Principal.
9. The Principal and the Department Heads share ideas and suggestions for revisions in orders.
10. The Principal forwards revised orders to the School Business Manager.
11. The School Business Manager sends collated orders to Vendors.
12. The School Business Manager updates relevant accounts.
13. Vendors send orders and invoices to the Department Heads.
14. Department Heads give signed invoices to the School Secretary.

15. The School Secretary gives an invoice summary by departments to the Principal.
16. The School Secretary sends signed invoices to the School Business Manager.
17. The School Business Manager sends payment checks to the Vendors.
18. The School Business Manager updates relevant accounts.
19. The School Business Manager sends the Principal periodic reports on updated accounts.

Information Flow Diagramming Exercise 2

Directions: Being able to describe the various pieces of information that are needed in order to make the decisions and carry out the activities that make up important organizational processes is an important skill. You must also be aware of information that is generated in the course of organizational activities, including the making of decisions, and be able to keep track of how this information is handled so that it is not lost. Since we use more information and use it more frequently than we sometimes realize, identifying and describing the movement of information in support of organizational processes is a detailed task. It is a kind of systems analysis.

In this exercise you are asked to examine a process you have seen before. It involves making telephone calls to establish a play reading committee (PRC) for a local community theater group (Decision Flow Diagramming Exercise 5, p. 143; see also, Fig. 9-18, p. 151). Now we want you to think about the steps in that process and to imagine what kinds of information you will need to carry out those steps. We also want you to think about what pieces of information are produced along the way and how they are used in the process. Then try to draw in appropriate information and output symbols (see, for example, Fig. 10-3) that describe the information co-flow of the process involved in putting together the PRC.

Answers to the Information Flow Diagramming Exercises

Exercise 1
See Figure 10-6.

Exercise 2
See Figure 10-7.

FIGURE 10-6 • *Diagram for Information Flow Diagramming Exercise 1*

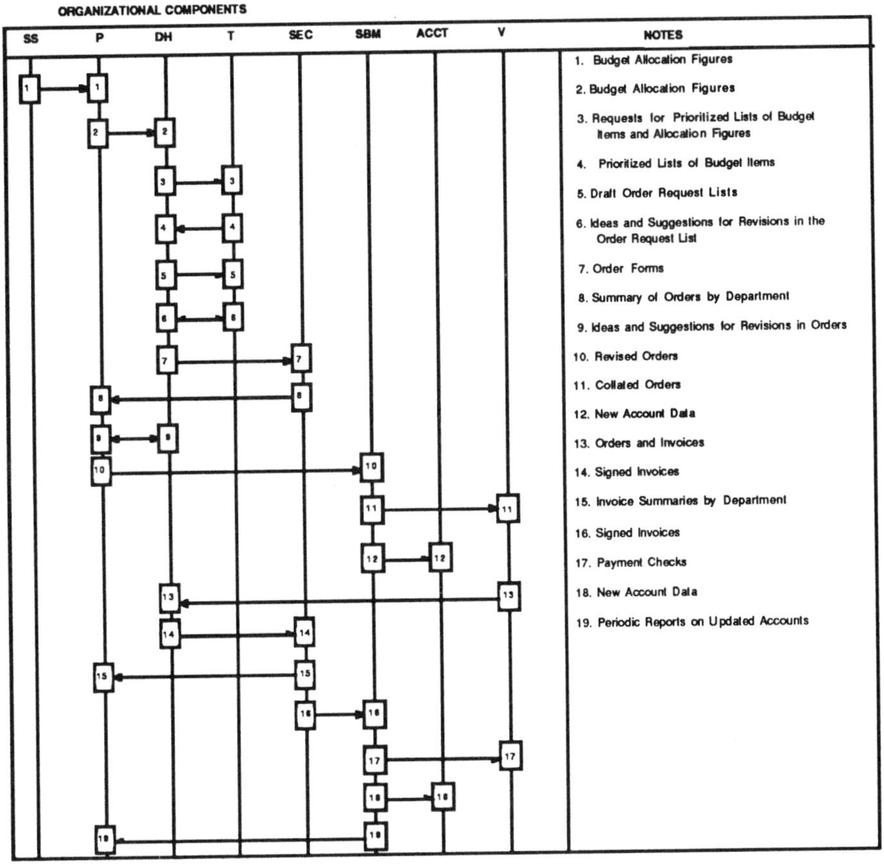

ORGANIZATIONAL COMPONENTS

SS	P	DH	T	SEC	SBM	ACCT	V	NOTES

1. Budget Allocation Figures

2. Budget Allocation Figures

3. Requests for Prioritized Lists of Budget Items and Allocation Figures

4. Prioritized Lists of Budget Items

5. Draft Order Request Lists

6. Ideas and Suggestions for Revisions in the Order Request List

7. Order Forms

8. Summary of Orders by Department

9. Ideas and Suggestions for Revisions in Orders

10. Revised Orders

11. Collated Orders

12. New Account Data

13. Orders and Invoices

14. Signed Invoices

15. Invoice Summaries by Department

16. Signed Invoices

17. Payment Checks

18. New Account Data

19. Periodic Reports on Updated Accounts

Doing Your Own Project

At the end of Chapter 9 we asked you to draw a decision flow diagram describing an important process in your project. Now examine the individual activities and decisions in this process to identify important pieces of information associated with them. Some of these pieces of information will be information inputs that are needed to carry out certain activities. Other pieces of information will be information outputs produced by certain activities. Also, every decision requires information and every decision is itself a piece of information. Include information symbols on your decision flow diagram to represent all of these information inputs and outputs.

Then draw an information flow diagram that shows where the

FIGURE 10-7 • *Diagram for Decision Flow Diagramming Exercise 3 with Information Input and Output Symbols Describing the Information Co-Flow (Information Diagramming Exercise 2)*

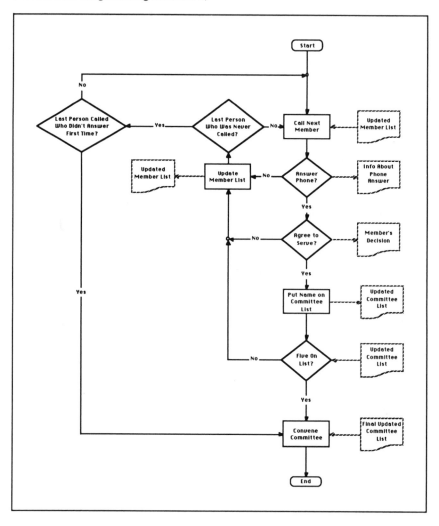

information inputs come from and where the information outputs go. Some information inputs are produced earlier in the process described by your decision flow diagram and are then used later in the process. Even in these cases, however, you must think through what happens to these pieces of information between the times they are produced and the times they are used. Other pieces of information come from or go to people, offices, or files inside or outside of your project or organization. Your information flow diagram should show all of the information transfers involved.

Remember that the actual transfer of information is shown by the graphics on the diagram (numbered boxes and arrows). Therefore, your note column should contain only information labels that tell what information is being transferred. These labels contain a noun, usually with a few descriptors to clarify it, but no verbs. For example, in Figure 10-6 the first two information transfers involve "Budget Information Figures." The essential noun in this label is *figures;* the additional words *budget information* are descriptors that tell what figures are meant. Look at the other information transaction labels in the note column of Figure 10-6. You will see that they all have this basic language structure.

Note

1. Holt, formerly Director of the Boston University Academic Computing Center, is currently Vice Chairman and Chief Technical Officer of Coordination Technology, Inc., Trumbull, CT.

CHAPTER ELEVEN

Documenting Activities and Building a Budget

A crucial piece of work in planning any project is preparing budget materials. The planning process you have gone through in the preceding chapters should be extremely helpful in building your project budget.

There are two basic components to consider in formulating a budget. The first component includes all the costs directly associated with the separate activities that make up your subsystems. The second component adds on to your activity costs the general costs of staff, facilities, materials, equipment, and other elements that support the project as a whole but that are not budgeted to individual activities. These costs are typically labeled *over head* or *indirect* costs.

The Elements of Activity Documentation

What we call *activity documentation* is a necessary step in preparing and supporting a project budget. Documenting the activities of the project also entails elements that focus on the managerial aspects of the activities as well as on the financial aspects. Following is a list of elements that we recommend you use as a guide in documenting project activities:

- PERT number and title
- Activity description
- Expected output
- Required input conditions
- Required resources and activity budget
- Management responsibilities

Going through and documenting project activities is the most detailed and time-consuming task in the planning process. In our classes and workshops we ask participants to practice the technique on only one or two activities. However, there is no choice in real organizational planning, outside of the classroom, but to ask certain questions about every project activity and to document your answers to those questions. As indicated in the preceding list, you need to describe six elements. In addition to the PERT number and title, you will describe: (1) what the activity is about, (2) what results it is intended to produce, (3) what conditions and resources must be in place for the activity to be successful, (4) what costs are associated with these resources, and (5) who is responsible for seeing that the activity is carried out and also that all of the necessary conditions and resources are in place to ensure a successful activity.

PERT Number and Title

It is helpful to think about documenting project activities as if you were making a notebook. You will have a page in the notebook for each activity. (If you need more than one page, that's all right.) The first thing you put on the page is the PERT number of the activity and its title from the PERT index. In this way every activity is clearly identified. Each activity is keyed to the earlier work you did in preparing your PERT diagram, Gantt diagrams, and slack table.

Activity Description

The next thing you write is a brief description of the activity. You want to describe, preferably in only a paragraph or two, the main steps of this activity. Explain just what people will be doing to achieve the desired results for the activity. You want to give your readers a good sense of what will actually be going on for each activity in the project you've planned.

Expected Output

Activities are intended to accomplish results. No activity is without a purpose. Each activity is designed to gain decisions; create materials; train personnel; alter political, financial, and cultural conditions, and so on. The products of activities may be the final products of the project, the ones that you described in your output specifications (see Chapter 4). Often, however, early activities develop results that are important to the success of later project activities. We sometimes call these *medial outputs* to distinguish them from the final outputs of the project. You should describe the results you expect from each activity in the project just as you specified the outputs for the project as a whole. The expected outputs described for your activities represent *production targets* for your activities. They determine how you will manage these activities, and they also provide criteria for judging when activities have failed and alternative activities must be implemented.

Required Input Conditions

Just as the expected outputs for an activity are analogous to the output specifications for the project, the required input conditions are comparable to the project's input specifications (see Chapter 5). There is, however, a very important difference. The input specifications for the project describe existing conditions. These are conditions that are given by historical circumstances not under the control of the project. They speak to what is, not at all to what should be. Therefore, any activities that you place at the beginning of the project must be designed to be successful given those existing conditions. You have no choice—you must start with what is given.

By contrast, however, what we call required input conditions for activities describe the conditions and resources that are necessary. If the conditions and resources for activity X don't exist when the project starts, then you must include activities in the project before activity X that create the necessary conditions and that produce or obtain the needed resources. Your only alternative is to redesign activity X so it can be carried out with different staff, facilities, equipment, materials, training, or cultural or political conditions.

Therefore, in this section of your activity documentation you should do two things. First, you should make a list of all the resources that you must have to do this activity and the important political, cultural, and individual readiness conditions that are required for the activity to be successful. Second, you should make a note for each of the resources and conditions on your list whether it was available at the outset of the project or whether it was obtained or created earlier in the project.

You should have described in your input specifications the important resources and conditions that were present at the outset of the project. Alternatively, you should identify where in the course of the project other conditions were created, where other resources were created or obtained. For each of these required conditions and resources, you should check to see whether it was listed in your input specifications or, otherwise, by what project activity or subsystem it was created or obtained. Such detailed checking is tedious work, but it is the only way you can be sure that you haven't left anything out.

An activity as common as putting on a management workshop depends on resources for its success. These include qualified trainers, supportive facilities and equipment, lighting, software in the form of printed materials, copied materials, slides, transparencies, and computer applications, right down to pads, pencils, newsprint, and magic markers. It may seem obvious to you, but every one of these resources requires a subsystem that has to be set up and managed to ensure that the resource is there when you need it. Often, too, political conditions such as bureaucratic support must be arranged in advance, participants recruited and selected, information disseminated, and so on. All these subsystems must be planned for and managed. Therefore, it is essential that you document for each activity all required conditions and resources.

Activity Budget

Having identified all the resources required for an activity, you can easily formulate an activity budget—or, simply put, a dollar figure next to each resource required to show what it will cost. Some resources, such as facilities, computers, or certain staff, may be shared items that are not charged activity by activity. These can be shown as indirect costs in the activity budgets. They will then be included in the project budget as overhead costs. In general, then, the project budget includes the sum of all the direct activity costs and the overhead or indirect costs.

You can see that this approach is a variation of *program budgeting*. Items contained within general cost categories such as personnel, equipment, materials and supplies, facilities, transportation, food, and lodging are displayed and summed across various project activities. Added to these are costs not allocated to individual activities. Showing the allocation of costs to different activities provides much detailed budget information; it takes the form of what we call a *matrix* budget.

Figure 11-1 shows the conceptual framework for activity budgeting. Think of each activity budget (i.e., each column in the maxtrix) as a page showing the types of costs for that activity. The cost items are grouped at the left side of the matrix under headings and subheadings. Accountants call these groupings *object cost categories*.

Management Responsibilities

The question you must answer in the final section of the activity documentation is "Who is responsible?" The question implies responsibility for (1) the project activity, (2) various parts of the activity, and (3) each and every one of the subsystems required to put the resources in place so that the activity can be implemented successfully. For a simple activity, one that is narrow in scope, you may identify a single person as having managerial

FIGURE 11-1 • An Illustrative Activity Budget

COST CATEGORY	ACTIVITY 1	ACTIVITY 2	ACTIVITY 3	ACTIVITY 4	ACTIVITY 5	. . .	ACTIVITY N	OVERHEAD	TOTAL
PERSONNEL	$$$	$$$	$$$	$$$	$$$	. . .	$$$	$$$	$$$$
EQUIPMENT	$$$	$$$	$$$	$$$	$$$	. . .	$$$	$$$	$$$$
MATERIALS & SUPPLIES	$$$	$$$	$$$	$$$	$$$	. . .	$$$	$$$	$$$$
FACILITIES	$$$	$$$	$$$	$$$	$$$	. . .	$$$	$$$	$$$$
TRANSPORTATION	$$$	$$$	$$$	$$$	$$$	. . .	$$$	$$$	$$$$
FOOD & LODGING	$$$	$$$	$$$	$$$	$$$	. . .	$$$	$$$	$$$$
TOTAL	$$$$	$$$$	$$$$	$$$$	$$$$	. . .	$$$$	$$$$	$$$$$

responsibility. However, management of larger, more complex activities is often shared among several people.

Typically one person may have general responsibility for the entire activity. This person may have responsibility for the entire subsystem of the project of which the activity is a part. At the same time other people may be responsible for subcomponents of the activity, including the subsystems required to obtain and deliver necessary resources. In your plan you should specify these managerial arrangements for *each* of your project activities and subsystems.

Moran's Activity Documentation

The following material was prepared by Moran as an example of documenting a major project activity. It illustrates the concepts just described.

1. *PERT Number and Title: 800-805. Conduct a kick-off meeting among writers, the operator of the desktop publishing system, the computer graphics person, the instructional designer, and the testing consultant.*
2. *Activity Description:*
   This project will involve more than 20 people, some of whom will be on loan from support organizations within the company. Many of these people have never met before. Most of them have never worked together on a project. The meeting will last about an hour and will take place on-site. Visuals will be shown using an overhead projector. Refreshments will be served. The group manager will give five minutes of opening remarks, emphasizing the importance of the project. As project manager, I will be the only other speaker, but I will invite the managers who are present to assist me in answering questions.
3. *Expected Outputs:*
   There will be:
   a. *Enthusiasm for the project and a sense of team spirit to get the job done. People leaving the meeting must have a clear picture of the project and understand their roles.*
   b. *Teams consisting of a writer and an instructor for each book.*
   c. *A final goal for each team, and a set of intermediate goals.*
   d. *Deadlines set by each team for meeting all goals.*
   e. *A follow-up meeting scheduled for these attendees for team progress reports.*
   f. *Understanding of the goal of the project and of each individual's role in meeting the goal.*
4. *Required Input Conditions:*
   a. *Management commitment to the resources to complete the project.*

b. *Management approval of the teams and the overall goals of the project.*

c. *A list of participants, their phone numbers, and electronic addresses.*

d. *A meeting room that can seat 25 people at tables arranged in a U-shape, with lights that can be dimmed, and window coverings that can be drawn.*

e. *Management approval to serve complimentary refreshments.*

f. *Fruit, crackers, cheese, juice, and soft drinks from the cafeteria, arranged in an attractive way on a table at the back of the room, including paper plates, napkins, plastic cutlery, and cups.*

g. *Wastepaper baskets around the room.*

h. *An overhead projector, spare bulb, and 4 × 6 foot projection screen set up in the room.*

i. *A lavaliere microphone with volume control and speakers arranged to avoid feedback.*

j. *A marker board with eraser, markers of at least three different colors, and a pointer.*

5. *Required Resources and Associated Costs (Activity Budget): [See Figure 11-2.]*

6. *Management Responsibilities:*

a. *The new hire sales training manager must make the writers, instructors, clerical staff, office environment, and computer equipment available for this project and must fund the outside resources, such as the graphics artist and editor.*

b. *The project manager must arrange for the production of computer graphics and the services of the editor. The project manager is responsible for a quality product, on time and on budget. This means monitoring the project full time, anticipating problems, and resolving conflicts.*

c. *The product experts are not within the control of this project; however, they have cooperated with similar efforts in the past.*

d. *The cafeteria staff will ensure that there are baskets for the crackers and slicers for the cheese. The clerical staff will ensure the refreshments are in the room prior to the start of the meeting.*

e. *The items listed as handouts for this meeting in the 800 subsystem will be put in a package, with a cover letter listing the contents and emphasizing the importance of the project. The clerical staff will make 40 copies of the package and have one copy at each seat at the start of the meeting.*

f. *The members of the clerical staff providing assistance will have copies of these input conditions as a checklist of pre-meeting duties.*

FIGURE 11-2 • *A Budget for One of Moran's Project Activities*

a. Writers - 5 for three months at $50/hr. (includes phone, copier usage, computer time, supplies, travel, office space, and associated overhead)	$ 132,000
b. Instructors' hours are not charged to this project	0
c. Product experts' hours are not charged to this project	0
d. Clerical staff - 2 for three months at $35/hr.	36,960
e. Computer graphics - 5 graphics per chapter for 37 chapters at $25 each	4,625
f. Editor for 144 hours at $48/hr.	6,912
TOTAL	$ 180, 497

Acquiring Necessary Resources

Typically project budgets are forced to fit predetermined financial constraints, a necessary fact of managerial life. This implies either promising more than one can deliver, which is certainly not unusual, or redefining project goals and activities to fit the resources that are available. In our planning language this implies trimming your output specifications and/or finding more cost-efficient ways of delivering them.

There is an alternative, however. You can purposefully set out to develop additional resources. You can build into your project activities to raise additional funds. You can also formulate plans to gain access to resources you need at no or little cost. The budgeting approach described in this chapter helps you to evaluate the resources you need, based on the activities required to achieve your output specifications. It helps you define the real costs of insufficient funding and it gives you a basis for acquiring additional support.

Summary Recaputulation

Developing documentation for each activity is a demanding but important step in the planning process. In doing so you clarify exactly what each activity is and what it is intended to accomplish. Equally importantly, the documentation process helps you to identify all of the many subsystems required to acquire and deliver the human, intellectual, technological, and material resources you will need to carry out successful project activities.

These descriptions provide a sound basis for assigning managerial responsibility and for building accountability into the project. Documenting your activities also forces you to make sure you have included in your project the prior activities necessary not only to create needed resources but also to shape the conditions needed to make subsequent activities successful. Finally, developing documentation at the level of individual project activities provides a sound basis of support for the project budget. It helps you to make a persuasive case for acquiring the resources that you need to do a quality project and deliver results.

Doing Your Own Project

Now it is your turn to practice. Choose an important and interesting activity in your project to work on by applying the ideas and techniques described in this chapter. Go through the steps described above for your activity so that when you are finished you will have identified all of the elements discussed:

1. PERT number and title
2. Activity description
3. Expected output
4. Required input conditions
5. Required resources and activity budget
6. Management responsibilities

When you have completed this task, you may wish to extend the process to other important activities in your project, possibly to all of them. A useful alternative to dealing with individual activities is to focus the same process on each of your project subsystems. While doing this will not give you the same level of detail, it will save you time and give you a basis for formulating a project budget.

CHAPTER TWELVE

Postscript

Some of our most experienced students have told us, after completing our course, that the individual planning techniques were very useful, but that the overall management concept was even more valuable to them. In general, participants indicate that the central organizing principles become apparent to them only as the course approaches its conclusion, after they have wrestled with applying the separate components from beginning to end.

Two insights seem crucial. The first is that the separate techniques are integrally connected. Students gain this realization as they proceed through the methodology, each step almost always forcing them to reconsider, and often revise, what they have done in the previous step. The emphasis throughout is on maintaining a logical consistency from the description of your values and goals, through the specification of desired results, the design of project subsystems and activities, to the design and analysis of micro-processes and information systems. The methodology exemplifies a problem-solving focus.

The second realization is that techniques presented in this course as planning tools derive from a basic theory of management. They are as useful for analyzing existing problems as they are for planning projects to bring about change. They are rooted in the belief that planning and management are not simply mechanistic processes.

Agendas must be described because the process of making them explicit forces reflection on underlying values and long-term goals. The knowledge you acquire in the process is useful not only for planning technical activities to achieve results, but is useful also as a basis for political negotiations and compromise. Knowing your own values and goals also provides a basis for becoming knowledgeable about and open to others' values and goals. Thus, the technique of formulating mission hierarchies causes the planner to reflect on deeper convictions and the politics of organizational development.

Making explicit the concrete results that will give life to abstract goals helps to clarify the goals, on the one hand, and provides a footing for effective action, on the other. A planner with practical vision must have an eye in the sky and feet on the ground. The specification of results also provides a basis for later evaluation. This represents a belief that the continuing cycle of evaluation, planning, management, and evaluation is fundamental to effective leadership at any level of organization.

Laying out a project plan in detail—in the form of PERT, Gantt, and decision flow diagrams—becomes a means of brainstorming project ideas, clarifying the nature of the support subsystems that often make the difference between success and failure, and managing the project. These diagramming techniques, too, go beyond the technical; they show a respect for the complexity of organizational development. Ultimately they become tools for thinking about the many operational and support systems that are required for achieving desired results.

Critical among these support systems are information systems. The concept of the information flow diagram is integration of information and activity. Information is the life blood of organizations. The analysis of how it is used, how it is generated, and how it is managed is crucial to leadership. Too often information for production and decision making is taken for granted and treated casually. Too often management information systems are thought of as data bases that are "out there" somewhere. Conceptually the information flow diagram reminds us that we, the users of information, are also the creators of information. It provides a tool for examining existing procedures and for thoughtfully designing more effective structures to handle information.

Perhaps most important is the idea of information co-flow. It ties together information with the organizational processes that require and generate information. The marriage of decision and information flow diagrams provides a conceptual map. With it, managers can think about how to organize people, paper, and computers to put the right information in the right place, in the right form, at the right time.

Throughout the book we have encouraged you to work on your own project. A place has been provided at the end of each chapter for you to take the ideas and formats discussed in the chapter and apply them to your own work. We hope that your efforts have proceeded well and that, like so many of the participants in our classes and workshops, you have a project plan or proposal to realize in your own organization. Following in the appendices are the complete planning documents written by Pat Moran, Mardella Lower, and George de George. These have been included as examples of the application of our planning methodology to corporate, health care, and educational projects. Hopefully, they have been helpful to you in providing different perspectives on the methodology and giving you ideas for your own work.

Related Readings

The General Context of Rational Planning

Carlson, R. V., and G. Awkerman (Eds.). *Educational Planning: Concepts, Strategies, Practices.* White Plains, NY: Longman, 1991.

Clay, K., S. Lake, and K. Tremain. *How to Build a Strategic Plan: A Step-by-Step Guide for School Managers.* San Carlos, CA: Ventures for Public Awareness, 1989.

Craig, D. *Hip Pocket Guide to Planning and Evaluation.* Ann Arbor, MI: University of Michigan, 1978.

Cunningham, W. G. *Systematic Planning for Educational Change.* Palo Alto, CA: Mayfield, 1982.

Easton, D. *A Systems Analysis of Political Life.* Chicago: University of Chicago Press, 1979.

Lindblom, C. *The Intelligence of Democracy.* New York: Free Press, 1965.

Peters, T. J., and R. H. Waterman, Jr. *In Search of Excellence,* ch. 2, "The Rational Model." New York: Harper & Row, 1983.

Shank, J. K., and V. Govindarajan. *Strategic Cost Analysis: The Evolution from Managerial to Strategic Accounting.* Homewood, IL: Irwin, 1989.

Problem Definition and Analysis

Kaufman, R. *Educational Systems Planning.* Englewood Cliffs, NJ: Prentice-Hall, 1972.

Kaufman, R. *Identifying and Solving Problems.* San Diego, CA: University Associates, 1982.

Richardson, G. P., and A. L. Pugh III. *Introduction to System Dynamics Modeling with DYNAMO.* Cambridge, MA: M.I.T. Press, 1981.

Stryker, P. "Can You Analyze This Problem?" *Harvard Business Review, 43*(3), May–June, 1965, pp. 73–78, and *43*(4), July–August, 1965, pp. 99–110.

Matrix Design Planning Method

Nadler, G. *The Planning and Design Approach.* New York: Wiley, 1981.

Nadler, G. *Work Design: A Systems Concept.* Homewood, IL: Irwin, 1970.

PERT/Network Analysis

Cook, D. L. *Educational Project Management.* Columbus, OH: Merrill, 1971.

Federal Electric Corporation. *A Programmed Introduction to PERT: Program Evaluation and Review Technique.* New York: Wiley, 1963.

PERT for Managers. Niles, IL: Preston Publications, n.d.

Wiest, J. D., and F. K. Levy. *A Management Guide to PERT, DCPM, and Other Networks* (2nd ed.). Englewood Cliffs, NJ: Prentice-Hall, 1977.

Flow Charting

Bohn, M. *Flowcharting Techniques.* Palo Alto, CA: Science Research Associates, 1971.

Boillot, M. H., et al. *Essentials of Flowcharting* (3rd ed.). Dubuque, IA: Brown, 1982.

Chapin, N. *Flowcharts.* New York: Van Nostrand Reinhold, 1971.

Farina, M. V. *Flowcharting.* Englewood Cliffs, NJ: Prentice-Hall, 1970.

I Know Flow Charting. New York: Dell, 1983.

Lane, G. H., and K. M. Cronin. *Flow Charts: Clinical Decision Making in Nursing.* Philadelphia: Lippincott, 1983.

McQuigg, J. D., and A. M. Harness. *Flowcharting.* Boston: Houghton-Mifflin, 1970.

Schriber, T. J. *Fundamentals of Flowcharting.* Melbourne, FL: Krieger, 1969.

Program Planning and Budgeting Systems

Haggart, S. A., et al. *Program Budgeting for School District Planning.* Englewood Cliffs, NJ: Educational Technology Publications, 1972.

Hartle, D. G. *A Theory of the Expenditure Budgetary Process.* Toronto: University of Toronto Press, 1976.

Novick, D. *Current Practices in Program Budgeting.* New York: Crane-Russak, 1973.

Sastry, K. S. *Performance Budgeting for Planned Development.* Atlantic Highlands, NJ: Humanities Press, 1980.

Schultze, C. L. *The Politics and Economics of Public Spending.* Washington, DC: The Brookings Institution, 1969.

Shaller, H. I. *Unified Planning and Budgeting in a Free Society.* Adelphi, MD: Oakview Book Press, 1977.

Shoup, D. C., and S. L. Mehay. *Program Budgeting for Urban Police Services: With Special Reference to Los Angeles.* New York: Irvington Publications, 1972.

Wildavsky, A. *The Politics of the Budgetary Process* (3rd ed.). Boston: Little, Brown, 1979.

Management Information Systems

Baldridge, J. V., and M. L. Tierney. *New Approaches to Management: Creating Practical Systems of Management Information and Management by Objectives.* San Francisco: Jossey-Bass, 1979.

Clowes, K. W. *The Impact of Computers on Managers.* Charlotte, NC: UMI Publications, 1962.

Dare, G. A., and K. G. Bakewell. *The Manager's Guide to Getting the Answers.* Phoenix, AZ: Oryx Press, 1981.

Dock, V. T. *MIS: A Managerial Perspective.* Palo Alto, CA: Science Research Associates, 1977.

Federico, P. A., et al. *Management Information Systems and Organizational Behavior.* New York: Praeger, 1980.

Lucas, H., and C. F. Gibson. *Casebook for Management Information Systems* (2nd ed.). New York: McGraw-Hill, 1980.

Lucas, H. C., Jr. *Why Information Systems Fail.* New York: Columbia University Press, 1975.

Westin, A. F. *Information Technology in a Democracy.* Cambridge, MA: Harvard University Press, 1971.

APPENDIX A

Moran's Paper

Updating Product Training Books

Boston University School of Education
AP762, Administrative Planning
Dr. Alan K. Gaynor
July 11–28, 1988

Executive Summary

This project will organize teams of instructors, product experts, and writers to update the product training books used by my company. The books are required reading for new hires into the sales force prior to their classroom training on the company's products.

Team members will have these responsibilities:

- The instructors currently teach about the products in class. They know the level of product knowledge that is prerequisite for class. Thus they will dictate the tables of contents of the books.
- The product experts are from the engineering and marketing groups within the company. They will provide in-depth technical knowledge of the products.
- The writers are educators who can explain products and the concepts behind them in familiar terms. They know how to create educationally sound objectives, and write text and tests to meet the objectives.

Updated books will enable new sales representatives to get the maximum benefit from the time spent in the classroom.

TABLE OF CONTENTS

I. Background Statement

This project will update the books that are part of the product training my company gives newly hired sales representatives. New sales representatives are required to read the books before attending two weeks of classroom training on the company's products. The books help them get the most from their classroom training by presenting product evolution, a sense of how the products complement one another, and the specifications of the individual products. The company's accelerating rate of new product introductions — 80% of the products sold today did not exist four years ago — has dated the existing product training books. Pressure to update the books comes from:

- The instructors, who now have to spend valuable classroom time covering those new products not yet in the books
- Sales managers and sales representatives, who seek the competitive advantage that knowledge of the newest products provides

Successful completion of this project will contribute to company productivity and profitability.

II. Mission Hierarchy

9. To contribute to company profitability.
8. To increase sales.
7. To return knowledgeable sales trainees to the field.
6. To maximize sales trainees' understanding of products during their two weeks of classroom training.
5. To prepare the sales trainees for their two weeks of classroom training on products.
4. *To update product training books.*
3. To gather product information from experts.
2. To identify experts with knowledge of the new products.
1. To identify products introduced since the existing product training books were written.

III. Mission Target and Rationale

This section describes why mission statement 4 (To update product training books) was chosen for this project rather than any other. The chosen mission is well within the charter of the corporate sales training organization of which I am a part. Our group has access to:

- The classroom instructors who decide which products will go into the books; and
- The experts in marketing and engineering who provide detailed product information.

The three mission statements lower in the hierarchy (To identify products . . . , To identify experts . . . , To gather product information . . .) are prerequisites of the target mission, and will be done as part of this project.

The mission statement immediately above the chosen statement (To prepare the sales trainees for their two weeks of classroom training on products) was not chosen because it is beyond the scope of my corporate sales training group. The product training books of mission statement 4 are only part of the preparations referred to in statement 5. Other preparations, such as interviews and sales calls, take place in the field.

IV. Output Specifications at the Target Mission Level and Below

Related Output Specifications:

1. There will be consistency in the level of detail and type of information in the books. For example, the books will have a stated objective, aim at a defined audience, assume a prior knowledge of concepts but not of products, and will avoid marketing information.
2. There will be a consistent look to the books, including covers, binding, page layout, format, type fonts, spacing, margins, and indentations.
3. There will be educationally sound behavioral objectives for each chapter.
4. There will be test questions, written in a consistent format, matching the objectives for each chapter.
5. There will be an introduction and summary in each chapter.
6. There will be tables, graphs, charts, and illustrations in the books.
7. There will be preparations made for a project kick-off meeting.
8. There will be a project kick-off meeting attended by the writers, the operator of the desktop publishing system, the computer graphics person, the instructional designer, and the testing consultant.
9. There will be chapters written by the writers.
10. There will be an assembling of individual chapters into preliminary books.
11. There will be a consistent editorial style throughout the books, including punctuation, grammar, structure, and use of trademarks.

12. There will be a table of contents, index, and glossary in each book.
13. There will be updated product training books.

**Mission Statement Below Target Statement:
To gather product information from experts**

Related Output Specifications:

• There will be product announcement brochures and articles provided by the product experts.
• There will be notes and audio tapes from interviews with the product experts.

**Next Lower Mission Statement: To identify
experts with Knowledge of the new products**

Related Output Specifications:

• There will be a list of experts provided by instructors.
• There will be by-lines in the product announcement articles.

**Lowest Mission Statement: To identify products
introduced since the existing product training
were written**

Related Output Specifications:

• There will be the existing product training books.
• There will be notes from interviews with instructors.
• There will be past issues of the updates the company sends to the sales force weekly.

V. Context Evaluation

A. Potential Facilitating and Hindering Factors and Their Implications for Project Activities

Potential Facilitating Factors and Their Implications
1. The instructors who conduct classroom training want students to be better prepared when they arrive for training.

Required project activity: Instructors will provide lists of product experts.

2. Product experts are anxious to get their messages in front of the sales force.
   Required project activities:
   a. Get schedule of product update seminars conducted by engineering.
   b. Write guidelines for product experts stating objective of project and defining the kind of product information needed.
3. All participants in this project can transmit documents to one another over a network.
   Required project activity: Compile and distribute a list of electronic addresses to project participants.

Potential Hindering Factors and Their Implications

1. New products will be announced during the project.
   Required project activity: Establish a design-freeze date for each chapter.
2. Each step of the writing, reviewing, revising, editing, and publishing process is subject to unexpected delays, which could cause the project to fall behind schedule.
   Required project activities:
   a. Meet with writers at least weekly to identify potential problems.
   b. Keep management informed with weekly status report on chapters.

B. Output-Input Specifications and Their Implications for Project Activities

Target Mission Statement: To update product training books

1. *Output Specification:* There will be consistency in the level of detail and type of information in the books. For example, the books will have a stated objective, aim at a defined audience, assume a prior knowledge of concepts but not of products, and will avoid marketing information.
   Required Project Activities:
   a. Interview instructors to get a profile of target audience.
   b. Give existing books to instructors, asking them to delete outdated or inappropriate information.
   c. Survey sales representatives in the field to determine positive and negative points of existing books.

     d. Attend the training that precedes this course in the curriculum to better understand the incoming audience.

     e. Consolidate comments made by instructors in step b.

     f. Write a product design document specifying the project objective, the detail of detail and type of information to be contained in books.

     g. Give project design document to instructors for their comments.

     h. Consolidate instructors' comments into final copy of project design document.

2. *Output Specification:* There will be a consistent look to the books, including covers, binding, format, type fonts, spacing, margins, and indentations.

  Input Specification: The existing product training books are not useful as a guide for the new books; however, publishing standards are available, and the project has its own desktop publishing system.

  Required Project Activities:

     a. Identify potential sources of publishing standards.

     b. Meet with the vendor who is providing the desktop publishing software.

     c. Get samples of output produced by vendor's software.

     d. Meet with the publishing group within the company.

     e. Get copies of corporate publishing standards that apply to this project.

     f. Get sample cover designs from the in-house design group.

     g. Decide on publishing standards.

     h. Write publishing standards.

3. *Output Specification:* There will be educationally sound behavioral objectives for each chapter.

  Input Specification: Chapter objectives in the existing books are not stated in behavioral terms; however, an instructional designer is available to help reword the objectives.

  Required Project Activities:

     a. Give instructional designer a copy of project design document.

     b. Meet with instructional designer to explain project.

     c. Get a list of acceptable verbs and sample objectives from instructional designer.

4. *Output Specification:* There will be test questions, written in a consistent format, matching the chapter objectives.

  Input Specification: Test questions in the existing books do not always match objectives and lack a consistent format; however, a testing consultant is available to work with the writers.

  Required Project Activities:

     a. Give the testing consultant the project design document.

    b. Meet with testing consultant to explain project.

    c. Obtain list of test writing guidelines.

5. *Output Specification:* There will be an introduction, summary, and glossary in each chapter.

  Input Specification: The introductions, summaries, and glossaries in the existing books will be inappropriate once the books are updated; however, the writers have guidelines for creating new introductions, summaries, and glossaries.

  Required Project Activities:

    a. Meet with instructional designer and agree upon guidelines for introductions, summaries, and glossaries.

    b. Draft guidelines with instructional designer.

    c. Review draft guidelines with instructional designer.

    d. Update guidelines as a result of review.

6. *Output Specification:* There will be tables, graphs, charts, and illustrations in the books.

  Input Specification: The graphics in the existing books are inappropriate for this project; however, there is money in the budget for new computer graphics.

  Required Project Activities:

    a. Identify a person within the group capable of creating computer graphics.

    b. Send the computer graphics person for training on the software to be used for this project.

    c. Ask the computer graphics person to create guidelines to be used by the writers in the creation of their graphics.

7. *Output Specification:* There will be preparations made for a project kick-off meeting.

  Input Specification: There is no precedent for a meeting of this kind; however, the material developed in the above required project activities provides a basis for the meeting.

  Required Project Activities:

    a. Complete required project activities listed previously as Potential Facilitating and Hindering Factors.

    b. Create project documents: PERT diagram, PERT index, PERT slack table, Gantt diagram, Decision Flow Diagram, and Information Flow Diagram.

8. *Output Specification:* There will be a project kick-off meeting attended by the writers, operator of the desktop publishing system, computer graphics person, instructional designer, and testing consultant.

  Input Specification: The writers are unaware of the scope of this project; however, there is a project design document, a table of contents for each book (developed at a lower mission level), lists of product experts (developed at a lower mission level), guidelines from the instructional designer and the testing consultant, and the information referred to in Output Specification 7.

Required Project Activities:

    a. Conduct a kick-off meeting among writers, operator of the desktop publishing system, computer graphics person, instructional designer, and testing consultant.

    b. Explain the project in terms of its objectives, the level of detail and type of information to be contained in books, as stated in the project design document.

    c. Distribute project design document.

    d. Distribute tables of contents, which were developed at a lower mission level.

    e. Distribute lists of product experts, which were developed at a lower mission level, to writers.

    f. Distribute publishing standards.

    g. Distribute list of verbs that are acceptable for use in writing chapter objectives, including samples of correctly written objectives, to writers.

    h. Distribute test writing guidelines to writers.

    i. Distribute guidelines for writing chapter introductions and summaries to writers.

    j. Distribute graphics guidelines to writers.

    k. Distribute information developed in Output Specification 7.

9. *Output Specification:* There will be chapters written by the writers.
Input Specification: The chapters of the existing books are out of date; however, the content of the chapters, lists of product experts, and writing guidelines are defined.

Required Project Activities:

    a. Review each chapter for compliance with project design document and guidelines.

    b. Meet with writers to resolve potential conflicts in comments returned by product experts.

    c. Arrange meetings between instructional designer and any writers having difficulties with objectives, chapter introductions, or chapter summaries.

    d. Arrange meetings between testing consultant and any writers having difficulties with test construction.

10. *Output Specification:* There will be an assembling of individual chapters into preliminary books.
Input Specifications: Books written to the specifications of this project do not exist; however, the processes of this project are in place to produce correctly structured, technically accurate preliminary books.

Required Project Activities:
    a. Review chapters for repetition, or contradiction, of material appearing in other chapters.
    b. Consolidate electronic versions of chapters into one book-length document.
    c. Merge graphics with text.
    d. Write preface to book.
    e. Write title page.
    f. Merge chapter tests into Appendix A.
    g. Merge test answers into Appendix B.
    h. Merge chapter glossaries into a single glossary at back of book.
    i. Transmit book to editor.

11. *Output Specification:* There will be a consistent editorial style throughout the books, including punctuation, grammar, structure, and use of trademarks.

    Input Specification: The project design document did not have a style sheet; however, there is a professional editor assigned to this project to apply the company's style standards.

    Required Project Activities:
        a. Receive edited, final copy from editor.
        b. Check that editor has applied style standards consistently.
        c. Verify that trademarks page created by editor includes all trademarks mentioned in text of book.
        d. Run program that checks spelling.
        e. Transmit finished copy to operator of desktop publishing system.

12. *Output Specification:* There will be a table of contents, index, and glossary in each book.

    Input Specification: The tables of contents and index in the existing books are inappropriate for the updated versions; however, the desktop publishing system can create tables of contents and indices automatically.

    Required Project Activities:
        a. Ensure that operator of desktop publishing system creates automatic table of contents.
        b. Ensure that operator of desktop publishing system creates automatic index.
        c. Ensure that operator of publishing system lays out page properly.

13. *Output Specification:* There will be updated product training books.

    Input Specification: The existing books are out of date; however, the process described in this project will result in up-to-date product training books.

    Required Project Activities:
        a. Print the books using the desktop publishing system.

b. Send books to the external organization that will reproduce, bind, box, warehouse, and distribute them.

VI. Activity Specifications

A. PERT Index

100 Subsystem	**Establishing Guidelines for Books**
100-110	Interview instructors to get a profile of target audience.
110-120	Collect comments from instructors on which parts of existing books are outdated or inappropriate.
110-130	Attend the training that precedes this course in the curriculum to better understand the incoming audience.
110-140	Survey sales representatives in the field to determine positive and negative points of existing books.
120-140	Consolidate comments made by instructors in activity 110-120.
130-140	Dummy Activity.
140-150	Write a design document specifying the project objective, the levels of detail and type of information to be contained in the books.
150-160	Collect comments on the design document from instructors.
160-300	Consolidate the instructors' comments into the final copy of the design document.

200 Subsystem	**Establishing Publishing Standards**
100-200	Identify potential sources of publishing standards.
200-210	Meet with vendor who is providing the desktop publishing software.
200-220	Meet with the publishing group within the company.
200-230	Get sample cover designs from the in-house design group.
210-230	Get samples of output produced by vendor's software.
220-230	Get copies of corporate publishing standards that apply to this project.
230-240	Decide on publishing standards.
240-700	Write publishing standards.

300 Subsystem	**Setting Guidelines for Chapter Objectives**
300-310	Give instructional designer a copy of the design document.
310-320	Meet with instructional designer to explain project.
320-700	Get a list of acceptable verbs and sample objectives from instructional designer.

400 Subsystem	**Setting Test Writing Guidelines**
300-400	Give the testing consultant the design document.
400-410	Meet with testing consultant to explain project.
410-700	Obtain list of test writing guidelines.

500 Subsystem	**Setting Guidelines for Chapter Introduction, Summary, and Glossary**
300-500	Meet with the instructional designer and agree upon guidelines for introductions, summaries, and glossaries.
500-510	Draft guidelines for writing introductions, summaries, and glossaries.
510-520	Review draft guidelines with instructional designer.
520-700	Update guidelines as a result of review.

600 Subsystem	**Establishing Guidelines for Tables, Graphs, Charts, and Illustrations**
100-600	Identify a person within the group capable of creating computer graphics.
600-610	Send the computer graphics person for training on the software to be used for this project.
610-700	Ask the computer graphics person to create guidelines to be used by the writers in the creation of their graphics.

700 Subsystem	**Preparing for Project Kick-Off Meeting**
700-710	Ask the instructors to provide lists of product experts.
700-720	Get schedules of product update seminars conducted by engineering.
700-730	Write guidelines for product experts stating objective of project and defining the kind of product information needed.

700-740	Compile a list of electronic addresses of project participants to facilitate transfer of documents.
700-750	Establish a design-freeze date for each chapter.
700-760	Create schedule of meetings to keep management updated on project status.
700-770	Create schedule for weekly meetings with writers.
710-770	Dummy Activity
720-770	Dummy Activity
730-770	Dummy Activity
760-770	Dummy Activity
740-770	Dummy Activity
750-770	Dummy Activity
770-800	Create project documents: PERT diagram, PERT index, PERT slack table, Gantt diagram, Decision Flow Diagrams, and Information Flow Diagrams.

800 Subsystem   **Conducting the Kick-Off Meeting**

800-805	Conduct a kick-off meeting among writers, the operator of the desktop publishing system, the computer graphics person, the instructional designer, and the testing consultant.
805-810	Explain the project in terms of its objectives, the levels of detail and type of information to be contained in books, as stated in the design document.
810-815	Distribute table of contents, which were developed at a lower mission level.
810-820	Distribute lists of product experts, which were developed at a lower mission level, to writers.
810-825	Distribute publishing standards.
810-830	Distribute list of verbs that are acceptable for use in writing chapter objectives, including samples of correctly written objectives, to writers.
810-835	Distribute test writing guidelines to writers.
810-840	Distribute guidelines for writing chapter introduction and summaries to writers.
810-845	Distribute graphics guidelines to writers.
810-850	Distribute information developed in Output Specification seven.
810-900	Distribute design document.

815-900	Dummy Activity
820-900	Dummy Activity
825-900	Dummy Activity
830-900	Dummy Activity
835-900	Dummy Activity
840-900	Dummy Activity
845-900	Dummy Activity
850-900	Dummy Activity

900 Subsystem   **Checking the Chapters**

900-910	Review each chapter for compliance with the design document and guidelines.
910-920	Meet with writers to resolve potential conflicts in comments returned by product experts.
920-930	Arrange meetings between testing consultant and any writers having difficulties with test construction.
920-940	Meet with writers at least weekly to identify potential problems.
920-1000	Arrange meetings between instructional designer and any writers having difficulties with objectives, chapter introduction, or chapter summaries.
930-1000	Dummy Activity
940-1000	Keep management informed with weekly status reports on chapters.

1000 Subsystem   **Assembling of Individual Chapters into Preliminary Books**

1000-1010	Review chapters for repetition or contradiction of material appearing in other chapters.
1010-1020	Merge graphics with texts.
1010-1030	Write preface to book.
1010-1040	Write title page.
1010-1050	Merge chapter tests into Appendix A.
1010-1060	Merge test answers into Appendix B.
1010-1070	Merge chapter glossaries into a single glossary at back of book.
1010-1080	Consolidate electronic versions of chapters into one book-length document.
1080-1100	Transmit book to editor.

1100 Subsystem   **Editing the Books**

1100-1100   Receive edited, final copy from the editor.

1110-1120   Check that editor has applied style standards consistently.

1110-1130   Verify that trademarks page created by editor includes all trademarks mentioned in text of book.

1120-1130   Dummy Activity

1130-1140   Run program that check spelling.

1140-1200   Transmit finished copy to operator of desktop publishing system.

1200 Subsystem   **Creating Table of Contents, Index, and Glossary**

1200-1210   Ensure that the operator of the desktop publishing system creates an automatic index.

1200-1220   Ensure that operator of desktop publishing system lays out pages properly.

1200-1300   Develop a glossary of terms.

1210-1300   Dummy Activity

1220-1300   Ensure that operator of desktop publishing system creates automatic table of contents.

1300 Subsystem   **Printing and Distributing the Books**

1300-1310   Print the books using the desktop publishing system.

1310-1320   Send books to the external organization that will reproduce, bind, box, warehouse, and distribute them.

B. PERT Diagram

See following pages.

C. PERT Slack Table

Project Event	$T(L)$	$T(E)$	Slack Time	Project Event	$T(L)$	$T(E)$	Slack Time
100*	0	0	0	815*	36	36	0
110*	3	3	0	820*	36	36	0
120	7	6	1	825*	36	36	0
130	8	7	1	830*	36	36	0

Continued

PERT Diagram—Part 1

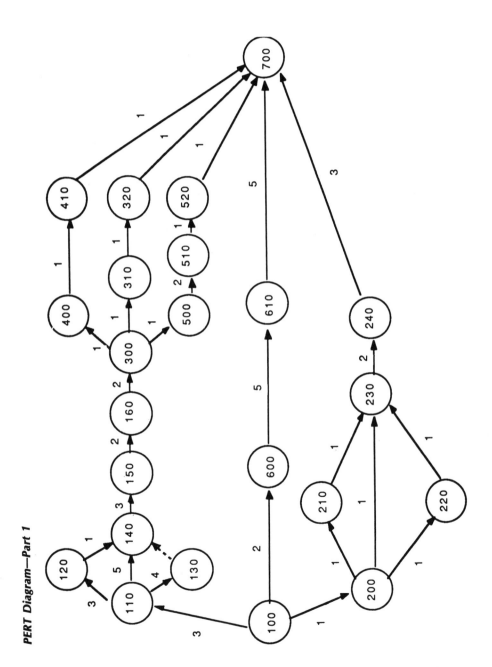

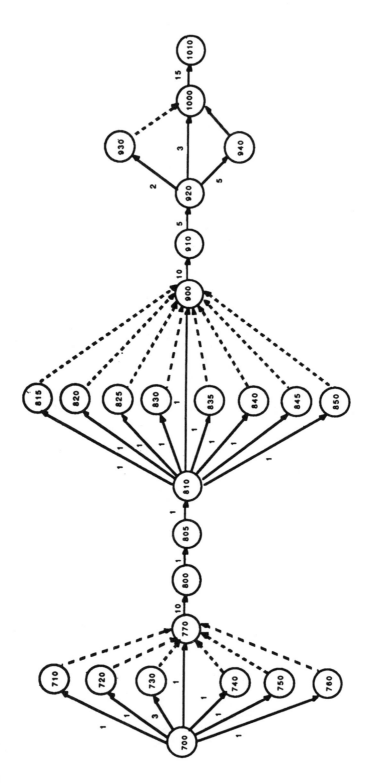

PERT Diagram—Part 2

PERT Diagram—Part 3

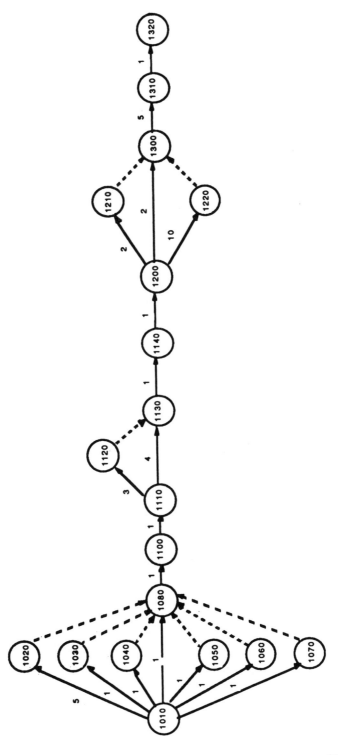

140*	8	8	0	835*	36	36	0
150*	11	11	0	840*	36	36	0
160*	13	13	0	845*	36	36	0
200	13	1	12	850*	36	36	0
210	14	2	12	900*	36	36	0
220	13	2	11	910*	46	46	0
230	15	2	13	920*	51	51	0
240	15	3	12	930	58	53	5
250	17	5	12	940*	56	56	0
300*	15	15	0	1000*	58	58	0
310	18	16	2	1010*	73	73	0
320	19	17	2	1020*	78	78	0
400	18	16	2	1030	78	74	4
410	19	17	2	1040	78	74	4
500*	16	16	0	1050	78	74	4
510*	18	18	0	1060	78	74	4
520*	19	19	0	1070	78	74	4
600	10	2	8	1080*	78	78	0
610	15	7	7	1100	79	79	0
700*	20	20	0	1110*	80	80	0
710	23	21	2	1120	84	83	1
720	23	21	2	1130*	84	84	0
730*	23	23	0	1140*	85	85	0
740	23	21	2	1200*	86	86	0
750	23	21	2	1210	96	88	8
760	23	21	2	1220*	96	96	0
770	23	21	2	1300*	96	96	0
800*	33	33	0	1310*	101	101	0
805*	34	34	0	1320*	102	102	0
810*	35	35	0				

T(S) for project is 102 days.

*Project events on the critical path are marked with an asterisk; these events have zero slack time.

D. Gantt Diagram

See page 205.

E. Decision Flow Diagram with Information Inputs and Outputs

See pages 206–210.

F. Information Flow Diagram (Activity 910-920) Keyed to the Information Inputs and Outputs Shown on the Decision Flow Diagram

See page 211.

Illustrative Gantt Diagram

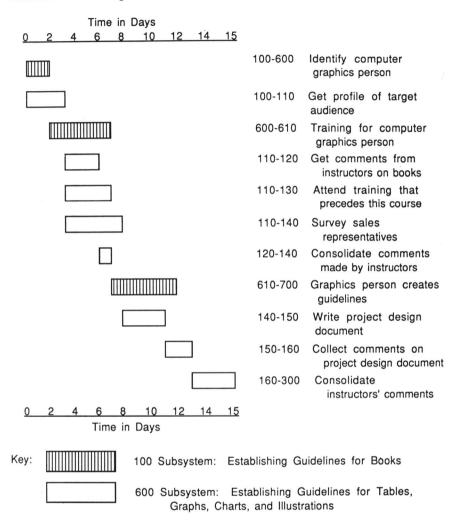

Time in Days

100-600	Identify computer graphics person
100-110	Get profile of target audience
600-610	Training for computer graphics person
110-120	Get comments from instructors on books
110-130	Attend training that precedes this course
110-140	Survey sales representatives
120-140	Consolidate comments made by instructors
610-700	Graphics person creates guidelines
140-150	Write project design document
150-160	Collect comments on project design document
160-300	Consolidate instructors' comments

Time in Days

Key: 100 Subsystem: Establishing Guidelines for Books

600 Subsystem: Establishing Guidelines for Tables, Graphs, Charts, and Illustrations

G. The Documentation of One Illustrative Project Activity

1. PERT Number and Title: 800-805. Conduct a kick-off meeting among writers, the operator of the desktop publishing system, the computer graphics person, the instructional designer, and the testing consultant.

Decision Flow Diagram—Part 1/5

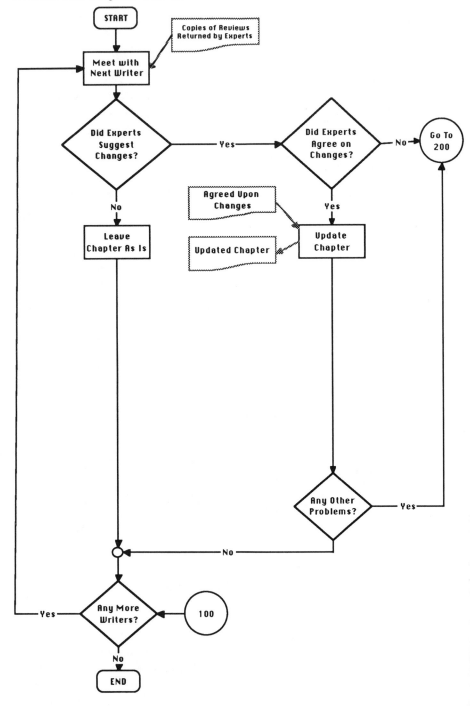

Decision Flow Diagram—Part 2/5

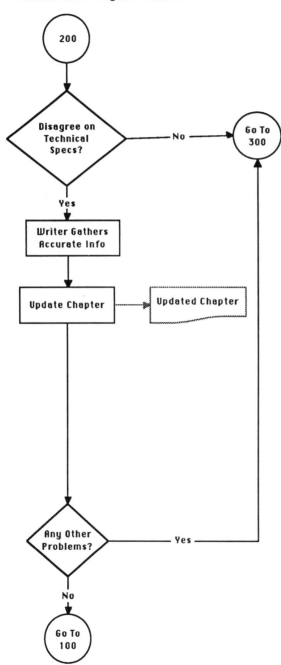

Decision Flow Diagram—Part 3/5

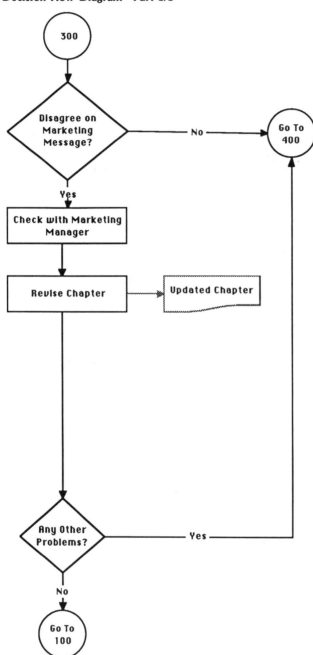

Decision Flow Diagram—Part 4/5

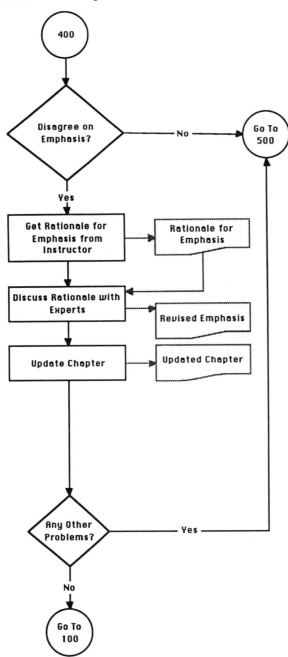

Decision Flow Diagram—Part 5/5

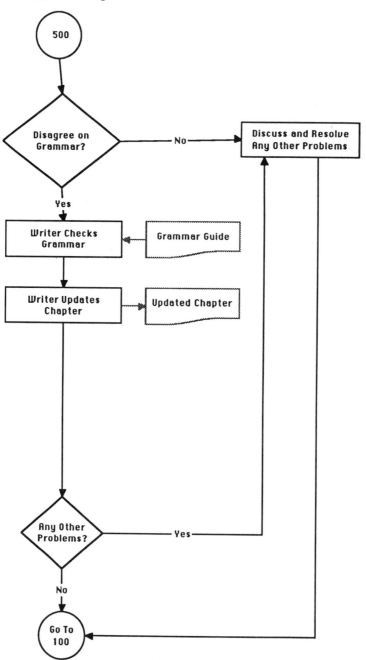

Illustrative Information Flow Diagram

Med. Rcds. Info. System   Unit Mgr.   3 Sister Hospitals   P. M. Info. Syst.   Task Force   P. M. Admin.

NOTES

1. Report on 10 Most Common Cancers Treated

2. 3 Sisters Hospital Report

3. Providence Hospital Information

4. Comparative Analysis

5. Comparative Analysis

6. Scope of Service Plan

211

2. Activity Description:

   This project will involve more than 20 people, some of whom will be on loan from support organizations within the company. Many of these people have never met before. Most of them have never worked together on a project. The meeting will last about an hour and will take place on-site. Visuals will be shown using an overhead projector. Refreshments will be served. The group manager will give five minutes of opening remarks, emphasizing the importance of the project. As project manager, I will be the only other speaker, but I will invite the managers who are present to assist me in answering questions.

3. Expected Outputs:

   There will be:

   a. Enthusiasm for the project and a sense of team spirit to get the job done. People leaving the meeting must have a clear picture of the project and understand their roles.

   b. Teams consisting of a writer and an instructor for each book.

   c. A final goal for each team, and a set of intermediate goals.

   d. Deadlines set by each team for meeting all goals.

   e. A follow-up meeting scheduled for these attendees for team progress reports.

   f. Understanding of the goal of the project and of each individual's role in meeting the goal.

4. Required Input Conditions:

   a. Management commitment to the resources to complete the project.

   b. Management approval of the teams and the overall goals of the project.

   c. A list of participants, their phone numbers, and electronic addresses.

   d. A meeting room that can seat 25 people at tables arranged in a *U*-shape, with lights that can be dimmed, and window coverings that can be drawn.

   e. Management approval to serve complimentary refreshments.

   f. Fruit, crackers, cheese, juice, and soft drinks from the cafeteria, arranged in an attractive way on a table at the back of the room, including paper plates, napkins, plastic cutlery, and cups.

   g. Wastepaper baskets around the room.

   h. An overhead projector, spare bulb, and 4 × 6 foot projection screen set up in the room.

   i. A lavaliere microphone with volume control and speakers arranged to avoid feedback.

   j. A marker board with eraser, markers of at least three different colors, and a pointer.

5. Required Resources and Associated Costs (Activity Budget):
    a. Writers—5 for three months at $50/hr. (includes phone, copier usage, computer time, supplies, travel, office space, and associated overhead) $132,000
    b. Instructors' hours are not charged to this project   0
    c. Product experts' hours are not charged to this project   0
    d. Clerical staff—2 for three months at $35/hr.   36,960
    e. Computer graphics—5 graphics per chapter for 37 chapters at $25 each   4,625
    f. Editor for 144 hours at $48/hr.   6,912
    TOTAL $180,497
6. Management Responsibilities
    a. The new hire sales training manager must make the writers, instructors, clerical staff, office environment, and computer equipment available for this project and must fund the outside resources, such as the graphics artist and editor.
    b. The project manager must arrange for the production of computer graphics and the services of the editor. The project manager is responsible for a quality product, on time and on budget. This means monitoring the project full time, anticipating problems, and resolving conflicts.
    c. The product experts are not within the control of this project; however, they have cooperated with similar efforts in the past.
    d. The cafeteria staff will ensure that there are baskets for the crackers and slicers for the cheese. The clerical staff will ensure the refreshments are in the room prior to the start of the meeting.
    e. The items listed as handouts for this meeting in the 800 subsystem will be put in a package, with a cover letter listing the contents and emphasizing the importance of the project. The clerical staff will make 40 copies of the package and have one copy at each seat at the start of the meeting.
    f. The members of the clerical staff providing assistance will have copies of these input conditions as a checklist of pre-meeting duties.

H. Internal Interface Analysis

This section looks back on the plan and considers where improvements could be made.

The PERT chart shows there is congestion at the 800 Subsystem—Conducting the Kick-off Meeting. The critical path fragments into nine segments in this subsystem; the PERT index shows that all nine activities start with the verb "Distribute" and involve handing out guidelines and standards. If the project could spread out these "Distribute" activities, it would flow more smoothly.

The 800 Subsystem of the PERT chart highlights a flaw in the project design, but also suggests ways to fix it:

- Nine elaborate lists of guidelines and standards are being handed to project participants at their first project meeting. This could negate the enthusiasm and positive feelings generated by the meeting.
- It is easier to follow examples than lists of guidelines and standards. Thus, in preparation for the meeting, the project manager should write a sample chapter that follows the guidelines and standards and use it for discussion at the meeting.
- Setting rules without the participation of the project members could jeopardize the success of the project by creating resentment. It would be better to let the discussion of the sample chapter be a guide, and to create guidelines and standards after the meeting.

Thus, this Internal Interface Analysis shows that the project should be modified. Project guidelines and standards should be created after the activities shown in the 800 Subsystem, but handed to project participants before the writing begins in the 900 Subsystem.

APPENDIX B

Lower's Paper

Establishing a Comprehensive Cancer Program

Mardella Lower
Education 692, Practical Administrative Techniques
Profs. Alan Gaynor and Jane Evanson
August 1987

Executive Summary

The purpose of this plan is to develop and provide a Comprehensive Cancer Program at Providence Hospital in Anchorage, Alaska. Cancer treatment has become highly specialized. We need a team approach to care for people with this dynamic disease. Staff members must have expertise to care for cancer patients and their families. We at Providence need to recognize cancer treatment as a specialization. We need to focus our energies on the development of a multidisciplinary team approach to cancer care.

Our hospital is fortunate to have many dedicated and knowledgeable professionals in the field of cancer. They have a great desire to work with cancer patients and families. The need for administrative support to designate cancer care as a specialization and assist with the development of a cancer program exists. A Comprehensive Cancer Program will allow for even more success in the treatment of this dynamic disease.

TABLE OF CONTENTS

I. Background Statement

Cancer covers the scope of practice from pediatrics to geriatrics and from medicine to surgery. An organized team approach is essential for treating all phases of the disease, from initial diagnosis through treatment, during follow-up, and at death. All team members involved with the cancer patient have a unique and collaborative role in the care and management of patient and family problems.

Historically, the Providence Hospital has been, and still is, the major referral center for the State of Alaska for cancer treatment. The cancer patient has been integrated with the general medical patient. Their care has been provided on a 46-bed medical unit. This unit functions at a 90% bed occupancy rate and is extremely busy. The staff are medical generalists, as medical nurses need to be. Often they are ill prepared to meet the special needs of the cancer patient, due to lack of specific training in the area of cancer treatment. Dealing with the special needs of a terminally ill patient is labor intensive and cannot be adequately accomplished while attempting to also serve the recovering medical patient.

The first Medical Oncologist joined the Providence Hospital staff in 1971. This individual brought the knowledge and ability to treat appropriate types of cancer without surgery. Providence had a Radiation Oncologist join the medical staff in 1978. This physician brought the latest in radiation treatment to the people of the State of Alaska. Providence now has several more oncologists in varying fields ready to participate in the medical treatment of cancer. Medical intervention of cancer has become more of the norm for the treatment of this disease instead of radical surgical procedures. These physicians have promoted the development of special courses in the care and treatment of cancer patients. Some nurses working on the medical unit have taken a very special interest in cancer treatment. They have taken additional training and certification in this field. They are few in number and their frustrations are many.

Currently there is no strategic plan for the care and treatment of the cancer patient's medical management at Providence Hospital. A definitive Comprehensive Cancer Treatment Program, involving administrative, fiscal, and clinical participation, is needed to provide the services and coordination necessary to engage this dynamic disease. The diagnosis of cancer generates tremendous stress in the patient/family system. Treatment may be long and difficult. Perhaps most stressful is the uncertainty of the outcome. The future, which held dreams and promises, may be tragically short. The threat of death is tangible. A Comprehensive Cancer Program is vital to assist the patient and family in understanding what is happening, help them manage the side effects of therapy and the disease, and maximize the quality of their lives.

Providence Hospital, like all hospitals in the country, is challenged to meet the future needs for cancer services. The wellness movement and the thrust to treat outside the traditional hospital as well as increasing numbers of survivors of cancer will shape the delivery of cancer services. An innovative hospital that combines clinical, marketing and business savvy with cancer program development shares the vision of cancer care evolution. Planning needs to begin immediately, and how the hospital's role will change by the year 2000 is predicted to be dramatic. An innovative, rather than responsive, comprehensive plan involving all related areas must be implemented at once to meet the current and future needs of cancer patients and their families. I believe that a Comprehensive Cancer Program will meet this need.

II. Mission Hierarchy

5. To enhance the quality of life for all patients suffering from cancer.
2. To meet the physical, emotional, educational and spiritual needs of cancer patients.
3. *To provide the cancer patient with a comprehensive cancer treatment program.*
2. To gain approval for hiring more staff to provide care for the cancer patients.
1. To increase administrative awareness of the need for a specific, designated cancer service.

III. Mission Target and Rationale

In order to provide the best possible environment for treating all people with cancer at Providence Hospital, a Comprehensive Cancer Program is needed.

Do all cancer patients feel alone? Must they endure the experience of diagnosis and therapy believing that their tumor creates a barrier that the "well" cannot penetrate? The treatment of cancer is a separate and unique science of its own. The medical profession sees it as that, and has developed special degrees and programs for cancer therapy called Oncology. Providence Hospital cannot continue to treat this dynamic and far-reaching disease as an ancillary addition to other nonfatal medical diseases. The multifocused impact of this disease on the patient, his family, job, quality of life and indeed, life itself requires that the treatment facility develop and implement a separate unit for the treatment of the cancer patient.

Special treatments, programs and equipment are now available to provide the cancer patient in Alaska the best possible medical outcome. The personnel and a program that pulls all these services together is needed. A Comprehensive Cancer Program to serve these people is essential. Let's not continue to deny that people with this devastating disease deserve and require a team of individuals who are skilled and specialized in the care of the cancer patient.

With the advent of more sophisticated diagnostic tests and more doctors specializing in the field of cancer treatment working at Providence Hospital, many more support services are needed to provide all the care requirements generated by these individuals. People are the support services; more qualified staff are needed to meet this dynamic field of care.

Level four cannot be achieved until level three is accomplished. Level two must be achieved and more staff provided to accomplish level three. A definitive, comprehensive cancer treatment program is essential to provide all services and coordination required for the care and treatment of the cancer patient with his unique and far-reaching needs.

IV. Output Specifications at the Target Mission Level and Below

Level 3.   **To provide the cancer patient with a comprehensive cancer program.**

3.1   There will be a clear statement of the mission of a comprehensive cancer program.

3.2   There will be a clear definition of the scope of services for an inpatient cancer program.

3.3   There will be specific educational programs for the cancer service.

3.4   There will be a multidisciplinary team approach to cancer patient care.

3.5   There will be a marketing strategy developed to provide information to the staff, community, State and the Providence Corporation that a specific Comprehensive Cancer Program exists.

Level 2.   **To gain approval for hiring more staff to provide cancer patient care.**

2.1   There will be a Comprehensive Cancer Program business plan.

2.2   There will be a financial system proposed to indicate cost and outcome for inpatient cancer services.

2.3   There will be a designated increase in the number of full-time employees to support a comprehensive cancer program.

Level 1.   **To increase Administration's knowledge of the need for a designated cancer service.**

1.1   There will be an increased awareness by Administration of the need to treat the cancer patient in a holistic way.

1.2   There will be information obtained from other Sister Hospitals in the Corporation that currently provide a designated cancer service to ascertain why they provide such a service.

V. Context Evaluation

A. Output-Input Specifications and Their Implications for Project Activities

Level 3.   **To provide the Cancer Patient a Comprehensive Cancer Program.**

Output Specifications	Input Specifications
3.1 There will be a clear statement of the mission of a Comprehensive Cancer Program at Providence Hospital.	3.1A. No mission currently exists; however, there is a mission statement for the entire facility describing the caring and healing of all patients in a compassionate way. The medical unit where cancer patients are treated has a unit practicum describing the mission of caring for all patients admitted to the service.
	3.1B. Project activities will include: 1. Cancer Nurse Coordinator will chair a task force to develop a mission statement. 2. Publish a pamphlet specifically for the cancer patient, beginning with the mission statement.
3.2 There will be a clear definition of the scope of services for an	3.2A. Presently there is not a clear definition of inpatient cancer service; however, one

inpatient cancer program.

does exist for outpatient cancer services.

3.2B. Project activities will include:

1. Obtain information from Medical Records Department for each type of cancer admitted to the medical unit.

2. Develop a list of the ten most common types of cancer treated to provide information to implement a program that meets the needs of the patient to be treated.

3. Engage Cancer Nurse. Coordinator and task force to write levels of care for each type of cancer to be treated, defining the scope of that care. Use supporting information from other Sister Hospitals that have designated cancer units.

4. Prepare nursing policies and procedures in the care of the cancer patient with models obtained from Sister Hospitals with cancer units.

5. Determine and assign specific hours of care for the cancer patient.

3.3 There will be specific educational programs for the cancer service.

3.3A. No formal comprehensive educational cancer program exists in the hospital; however, programs have been developed by the medical unit nursing staff. Some free pamphlets are made available to patients and family from the American Cancer Society.

3.4 There will be a multi-disciplinary team approach to cancer patient care.

3.5 There will be a marketing strategy developed to provide information to the staff, community, State and

3.3B. Project activities will include:
1. Cancer Nurse Coordinator, task force and Continuing Education Department wil develop written educational programs for staff with supporting information from the National Oncology Nursing Society.
2. Cancer Nurse Coordinator, task force and Continuing Education Department will write cancer education programs for patients/families.

3.4A. No formal process exists for each member to meet and discuss patient care issues with the frequency needed; however, weekly rounds are held presently for the purpose of communication, planning and information sharing.

3.4B. Project activities will include:
1. Identify the members of the Multidisciplinary Team.
2. Have each member of the team write a description of his or her role in the care of the patient.
3. Team members will write a process for describing the plan for each patient's care.
4. Develop a form used in the patient's medical record to convey information.

3.5A. No marketing strategies exist for a cancer program; however, a successful Community Relations Depart-

the Providence Corporation that a specific Comprehensive Cancer Program exists.

ment is in place that has demonstrated the ability to provide services to accomplish this goal.

Output Specifications

Input Specifications

3.5B. Project activities will include:
1. Cancer Nurse Coordinator and the Community Relations Department will develop a brochure describing a comprehensive cancer program.
2. Publish human interest stories in the community newspapers describing cancer patient care at Providence Hospital.
3. Develop television advertisements describing the cancer program.
4. Patients and families will refer other patients to the program through established networking with Anchorage Hospice and other organizations.

Level 2.   To gain administrative approval for hiring more staff to provide cancer patient care.

Output Specifications

Input Specifications

2.1 There will be a Comprehensive Cancer Program business plan.

2.1A. Presently there is not a hensive Cancer Program business plan; however, most of the information needed is available through our Medical Records Department, Accounting and Hospital statisticians reports that provide information about financial reimbursement.

2.1B. Project activities will include:

1. Obtaining and reviewing statistical information from our Medical Records Department regarding the number of cancer patients treated medically in the last two years on the medical unit.

2. Review and prepare a report of the top ten types of cancer treated, their length of stay and the reimbursement provided for their hospitalization.

3. Review and determine the major modes of treatment for the top ten diagnoses.

4. Review Hospital Information System reports and determine the major physicians who admit and treat patients medically with cancer.

5. Prepare a comprehensive business plan with information obtained to support a cancer program.

6. Present information in the form of a report supporting a Comprehensive Cancer Program business plan to Administration.

2.2 There will be a financial system proposed to indicate cost and outcome for inpatient cancer services.

2.2A. There is no financial system available at present to indicate cost and outcome for inpatient cancer services; however, there is a billing and accounting system in place that could provide computerized billing for costing out inpatient cancer services.

2.2B. Project activities will
include:
1. Determine the ten major
types of cancer treated.
2. Determine reimbursement
systems for those diagnoses
based on information available through Accounting.
3. Develop a charge system
for specific care provided
with help from the Finance
Department.
4. Develop policies and procedures for charging and
biling for services provided.
5. Incorporate the billing
and reimbursement system
into Providence Hospital's
accounting system.
6. Develop, and have
printed, a formal charge
and billing schedule and
have available to both
physicians and patients.

2.3 There will be a designated
increase in the number of
full-time employees to support a comprehensive
program.

2.3A. There is no plan for a
designated increase in the
number of full-time em-
ployees to support a com-
prehensive cancer program;
however, there are Sister
Hospitals in the Corporation
with designated cancer units
that can be used as sources
of information on the ratio
of patients to nurses.

2.3B. Activities to demonstrate the
need to increase the number
of full-time employees
include:
1. Obtain information from
three Sister Hospitals with
designated cancer units
regarding the nurses-per-

patient ratio in their cancer units.

2. Ask three Sister Hospitals if they have an acuity-based staffing system. Request reports on their hours of care provided in these units.

3. Compare their staffing budget with the existing medical unit.

4. Monitor the cancer patients' average acuity level on the medical unit for two months to determine the "average standard hour of care" per patient day.

5. Establish an average acuity level for the cancer patient using the existing measuring tool used for the medical patient.

6. Prepare a budget proposal change for a new "hour of care" for cancer patients.

7. Present new "hour of care" budget proposal for hiring more staff for cancer patient care.

8. Gain administrative approval for hiring more staff to provide cancer patient care.

Level 1.   To increase Administration's knowledge of the need for a designated cancer service.

Output Specifications	**Input Specifications**
1.1 There will be an increased awareness of the need to treat the cancer patient in a Comprehensive Cancer Program approach.	1.1A. There is no administrative approval for a designated cancer service; however, some of the individual administrators are very

interested in further development of a designated approach to care.

1.1B. Activities to gain administrative approval for a designated cancer service include:

1. Identify inpatient cancer care as a designated service with specific goals.

2. Identify cancer care as a specialization.

3. Obtain supportive statements from the Radiation Oncologists and the Medical Oncologists who care for the cancer patients.

4. Define for Administration our current number of patients treated with cancer on the general medical unit. Provide and analyze a report of statistical data to outline this information.

5. Meet with Administration to review this information.

6. Obtain approval for a designated service.

1.2 There will be information obtained from Sister Hospitals in the Corporation currently providing a designated cancer service to ascertain why they provide such a service.

1.2A. There is no information currently available from Sister Hospitals in the Corporation that currently provide a designated cancer service; however, there are many contacts available within the Corporation.

1.2B. Activities to obtain information about designated programs will include:

1. Contact managers of three Sister Hospitals and ask for specific information about their programs.

2. Develop a short survey that will provide information about their service and why they provide it.

3. Analyze information and develop a plan for a Comprehensive Cancer Program to be presented to Providence Hospital Administrative Team.

B. Potential Facilitating and Hindering Factors and Their Implications for Project Activities

Below are factors that can facilitate and hinder the mission of developing a Comprehensive Cancer Program for cancer patients. In addition, each facilitating factor has one or more activities. Likewise, for each potential hindering factor are activities that purport to deal with those factors. These activities have been integrated into the project design and appear explicitly in the PERT Index and PERT Diagram.

Facilitating Factors

1. a. Currently there are four Registered Nurses working on the medical unit who are certified in Oncology nursing. They are willing to assist in any way to develop and provide more knowledgeable nurses working with the cancer patient.
    b. In order to take advantage of the knowledge of the nurses with special certification, paid time will have to be provided for those people to assist in the development of further teaching programs for nurses who care for the cancer patient.
2. a. There are educational programs already in place in the facility to assist the nurse specializing in cancer care.
    b. In order to take advantage of these programs, a more frequent scheduling of the programs will have to exist and an increase in the number of educational hours will be necessary to accommodate this needed education.
3. a. there are many hospital employees at all levels who have a good understanding of the special needs and skills required for the cancer patient.
    b. These employees need to be unified and mobilized and a comprehensive Cancer Program could be defined by these individuals.

4.   a. The medical unit has a nurse who acts as a Cancer Nurse Coordinator for a segment of cancer patients; time is provided once a week for her to act in this role.

b. In order to take advantage of this individual's knowledge and expertise, more time needs to be provided for more than one day a week to perform in this role. She has the education and background to pull all these services together and develop a more comprehensive program.

Hindering Factors

1.   a. Educational programs do not exist in Alaska for cancer nursing education other than programs currently provided at Providence Hospital. All formal cancer education programs are offered out of State.

b. Providence Hospital has the ability to be the major educational provider in cancer nursing care in the state. The staff with the knowledge, expertise and certification are available in the facility. Providence Hospital's Continuing Education Department and the cancer care staff could provide such a program. Those who attend could be charged a fee to cover the costs. This offering would also assist in marketing the services provided in the facility.

2.   a. Many physicians and staff are against a designated cancer unit because of the connotation of "death row."

b. There are three Medical Oncologists and two Radiation Oncologists currently practicing medical care at Providence Hospital. The physician could assist in conveying the importance of a designated service and in gaining the support from other physicians and staff in the need for the service. A task force, to include doctors and staff, should be used as an incentive in getting them to buy into this plan.

3.   a. There are no qualified personnel available to hire for jobs that are already specialized in cancer nursing.

b. The importance of designating a cancer treatment unit at Providence Hospital will have to be communicated to Administration and the Personnel Department in order to recruit trained and experienced staff.

VI. Activity Specifications

A. PERT Index

100 Subsystem: Identifying Task Force and Support Group for Service
100-110   Identify key professional staff from all hospital disciplines that

currently work with the medical management of the cancer patients at present.

100-120	Define the members of the medical management team as the multidisciplinary cancer patient team.
100-130	Obtain description of each member's role in the care of the patient.
110-140	Dummy Activity
120-140	Solicit support of medical Oncologist to act as advisor of program development.
130-140	Dummy Activity
140-150	Obtain support and time of the multidisciplinary team members to assist in the work of a task force to develop a Comprehensive Cancer Program plan.
150-160	Identify specific responsibilities for the task force.
150-170	Plan task force meetings and development of time line for project.
160-200	Conduct ongoing meetings with task force to develop a clear mission statement of services.
160-170	Dummy Activity
170-180	Engage task force in program development.
180-190	Review information and outcome of program plan.

200 Subsystem Defining the Scope of Service

200-210	Develop goals and objectives for the service.
210-220	Engage Cancer Nurse Coordinator and task force to write plan for scope of service for cancer patients.
210-230	Research and identify at least ten of the most common types of cancer treated on the Medical Unit through information requested and received from Medical Records and Hospital Information System.
210-600	Assign Oncology Nurse Coordinator to develop and coordinate cancer nursing education.
220-240	Dummy Activity
230-240	Request reports from Medical Records tracking at least the ten most common types of cancer treated on the medical unit for one year.
230-300	Develop levels of care for each type of cancer patient most commonly treated, define scope of care.
240-250	Develop standards of nursing care for the medical management of the cancer patient service.

240-260   Write policies and procedures for cancer patient care.

250-270   Dummy Activity

260-270   Define the role of the multidisciplinary team in the care of the cancer patient.

300 Subsystem: Planning for a Comprehensive Cancer Program

300-310   Obtain information from the Hospital Information System indicating the insurance, Medicare, Medicaid and private pay financial reimbursement to the hospital for the past year for cancer patients treated medically on the medical unit.

300-320   Obtain information from three Sister Hospitals that have designated cancer units regarding their scope of service, financial reimbursement, labor budget (staffing), policies and procedures and integration of the program with their facility.

310-320   Analyze information obtained from Medical Records and the Providence Hospital Information System and prepare a report of findings indicating the high and low reimbursement to the hospital by diagnosis.

320-330   Compare information obtained from three Sister Hospitals with the current medical management of the cancer patient at Providence Anchorage to assist in defining a new scope of service.

330-400   Develop plan for Scope of Service.

400 Subsystem: Administrative Approval

400-410   Develop a proposal statement to include information about what the scope of service for a Comprehensive Cancer Program would entail.

400-420   Identify cancer care as a specialization.

410-440   Obtain supportive statements for a Comprehensive Cancer Program from Radiation Oncologist and Medical Oncologist to submit to Administration.

420-430   Analyze and review statistical information regarding the number of cancer patients treated medically and present information to Administration.

430-440   Provide a comparative analysis with information received from three Sister Hospitals that have designated cancer units and the service provided to cancer patients on the medical unit at Providence Anchorage.

440-450   Identify variable fixed costs, submit cost and benefit comparative analysis for service.

440-700	Incorporate the billing and reimbursement system for the cancer program into Providence accounting system.
450-460	Review formal proposal with administrative representatives.
450-500	Submit staffing levels projected to support program.
460-500	Obtain administrative approval for the project.

500 Subsystem: Increasing Labor Budget

500-510	Establish the average acuity level for the cancer patient using the existing measuring tool.
500-520	Monitor the acuity level of the cancer patient on the medical unit for two months to determine the "average standard hours of care" per patient day.
510-520	Prepare a report defining the hours of nursing time needed for the average cancer patient.
520-530	Identify education time needed per staff member for programs and budget for it.
520-540	Budget planning time for Oncology Nurse Coordinator to be full-time.
520-550	Plan marketing program.
540-560	List needed budget increase in the number of full-time employees needed to support program.
540-570	Submit budget proposal for change in standard hours of patient care to Administration.
560-570	Dummy Activity
550-800	Budget time for marketing program.
570-580	Obtain administrative approval for hiring more full-time employees to provide comprehensive cancer patient program.

600 Subsystem: Organizing and Revising Education and Training

600-610	Determine staff educational needs.
600-620	Plan for providing in-service training to staff.
610-630	Dummy Activity
620-630	Establish cancer nursing education program development with the support of the Providence Continuing Education Department.
630-640	Develop and provide a mandatory course for all nurses caring for cancer patients in "Basic Concepts in Cancer Nursing" course.
630-650	Determining staff self-training needs.
640-660	Provide a mandatory course for all nurses caring for cancer patients in "Basic Concepts in the Care of the Patient Receiving Radiation Therapy" course.

650-670   Develop self-training modules for all staff education.

660-690   Establish nurse instructor course for the patient education program for the cancer patient who is receiving chemotherapy.

670-690   Establish nurse instructor course for the patient education program for the cancer patient who is receiving radiation therapy.

700 Subsystem: Establishing Systems for Charges and Billing

700-710   Review charging, billing and reimbursement systems established by three Sister Hospitals for services they provide in their Comprehensive Cancer Program.

700-720   Determine, with the help of the Accounting Department, which insurance companies are willing to pay for outlined services for cancer patient care.

700-730   Determine, with Accounting's help, the appropriate charges for the nursing services provided.

710-740   Dummy Activity

720-740   Determine, with Accounting's help, the best type of billing and reimbursement to use.

730-740   Dummy Activity

740-750   Develop, and have printed, a formal charge and billing schedule; have available to physicians and patients.

800 Subsystem: Promoting and Marketing the Program

800-810   Identify service strengths and match to user requirements.

800-820   Develop a pamphlet describing the purpose and scope of service.

800-830   Develop articles for hospital paper.

810-840   Dummy Activity

820-840   Obtain assistance from Community Relations in developing advertisements for all media promoting the program.

830-840   Dummy Activity

840-850   Identify key support groups and ensure referral group awareness.

850-860   Publish human interest stories in the community newspapers.

860-900   Patients and families will refer other patients to the program through Anchorage Hospice and other organizations.

900 Subsystem: Evaluating the Program

900-910   Provide Job Satisfaction Questionnaires.

900-920	Plan to audit Patient Satisfaction Questionnaires.
910-920	Obtain market share statistical analysis and projections.
920-930	Monitor and identify service improvements.
930-940	Analyze financial reimbursement statements once program is in place to determine profit and loss.
940-950	Develop quality assurance monitoring of program service.
950-960	Provide monthly reports to Administration on quality of service.

B. PERT Chart

See pages 236–238.

C. Slack Table in Weeks

Event	TL	TE	Slack	Event	TL	TE	Slack
100	2	0	2*	500	20	18	2*
110	4	1	3	510	21	19	2*
120	3	1	2*	520	22	20	2*
130	4	2	2*	530	34	21	13
140	4	2	2*	540	34	21	13
150	5	3	2*	550	23	21	2*
160	6	4	2*	560	35	22	13
170	34	4	30	570	35	22	13
180	35	5	30	580	36	23	13
190	36	6	30	600	31	7	24
200	7	5	2*	610	33	8	25
210	8	6	2*	620	32	8	24
220	34	7	27	630	33	9	24
230	9	7	2*	640	34	10	24
240	34	8	26	650	34	10	24
250	36	9	27	660	35	11	24
260	35	9	26	670	35	11	24
270	36	10	26	690	36	12	24
300	11	9	2*	700	33	17	16
310	13	10	3	710	35	18	17
320	12	10	2*	720	34	18	16
330	13	11	2*	730	35	18	17
400	14	12	2*	740	35	19	16
410	17	13	4	750	36	20	16
420	15	13	2*	800	24	22	2*
430	16	14	2*	810	26	23	3
440	17	15	2*	820	25	23	2*
450	18	16	2*	830	26	23	3
460	19	17	2*	840	26	24	2*

Continued

PERT Diagram, Part I

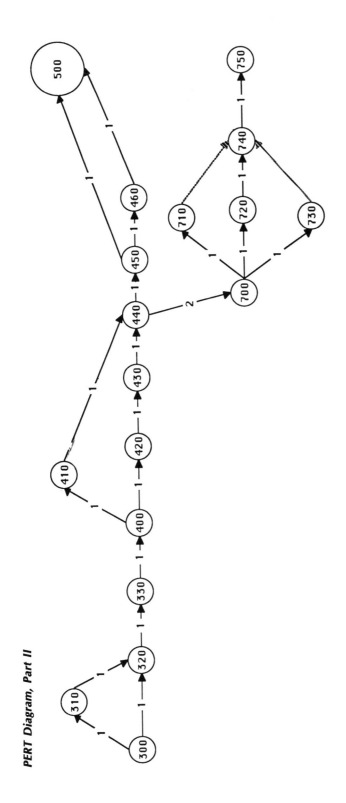

PERT Diagram, Part II

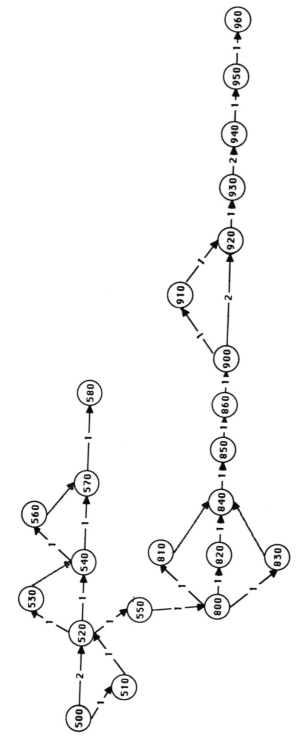

PERT Diagram, Part III

Event	TL	TE	Slack	Event	TL	TE	Slack
850	27	25	2*	930	32	30	2*
860	28	26	2*	940	34	32	2*
900	29	27	2*	950	35	33	2*
910	30	28	2*	960	36	34	2*
920	31	29	2*				

*Events along the critical path

D. Gantt Diagram

Illustrative Gantt Diagram

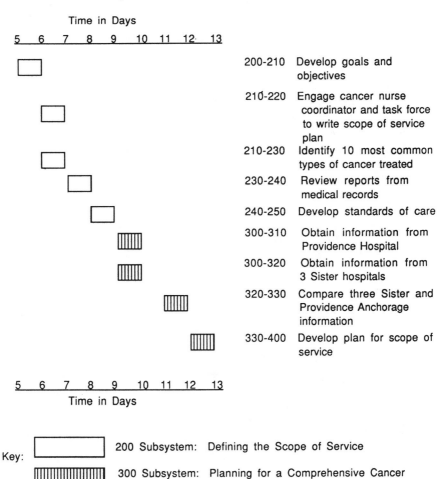

Time in Days

| 5 | 6 | 7 | 8 | 9 | 10 | 11 | 12 | 13 |

200-210 Develop goals and objectives

210-220 Engage cancer nurse coordinator and task force to write scope of service plan

210-230 Identify 10 most common types of cancer treated

230-240 Review reports from medical records

240-250 Develop standards of care

300-310 Obtain information from Providence Hospital

300-320 Obtain information from 3 Sister hospitals

320-330 Compare three Sister and Providence Anchorage information

330-400 Develop plan for scope of service

| 5 | 6 | 7 | 8 | 9 | 10 | 11 | 12 | 13 |

Time in Days

Key:

200 Subsystem: Defining the Scope of Service

300 Subsystem: Planning for a Comprehensive Cancer Care Program

E. Decision Flow Diagram

300 Subsystem: Planning for a Comprehensive Cancer Program
The subsystem illustrated in the decision flow diagram is the *300 Subsystem:* Planning for a Comprehensive Cancer Program.

Obtaining from our Hospital Information System information indicating the insurance, Medicare, Medicaid and private pay financial reimbursement to the hospital for the past year for cancer patients treated medically on the medical unit will assist in determining where the hospital may be making money, breaking even or losing money on our current approach to hospital care. This, in conjunction with information from our Medical Records Department tracing the ten most common types of cancer treated medically on the medical unit for one year, will help in determining what we are treating and what our reimbursement has been. After information has been received from our Medical Records Department and our Hospital Information System, it will be analyzed and a report of findings indicating high and low reimbursement to the hospital by diagnosis will be indicated.

Information from three Sister Hospitals in the Corporation that have designated cancer units will be requested. The information will include their Scope of Service, Financial Reimbursement, Labor Budget (staffing pattern), Policies and Procedures and integration of the program with their facility. A comparison of information from the three Sister Hospitals with the current medical management of the cancer patient at Providence Anchorage will be made to assist in defining a new Scope of Service. The plan for the Scope of Service will then be developed.

F. Information Flow Diagram

See page 243.

G. Activity Documentation

Title: PERT Activity 500-510:
Monitor the acuity level of the cancer patient on the Medical Unit for two months to determine the "average standard hour of care" per patient day.

Description of Activity:
This activity will take two months to perform. The form that will be used by the staff nurse to do this exercise is already in existence. The form has a list of activities that will help the nurse to define how many hours each patient's care requires. The hours of care are then defined by assigned levels. The assigned levels are then converted into the number of staff nurses working

Decision Flow Diagram, Part I

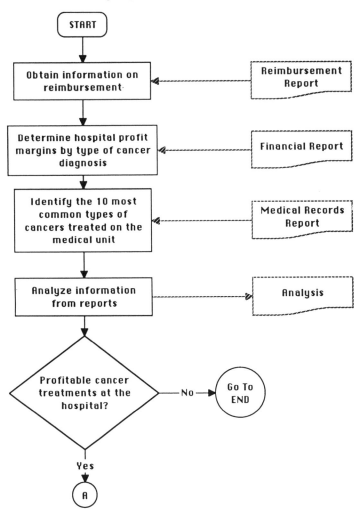

in the department to provide nursing care. All staff nurses have been trained on the use of this form and all newly hired nurses are also provided instructions on the use of the form during orientation.

The form used to monitor the acuity level of the cancer patient on the medical unit to determine the "average standard hour of care" per patient day will be reviewed every 24 hours. The level of care determined for each patient will be placed in the nursing office computer by the Nursing Office Secretary. The Nursing Office Secretary will generate a report to the Unit

Decision Flow Diagram, Part II

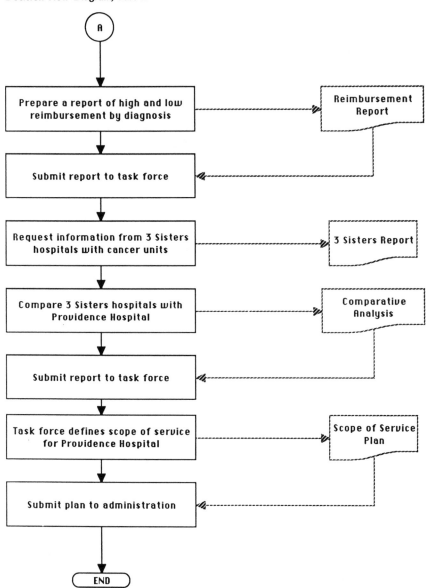

Manager every morning with the previous day's activities. This process is already in place. It was a major project performed by the Nursing Administration with the help of a consulting firm. This activity is the key to the success

Illustrative Information Flow Diagram

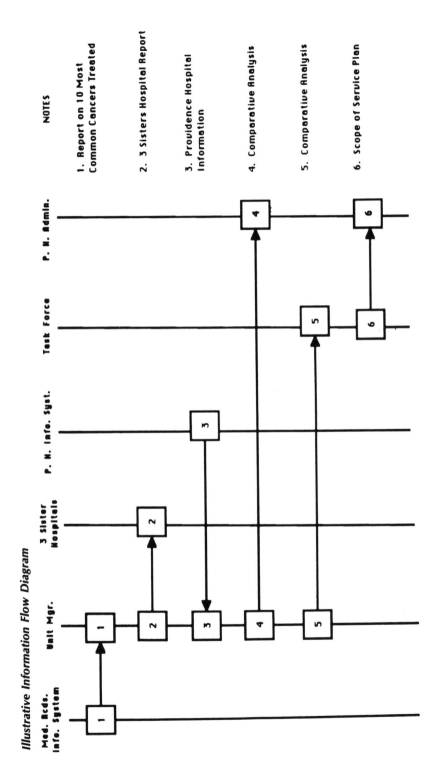

NOTES

1. Report on 10 Most Common Cancers Treated

2. 3 Sisters Hospital Report

3. Providence Hospital Information

4. Comparative Analysis

5. Comparative Analysis

6. Scope of Service Plan

in hiring more staff for the department to provide nursing care. The levels of care and hours of nursing time are converted into the labor budget.

Activity Outputs:

The form used by the staff for determining the acuity level of the cancer patient on the medical unit to determine the "average standard hour of care" for the cancer patient already exists. The staff are prepared to use the tool. The Nursing Office Secretary is already entering the information into the computer and generating a report to the Unit Manager on the medical unit. The difference in this activity will be separating the report information. The general medical patient and the cancer patient's acuity levels will be identified separately. This will be very easy to do. The form has the diagnosis of the patient on it already.

The expected outcome will be that the hours of care for the cancer patient will be higher and more hours of care will be needed. This will assist in substantiating more staff be hired and the labor budget will be adjusted.

Required Input Conditions:

1. Staff nurses determine daily the level of care for cancer patients.
2. Report submitted to the Nursing Office Secretary.
3. Nursing Office Secretary generates a report to the Unit Manager of the medical unit every day.
4. Unit Manager reviews and compiles information.
5. Unit Manager submits summary report to Nursing Administration.
6. Nursing Administration reviews information with Assistant Administrator of Hospital for approval of increase in labor budget for cancer patient care.

Required Resources:

The documentation of acuity levels already exists. Secretarial support and the computer-generated reports are already in place. Time for the staff nurses to evaluate the level of care for their patients is already integrated into their daily activities.

The human resources are the Staff Nurse, Nursing Office Secretary and the Unit Manager.

Activity Budget for 24 Hour Process:

1. Staff Nurse time	cost	$16.00 per hour
2. Nursing Office Secretary	cost	11.00 per hour
3. Unit Manager	cost	23.00 per hour
4. Report copying	cost	Indirect
5. Paper	cost	Indirect
6. Acuity form	cost	Indirect
7. Nursing office computer	cost	Indirect
		$50.00 per hour

H. Interface Analysis

1. Internal Interface

Since this project will require the staff nurse to separate the process of defining the level of care for the cancer patient from that of the general medical patient (500-510), it will be important to monitor the acuity forms to be certain that the diagnosis of the patient is included on each form every day. This will assist in keeping our data as accurate as possible.

This project has a wide spectrum of key players, including the Unit Manager, the Multidisciplinary Team and the Medical Oncologist. The Oncology Nurse Coordinator (210-600), the Medical Records Department (300-320), the Hospital Information System (300-310), and the other Sister Hospitals with designated cancer units (310-330) all play roles in obtaining information for the development of a Comprehensive Cancer Program at Providence Hospital Anchorage. The Unit Manager and task force will be key individuals in keeping this project online until completion. The final evaluation of the program in the 900 Subsystem will provide a basis for review and revision.

APPENDIX C

De George's Paper

Developing a Bilingual/ESL Management Training Program

George P. De George
EL792, Practical Administrative Techniques
Dr. Alan Gaynor
May 1987

Executive Summary

In comparison with the area of instructional methods, the area of bilingual/ESL program management receives little focus in graduate programs funded to train bilingual/ESL personnel. Part of the problem is that there are few individuals who are aware of the needs of such program managers, and who, at the same time have the expertise to organize the type of training that will address their needs. Program managers have typically been recruited from among experienced teaching staff, i.e., individuals who are usually not professionally trained to be managers on a prior basis.

The need for training bilingual/ESL program directors has not gone unrecognized. Throughout the 1970s the Office of Bilingual Education and Minorities Languages Affairs conducted several national management institutes for Title VII program directors. The emphasis, however, was in imparting information, especially about relevant federal regulations, rather than on skills development. More recent efforts across the nation have been more systematic and comprehensive; however, they are far from complete and their written record is not as extensive and accessible as it could be.

What is needed in the field at this time is a complete and detailed syllabus of all the critical content/skill areas which ought to be covered in the training of bilingual/ESL program directors. This project will prepare such a syllabus based upon the requirements of state and local educational agencies, an analysis of college and university training programs in bilingual program administration, interviews with experts in the field, and an extensive search of the literature on content and skills. Marketing, advertising, sales, and distribution strategies will also be developed.

TABLE OF CONTENTS

I. Background Statement

In comparison with instructional methods, the area of bilingual/ESL program management receives little focus in graduate programs funded to train bilingual/ESL personnel. On an in-service basis, whether through training programs organized in school districts or through statewide, regional, or national conferences for bilingual/ESL educators, the real needs of bilingual/ESL program managers for training are dealt with occasionally, often unsystematically, and with a focus on informing rather than on skill training. Part of the problem is that there are few individuals who are aware of the needs of such program managers and who, at the same time, have the expertise to organize the type of training that will address their needs.

The other part of the problem is that the specialized nature of bilingual/ESL education requires that directors of such programs have an intimate knowledge of the instructional and curriculum aspects of the programs, be proficient in at least one of the relevant program languages, be skilled in a variety of technical management functions such as proposal writing and program evaluation, and be able to manage staff, parents, students, and others of diverse cultural backgrounds. Because of these demands, such program managers have typically been recruited from among experienced teaching staff, i.e., individuals who are usually not professionally trained to be managers on a prior basis. This situation has existed since 1968 when federal legislation was enacted to fund programs for limited English-speaking students and subsequent to which many states enacted laws that mandated or encouraged the establishment of bilingual/ESL programs. The result of this national and state support, the constant influx of limited English-speaking student populations, and the recognition of non- or limited English-speaking groups already living here has been the proliferation of such programs on a national basis. At the present time, there are about 800 federally funded bilingual/ESL programs throughout the country. State and locally funded programs greatly outnumber these. The Commonwealth of Massachusetts alone has forty-six state and local funded bilingual/ESL programs servicing eighteen language groups as opposed to fourteen Title VII federal funded programs servicing twelve language groups. In summary, there are many current directors, especially those newly appointed, who need some effective in-service training and the benefit of well-organized educational administration programs at colleges and universities that are responsive to their needs.

The need for training bilingual/ESL program directors has not gone unrecognized. Throughout the 1970s the Office of Bilingual Education and Minorities Languages Affairs conducted several national management institutes for Title VII program directors, but typically such institutes were informational in nature, that is, they dealt with federal rules and regulations, federal funding and grant applications. Rarely was there any training in such areas as staff evaluation and management and relating to groups external to one's program. Attempts were made to clarify matters of proposal writing, federal budgets, and program evaluation. The emphasis, however, was in imparting information, especially about relevant federal regulations, rather than on skills development.

By the late 1970s and early 1980s, the need for more focused management training began to be recognized. In 1978–1979, small Title VII federal grants for management training were authorized and led to such efforts as the Institutes for Program Improvement, which were funded through the Evaluation, Dissemination and Assessment Center in Cambridge, Massachusetts, and two large-scale bilingual program management institutes by the same organization in 1981 and 1984. The focus of these efforts was professional management skills training such as evaluation planning, leadership styles, strategies for staff management, organizing parental involvement, and managing task-oriented groups. The same organization contributed two publications to the field: *Improving Bilingual Program Management: A Handbook for Title BII Managers* (1980), and *Bilingual Program Management: A Problem-Solving Approach* (1985).

While these more recent efforts and similar ones across the nation have been more systematic and comprehensive, they are far from complete and their written record is not as extensive and accessible as it could be. What is needed in the field at this time to assist educational administration faculty and coordinators of in-service training, therefore, is as complete and as detailed a syllabus as possible of all the critical content/skill areas that ought to be covered in the training of bilingual/ESL program directors. Such a syllabus could serve as the basis for further needs assessment. It could suggest content/skill areas to be incorporated into existing educational administration course structures and into workshops and seminars of in-service trainers. It could suggest to researchers further areas for investigation and to writers ideas for textbooks and other publications. The existence of such a syllabus, along with several existing publications, would serve as a ready reference to interested faculty and trainers, eliminate the need to "reinvent the wheel," and leave more time for development as opposed to time-consuming research.

II. Mission Hierarchy

LEVEL 10:   To improve the quality of instruction, effectiveness, and morale of bilingual/ESL education programs.

LEVEL 9:   To enhance the quality of management in bilingual/ESL programs.

LEVEL 8:   To produce more and better trained managers of bilingual/ESL education programs.

LEVEL 7:   To support the development of quality pre-service and in-service management training programs for directors of bilingual/ESL education programs.

LEVEL 6:   *To develop a comprehensive syllabus for pre-service and in-service management training programs for bilingual/ESL program directors.*

LEVEL 5:   To determine the training needs of directors of bilingual/ESL education programs in terms of content and skill areas.

LEVEL 4:   To determine the content/skill areas in which LEA directors feel they need to be trained on a pre-service and in-service basis; the perceptions of SEA bilingual/ESL coordinators of the training needs of LEA bilingual/ESL directors; the content/skills areas taught in courses at colleges and universities in programs leading to degrees and certification in elementary/secondary program direction and, where possible, in bilingual/ESL program direction; the basic requirements of key states with respect to certificates for the position of elementary/secondary program directors and, where possible, that of bilingual/ESL program director.

LEVEL 3:   To ascertain from experts the key content/skill areas that constitute the domain of training for directors of bilingual/ESL programs.

LEVEL 2:   To extract from the literature the key content/skill areas that constitute the domain of training for directors of bilingual/ESL programs.

LEVEL 1:   To develop an organizational structure or substructure and resources to undertake the mission.

III. Mission Target and Rationale

At the present time there is no comprehensive, systematic, updated syllabus for the domain of management training for directors of elementary and secondary bilingual/ESL education programs. There is a body of literature that discusses various facets of the domain and there are in some colleges and universities general programs in educational administration and program and courses for bilingual/ESL program management. In addition, professional workshops and seminars have been developed and delivered by private consulting firms and various federal, state, and local training agencies.

In contrast to Level 6, Level 7 presents a long-range goal. Development of a syllabus for use by educational administration faculty and in-service trainers would be a valuable first step toward realizing the long-range goal stated in Level 7. The need for a syllabus is widespread across the country. Level 6 is doable and, if accomplished, would be reproducible and accessible to those who need it.

IV. Output Specifications

LEVEL 6:   To develop a comprehensive syllabus for pre-service and in-service management training programs for bilingual/ESL program directors.

6.1 There will be a clear statement of purpose for the syllabus.

6.2 There will be a brief history of the development of bilingual/ESL education in the U.S. and of the evolution of the role of the bilingual/ESL director.

6.3 There will be presented several typical scenarios illustrating the work of the bilingual/ESL director and a description of the qualities of an effective director.

6.4 There will be a summary of the relevant literature, resources, and sources of information and assistance for bilingual/ESL program management.

6.5 There will be a detailed, comprehensive breakdown of the content/skill areas that constitute the domain of bilingual/ESL management training.

LEVEL 5:   To determine the training needs of directors of bilingual/ESL educational programs in terms of content and skill areas.

There will be a detailed, comprehensive, written meta-analysis of all the previous written analyses and descriptions of the content and skills that constitute the domain of bilingual/ESL program administration.

LEVEL 4:   To determine the content/skill areas in which LEA directors feel they need to be trained on a pre-service and in-service basis; the perceptions of SEA bilingual/ESL coordinators of the training needs of LEA bilingual/ESL directors; the content/skill areas taught in courses at colleges and universities in programs leading to degrees and certification in elementary/secondary program direction and, where possible, in bilingual/ESL program direction; the basic requirements of key states with respect to certificates for the position of elementary/secondary program director and, where possible, that of bilingual/ESL program director.

4.1 There will be a written analysis and description of the content and skills that constitute the domain of bilingual/ESL administration based on questionnaires and interviews of a sample of LEA bilingual/ESL program directors.

4.2 There will be a written analysis and description of the content and skills that constitute the domain of bilingual/ESL administration based on questionnaires and interviews of a sample of SEA bilingual/ESL coordinators.

4.4 There will be a written analysis and description of the content and skills that constitute the domain of bilingual/ESL administration based on the courses taught at a sample of colleges and universities having programs leading to degrees and certification in elementary/secondary program administration and, where possible, in bilingual/ESL program administration.

4.5 There will be a written analysis and description of the content and skills that constitute the domain of bilingual/ESL administration based on the requirements of key states for certificates in elementary/secondary program administration and, where possible, for bilingual/ESL program administration.

LEVEL 3: To ascertain from experts the key content/skill areas that constitute the domain of training for bilingual/ESL program directors.

There will be a written analysis and description of the content and skills that constitute the domain of bilingual/ESL program administration based on interviews of a sample of recognized experts.

LEVEL 2: To ascertain from the literature the key content/skill areas that constitute the domain of training for bilingual/ESL program directors.

There will be a written analysis and description of the content and skills that constitute the domain of bilingual/ESL program administration based on a reading of the relevant literature.

LEVEL 1:   To develop an organizational structure or substructure and resources to undertake the mission.

    1.1   There will be a market search providing data on potential project sponsors and product consumers.

    1.2   There will be a plan and criteria for sponsor selection.

    1.3   There.will be a plan for project organization, integration into a greater organization, and initial implementation.

V. Context Evaluation

A. Input Specifications

LEVEL 6:   To develop a comprehensive syllabus for pre-service and in-service management programs for bilingual/ESL program directors.

Output Specifications	Input Specifications
6.1 There will be a clear statement of purpose for the syllabus.	There is no definitive statement of purpose, but the background statement outlines several reasons.
6.2 There will be a brief history of the development of bilingual/ESL education in the U.S. and of the role of director.	There are accounts of the development of bilingual/ESL education in the U.S., but no known accounts of the evolution of the role of bilingual/ESL program director. However, there are accounts of specific events and training programs that can be searched, and agencies and individuals who can be queried.
6.3 There will be presented several typical scenarios illustrating the work of the bilingual/ESL director and a description of the qualities of an effective director.	There are few recorded scenarios and descriptions of what are the qualities of a good bilingual director. However, there are training personnel, written sources, and program directors who can provide information.
6.4 There will be a summary of the relevant literature, resources, sources of information and assistance for	There is no comprehensive summary of the relevant literature, resources, and sources of information and assistance for program

the area of bilingual/ESL program management.

management. However, there are searches of the literature, professional organizations, clearinghouses, federal and state agencies, bibliographies, and published hand-out materials that can supply information.

6.5 There will be a detailed, comprehensive breakdown of the content/skill areas that constitute the domain of bilingual/ESL management.

There is no syllabus at the present time. However, several published works survey the domain, and programs of past and present conferences can provide information, as well as consultants and trainers in the field, and experts and faculty of college and university training programs.

LEVEL 5:   To determine the training needs of directors of bilingual/ESL education programs in terms of content and skill areas.

Output Specifications

There will be a detailed, comprehensive, written meta-analysis of all the previous analyses and descriptions of the content and skills that constitute the domain of bilingual/ESL program administration.

Input Specifications

There is currently no written, detailed, comprehensive meta-analysis of the content and skills that constitute the domain of bilingual/ESL program administration. However, there is a literature on educational experts administration, requirements for administrative certification that can be reviewed, ongoing pre-service and in-service programs that can be analyzed, and SEA coordinators and LEA directors who can be interviewed.

LEVEL 4:   To determine the content/skill areas in which LEA directors feel they need to be trained on a pre-service and in-service basis; the perceptions of SEA bilingual/ESL coordinators of the training needs of LEA bilingual/ESL directors; the content/skill areas taught in courses at colleges and universities in programs leading to degrees and certification in elementary/secondary program direction and, where possible, in bilingual/ESL program direction; the basic requirements of key states with respect to certificates for the position of elementary/secondary program director and, where possible, that of bilingual/ESL program director.

Output Specifications

There will be a written analysis description of the content/skill areas that constitute the domain of bilingual/ESL administration based on questions and interviews of a sample of SEA bilingual/ESL coordinators; based on interviews of a sample of LEA bilingual/ESL directors; based on the courses taught at a sample of colleges and universities having programs leading to certification elementary/secondary program administration and, where possible, bilingual/ESL program administration; based on the requirements of key states for certification in elementary/secondary program administration and, where possible, for bilingual/ESL program administration.

Input Specifications

There is no such analysis and description of the content/skill areas based on questionnaires and interviews conducted with SEA coordinators; however, there are some relevant research studies and data available as a result of needs assessments done for regional and bilingual management conferences. There is no such analysis and description of the content/skill areas based on questionnaires and interviews conducted with LEA in directors; however, there are some relevant research studies and data available as a result of needs assessments done for regional bilingual management conferences. There are no such analyses and descriptions based on courses taught; however, there are some research studies, general and bilingual administration courses that can be examined and faculty that can be interviewed. There are no such analyses and descriptions based on the requirements of key states; however, there are some research studies and states do issue requirements that can be studied and state-level certification officers can be interviewed.

LEVEL 3:   To ascertain from experts the key content/skill areas that constitute the domain of training for directors of bilingual/ESL programs.

Output Specifications

There will be a written analysis description of the content/skills that constitute the domain of bilingual/ESL program administration based on interviews of a sample of recognized experts.

Input Specifications

There is no such analysis and description of the content/skills that constitute the domain of bilingual/ESL administration based on the interviews of a sample of recognized experts. However, there are bilingual/ESL management experts, whether writers, trainers, or other practitioners, that can be identified and interviewed.

LEVEL 2:   To ascertain from the literature the key content/skill areas that constitute the domain of training for directors of bilingual/ESL programs.

Output Specifications	**Input Specifications**
There will be a written analysis and description of the content/skills that constitute the domain of bilingual/ESL program administration based on a reading of the relevant literature.	There is no such analysis and description of the content/skills that constitute the domain of bilingual/ESL administration based on the literature. However, there are some relevant research studies and extant literature that can be examined.

LEVEL 1:   To develop an organizational structure or substructure and resources to undertake the mission.

1.1 There will be a market search providing data on potential project sponsors and product consumers.	There is no specific market search providing data for this project; however, it is known what types of data ought to be collected, and which potential sponsors and product consumers ought to be queried.
1.2 There will be a plan and criteria for sponsor selection.	There are no such plan and criteria; however, the requirements for getting the project done suggest the selection criteria and the literature on grantsmanship will supply information on sponsor selection.
1.3 There will be a plan for organization, integration into a greater organization, and initial implementation.	There is no such plan, but the project literature on organizational analysis and profit/nonprofit organizations and business administration will supply information; in addition, an analysis of the output specifications suggests the type of structure required of the project and what initial implementation consists of and, to some extent, the ways in which the project must be integrated into a greater structure.

B. Potential Facilitating and Hindering Factors and Implications of Context Evaluation for Project Design

Below are listed factors that potentially can facilitate and hinder the mission of developing a comprehensive syllabus for pre-service and in-service management training programs for bilingual/ESL program directors. In addition there are listed for each facilitating factor one or more activities that take advantage of those factors toward mission accomplishment. Likewise, for each potential hindering factor are listed activities that purport to deal with those factors. These activities have been integrated into the project design and appear explicitly or implicitly in the PERT index and PERT diagram.

Facilitating Factors

1. A variety of agencies and institutions is likely to be willing to sponsor this project including college/universities, federally funded agencies, private contractors, and publishers.

Activity: Seek an agency or institutional sponsor utilizing the following criteria:

   a. Interest the organization has in the project
   b. Interest qualified staff of the agency or institution have in working on or supporting the project
   c. Potential qualified professional staff available to work on the project
   d. Number and quality of support staff the organization is willing to commit to the project
   e. Material resources and equipment essential to the project that the organization is willing to commit or acquire and access of resources to the project staff
   f. Willingness of the organization to commit and seek financial resources
   g. Capability of the organization in research, development, marketing, and distribution of print products
   h. Willingness of the agency or institution to integrate project into its structure and ongoing activities

2. A variety of potential funding sources is available to this project including federal funds, state, and private/foundation sources.

Activity: Conduct a search of the elibibility of the project for outside funds including federal, state, and private/foundation funding sources.

3. There is at least an even chance of finding a sponsoring agency or institution that has or can acquire the requisite human, material, and financial resources to undertake this project.

Activity: In seeking a sponsor, incorporate into the criteria the requisite resources.

4. Because of the need for this syllabus and its practicality, institutions that are desirous of publishing, such as universities, will be particularly open to sponsoring the project.

Activity: Use this as a criterion and as a selling point in choosing a sponsor.

5. The project can conceivably be performed by a small team of individuals on their own time and at their own expense.

Activity: In formulating alternate strategies to that of employing a sponsoring agency, incorporate this factor as one of the alternate strategies.

6. The project can easily be incorporated into most sponsoring agency and institutional schedules and structure.

Activity: Draw up alternative staffing patterns for the project and corresponding cost estimates; include options for in-house staff only, combinations of in-house staff and outside consultants/contractors, and short and long-term staff; devise a plan whereby project can be integrated into the agency/institution's structure and ongoing activities.

7. In several agencies/institutions, some qualified staff are apt to want to participate in the project or lend significant types of support.

Activity: In seeking a sponsor, choose one in which several staff are willing to participate or lend support to the project. Before approaching a sponsor, endeavor to ascertain whether any of its staff are qualified to work on the project and make the same inquiry after approaching a potential sponsor, if necessary.

8. A variety of agencies and institutions is likely to be willing to lend the use of their resources and facilities for such a project, e.g., telephones, computers, etc., as opposed to hiring the project staff.

Activity: During the market search, ascertain which sponsors would be so willing, include this concept when drawing up alternative sponsor and staffing patterns, and identify the types of qualified staff that would be willing to work under such an arrangement.

9. Flexible and cost-effective staffing arrangements are possible for this project including the use of a small internal staff coupled with outside consultants and contractors.

Activity: Incorporate this concept when drawing up alternative staffing patterns for the project and use it as a selling point when seeking a sponsor.

10. There is a definable, national market for the syllabus.

Activity: Conduct a brief but well focused and well-thought-out market search in order to:

    a. Determine more precisely what are the principal and wider markets for the syllabus

    b. Determine how great the interest in such a product is and how it would compete against somewhat similar products

    c. Determine what price, if any, the market is willing to pay for such a product

    d. Ascertain the product format most appealing to the market

    e. Determine which organizations or types of organizations are most likely to be interested in sponsoring such a project

    f. Have a basis for formulating a marketing, selling and distribution strategy

11. The major market for this product is concentrated in several key states, e.g., California, New York, Texas.

Activity: Determine the key states and regions within them more precisely through the market search and use this information in seeking a sponsor, and in devising selling and distribution strategies.

12. Production of the syllabus will not require expensive printing, layout, cover design, print and cover stock — good quality word processing and electronic duplication will suffice.

Activity: Use this as a selling point in seeking a sponsor; seek a sponsor that has the requisite resources.

13. The existence of relevant information clearinghouses and computer search capability makes thorough, accurate, and rapid research possible.

Activity: Determine computer needs for the project, seek sponsors that have them or are willing to acquire them; provide for them in the project budget; determine and use from the outset clearinghouses and other sources of information.

14. Experts in bilingual/ESL program administration can be readily identified through the literature, the network of federal and state bilingual agencies, professional organizations and college/university bilingual training programs.

Activity: Begin identifying and using these sources of information at the beginning of the project and identifying experts in the course of the search of the literature.

15. With respect to SEA administrative certification requirements, compendia are available and a closer scrutiny of 10–15 key states will suffice.

Activity: Identify these compendia at the beginning of the project and obtain SEA information available from the Office of Bilingual Education and Minorities Languages Affairs (OBEMLA) and the National Clearinghouse for Bilingual Education (NCBE).

16. Identification of colleges/universities having bilingual education training programs can easily be done through OBEMLA, SEA bilingual/ESL coordinators, and NCBE.

Activity: Contact these sources of information early in the project.

17. SEA bilingual/ESL coordinators are easily identified through OBEMLA and NCBE; LEA directors are easily identified through OBEMLA and SEA coordinators.

Activity: Contact these sources of information early in the project.

18. The availability of computer hardware and software, particularly word processing, filing, and data base packages, greatly facilitates the execution of a project of this type.

Activity: Choose a sponsor that has or is willing to acquire requisite computer capability and provide for same in the project budget.

Hindering Factors

1. There is a potential difficulty in assembling or finding in one sponsoring agency or institution all of the required human, material, and financial resources needed to accomplish the project; even if these are there, access problems may arise and thus slow the project or affect staff morale adversely.

Activity: Leave ample time to seek out willing sponsors that have all or most of the necessary resources and are willing to acquire them; provide for such resources in the project budget; and include access to resources as one of the criteria in choosing a sponsor.

2. Offering this publication for sale may hinder its marketability and will necessitate time and expense in formulating and implementing marketing and advertising strategies and distribution procedures.

Activity: Use the market search results as a basis for deciding these issues.

3, A significant and needy segment of the market for this product is spread thinly over a vast geographical area that includes not only the continental United States, but outlying areas such as Alaska, Hawaii, the Trust Territories, Puerto Roco, and the Virgin Islands.

Activity: Plan for this by using the market search results in devising an effective marketing, sales, and distribution strategy. Use of relevant national conferences for marketing is usually helpful.

4. The project is potentially time-consuming and labor-intensive.

Activity: Deal with this factor by choosing a sponsor with the necessary resources to overcome these, by maintaining master lists of all information and technical support services; by careful construction and piloting of telephone scripts, interview protocols, and questionnaires; by optimum use of computers and computer software; by delegating appropriate tasks to support staff; by allowing ample slack time; and by devising early on an orderly, logical, and systematic set of categories for storing and classifying information collected by the various sub-studies.

5. The project could entail some high costs due to the need for extensive telephone interviewing and networking, secretarial support and word processing, electronic duplication, proof reading, cover design, mailing, and long-range warehousing and distribution.

Activity: In addition to the activities outlined for factor 2 above, make sure that the sponsoring agency chosen has adequate warehousing facilities, distribution capability, and a long-range commitment to marketing the syllabus; endeavor to bring in the necessary financial resources to cover these costs.

6. Some key words identified in the literature search may be unavailable or difficult to obtain in hard copy or microfiche form.

Activity: Identification and use of information sources early on will minimize this potential hindering factor.

7. Some key works may be difficult to identify because of the unsystematic manner in which the products of federally funded projects are handled after the termination of a project.

Activity: The potential effects of this factor can be minimized by use of the types of information sources mentioned under factor 2 and by contacting the Office of Bilingual Education and Minorities Languages Affairs (OBEMLA) and the National Clearinghouse for Bilingual Education (NCBE).

VI. Activity Specifications

A. PERT Index

100 Subsystem	Conducting the Market Search
100-110	Prepare market search design
110-120	Prepare questionnaire
120-130	Prepare list of respondents
130-140	Conduct search
140-200	Compile, analyze and summarize data

200 Subsystem   **Planning for Sponsor* Selection**

200-210   Determine essential project needs: professional and support staff, computers, other equipment, materials, space, and funding
210-220   Determine alternate staffing patterns and options
220-230   Prepare list of potential project professional staff
230-240   Identify potential outside funding sources**
240-300   Obtain eligibility requirements and application forms from various funding agencies.

300 Subsystem   **Selecting a Sponsor**

300-310   Develop criteria for sponsor selection
310-320   Develop list of sponsorship options
320-330   Draw up list of potential sponsors
330-340   Conduct sponsor search
340-350   Negotiate with interested, qualified potential sponsors
350-360   Select best sponsorship offer
360-370   Secure sponsor commitment
370-380   Negotiate with sponsor the writing of grant proposal(s)
380-390   Write grant proposal(s)
390-400   Obtain grant award

400 Subsystem   **Organizing and Integrating the Project**

400-410   Employ project professional and support staff
410-420   Devise staff working relationships
420-430   Assign work functions among professional and support staff
430-440   Develop work systems, schedule, and time lines
440-450   Establish guidelines for staff supervision and management
450-460   Devise plan for internal coordination of project with sponsoring agency/institution
460-500   Implement internal coordination plan

500 Subsystem   **Implementing the First Stages of the Project**

500-510   Arrange for use of relevant sponsor resources
510-520   Construct inventory of all external organizational, individual, print, media, and electronic informational and technical assistance resources

*Sponsor: agency or institution that undertakes the project.
**Funding source: agency which provides funding to project sponsor.

520-530	Devise plan for use of all internal and external resources
530-600	Devise initial taxonomy and system for collecting, organizing, storing, and retrieving data
530-700	Write statement of purpose for syllabus

600 Subsystem **Surveying the Literature**

600-610	Prepare lit of topics for literature search
610-620	Conduct computerized literature search
610-630	Conduct library search
610-640	Conduct search of other sources and agencies
620-650	Prepare list of works from computerized literature search
630-650	Prepare list of works from library search
640-650	Prepare list of works from other sources and agencies
650-660	Collapse lists into one bibliography
660-670	Obtain copies of works listed in bibliography
670-680	Read and extract relevant information on content/skills
680-690	Revise taxonomy and system for organizing data collection and incorporate into report
690-800	Analyze and summarize information on content/skills into report.

700 Subsystem **Writing an Introduction to the Syllabus**

530-700	Write statement of purpose for syllabus
700-710	Conduct research for history of bilingual/ESL education
710-720	Compose short history of bilingual/ESL education
720-730	Conduct research for history of evolution of role of bilingual/ESL director
730-740	Compose short history of evolution of role of bilingual/ESL director
740-750	Compose scenarios and list of desirable qualities
750-760	Assemble first draft of introduction
760-1420	Prepare second draft of introduction

800 Subsystem **Interviewing Experts**

800-810	Construct interview protocol
810-820	Prepare lists of experts
820-830	Contact experts and make interview appointments
830-840	Conduct interviews
840-850	Compile data from interview protocols
850-860	Revise taxonomy and system for organizing data collected and incorporate into report
860-900	Analyze and summarize data into report

900 Subsystem   **Analyzing Requirements of SEAs**

900-910   Identify key SEAs
910-920   Contact SEAs and request certification requirements
920-930   Extract all pertinent information regarding content/skills
930-1300   Compile, analyze, and summarize data into written report

1000 Subsystem   **Analyzing Requirements of Colleges and Universities**

900-1000   Identify colleges and universities having training programs/courses in bilingual program administration
1000-1010   Contact and request requirements for certification and degrees for elementary and secondary program direction and for bilingual/ESL program direction
1010-1020   Extract all pertinent information from written requirements, course descriptions, etc.
1020-1300   Compile, analyze, and summarize data into written report

1100 Subsystem   **Interviewing LEA Directors**

900-1100   Construct interview protocol
1100-1110   Prepare a list of LEA directors to contact
1110-1120   Contact LEA directors and make interview appointments
1120-1130   Conduct interviews
1130-1140   Compile data from interview protocols
1140-1300   Analyze and summarize data into report

1200 Subsystem   **Interviewing SEA Directors**

900-1200   Construct interview protocol
1200-1210   Prepare list of SEA directors to contact
1210-1220   Contact SEA directors and make interview appointments
1220-1230   Conduct interviews
1230-1240   Compile data from interview protocols
1240-1300   Analyze and summarize data into report

1300 Subsystem   **Doing a Meta-Analysis and Writing the Main Body of the Syllabus**

930-1300   Compile, analyze, and summarize SEA requirements into report

1020-1300	Compile, analyze, and summarize requirements of colleges and universities into report
1140-1300	Analyze and summarize LEA director interviews into report
1240-1300	Analyze and summarize SEA director interviews into report
1300-1310	Write meta-analysis
1300-1500	Develop marketing strategy
1310-1320	Write main body of syllabus
1320-1400	Prepare second draft of syllabus

1400 Subsystem	**Completing the Syllabus**
760-1420	Prepare second draft of introduction.
1400-1410	Prepare cover design
1410-1420	Prepare final layout
1420-1430	Assemble entire text of syllabus and proof
1430-1440	Prepare final draft of syllabus
1440-1450	Choose cover stock, paper, and binding
1450-1550	Reproduce syllabus and bind copies

1500 Subsystem	**Marketing, Advertising, Selling, and Distributing the Syllabus**
1300-1500	Develop marketing strategy
1500-1510	Develop advertising strategy
1510-1520	Develop sales/distribution stratgegy
1520-1530	Arrange for storage and distribution
1530-1540	Implement advertising strategy
1540-1550	Initiate marketing, selling, and distribution of syllabus

B. PERT Diagram

See pages 268–271.

C. Slack Table (in weeks) [T(S) = 156]

Event	T(L)	T(E)	Slack	Event	T(L)	T(E)	Slack
100	12	0	12*	220	19	7	12*
110	13	1	12*	230	20	8	12*
120	14	2	12*	240	21	9	12*
130	15	3	12*	300	22	10	12*
140	16	4	12*	310	23	11	12*
200	17	5	12*	320	24	12	12*
210	18	6	12*	330	25	13	12*

Continued

PERT Diagram, Part I

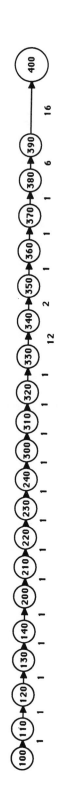

PERT Diagram, Part II

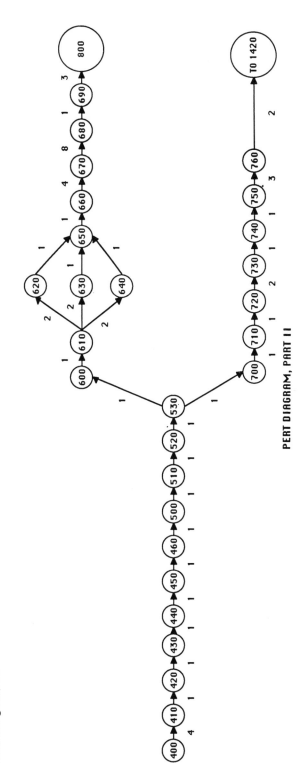

PERT DIAGRAM, PART II

270

PERT Diagram, Part III

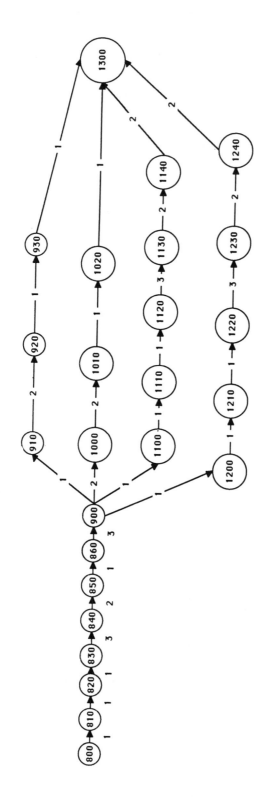

PERT Diagram, Part IV

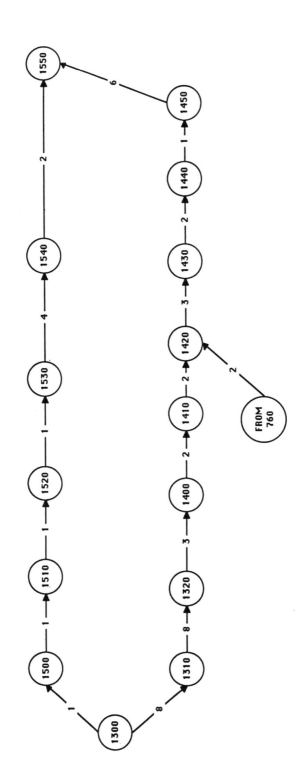

Slack Table (Continued)

Event	T(L)	T(E)	Slack	Event	T(L)	T(E)	Slack
340	37	25	12*	820	101	89	12*
350	39	27	12*	830	102	90	12*
360	40	28	12*	840	105	93	12*
370	41	29	12*	850	107	95	12*
380	42	30	12*	860	108	96	12*
390	48	36	12*	900	111	99	12*
400	64	52	12*	910	117	100	17
410	68	56	12*	920	119	102	17
420	69	57	12*	930	120	103	17
430	70	58	12*	1000	117	101	16
440	71	59	12*	1010	119	103	16*
450	72	60	12*	1020	120	104	16
460	73	61	12*	1100	112	100	12*
500	74	62	12*	1110	113	101	12*
510	75	63	12*	1120	114	102	12*
520	76	64	12*	1130	117	105	12*
530	77	65	12*	1140	119	107	12*
600	78	66	12*	1200	112	100	12*
610	79	67	12*	1210	113	101	12*
620	81	69	12*	1220	114	102	12*
630	81	69	12*	1230	117	105	12*
640	81	69	12*	1240	119	107	12*
650	82	70	12*	1300	121	109	12*
660	83	71	12*	1310	129	117	12*
670	87	75	12*	1320	137	125	12*
680	95	83	12*	1400	140	128	12*
690	96	84	12*	1410	142	130	12*
700	129	66	63	1420	144	132	12*
710	130	67	63	1430	147	135	12*
720	131	68	63	1440	149	137	12*
730	133	70	63	1500	147	110	37
740	134	71	63	1510	148	111	37
750	135	72	63	1520	149	112	37
760	138	75	63	1530	150	113	37
800	99	87	12*	1540	154	117	37
810	100	88	12*	1550	156	144	12*

*Critical Path

D. Gantt Diagram

See on page 273.

Illustrative Gantt Diagram

Illustrative Gantt Diagram

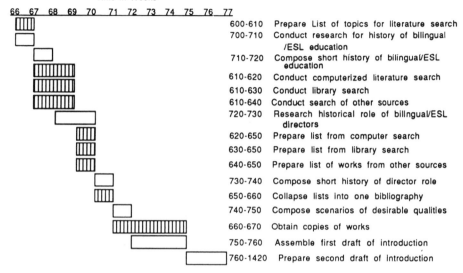

Time in Weeks

66	67	68	69	70	71	72	73	74	75	76	77		

600-610	Prepare List of topics for literature search
700-710	Conduct research for history of bilingual /ESL education
710-720	Compose short history of bilingual/ESL education
610-620	Conduct computerized literature search
610-630	Conduct library search
610-640	Conduct search of other sources
720-730	Research historical role of bilingual/ESL directors
620-650	Prepare list from computer search
630-650	Prepare list from library search
640-650	Prepare list of works from other sources
730-740	Compose short history of director role
650-660	Collapse lists into one bibliography
740-750	Compose scenarios of desirable qualities
660-670	Obtain copies of works
750-760	Assemble first draft of introduction
760-1420	Prepare second draft of introduction

66 67 68 69 70 71 72 73 74 75 76 77

Time in Weeks

Key:

600 Subsystem: Surveying the Literature

700 Subsystem: Writing the Introduction

E. Illustrative Decision Flow Diagram

The subsystem illustrated in the decision flow diagram is the *800 Subsystem: Interview Experts.*

Obtaining from recognized experts in the field their direct input regarding what ought to be covered in the training of bilingual/ESL program directors is the work of this subsystem. The first step in the process is to construct an interview protocol that will solicit their input effectively, efficiently, and accurately. Two documents generated previously, the initial taxonomy for classifying project data and the report on the survey of the literature on bilingual/ESL program management, are to be used in protocol development. To ensure that the protocol elicits the requisite data effectively, efficiently, and accurately, it must be pilot tested with five qualified volunteers. Pilot testing and revising the protocol three times will produce a relatively valid and reliable protocol within a reasonable span of time. When

Decision Flow Diagram, Part I

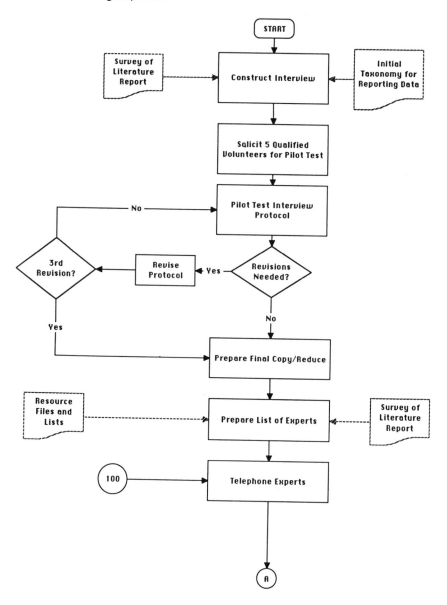

Decision Flow Diagram, Part II   **Decision Flow Diagram, Part III**

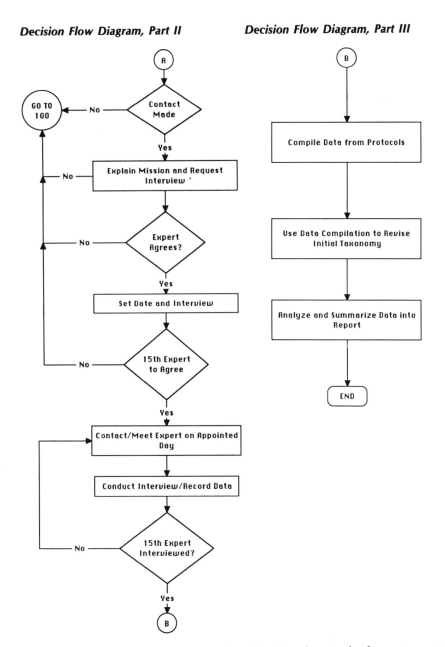

the final copy is drawn up and reproduced, a list of recognized experts must be compiled. Project resource files and lists and the survey of literature report will provide input for this task. Each expert is then to be telephoned. If contact is made, the mission is to be explained and an interview is to be requested.

If the expert contacted does not agree, then the next expert on the list is to be telephoned. If the expert agrees to an interview, a date is then to be set. This process is continued until interview dates have been set with fifteen experts. Each expert is then to be contacted by telephone or met on the appointed day and the interview is to be conducted and the data recorded on the interview protocol. This process continues until all fifteen experts have been interviewed. The data from the protocols are then to be compiled, analyzed, and summarized into a report. The contents of this report are then to be used in revising the initial taxonomy for classifying project data.

F. Illustrative Information Flow Diagram

See page 277.

G. Illustrative Project Activity Documentation

PERT Activity 730-740:
Compose short history of evolution of role of bilingual/ESL director.

Description of Activity
The act of writing a short history of the evolution of the role of bilingual/ESL director will be the final act of synthesis following a series of research activities and investigations. Some of the principal research activities feeding into the writing of this history have been built into the project itself. These activities are the survey of the literature and the interviewing of LEA and SEA directors.

The data gathered from these sources will be analyzed chronologically on the federal, state, and local levels, starting with the statutory and regulatory bases for the establishment of the director's position. On all three levels, trends in the development of the roles and functions of local bilingual/ESL directors will be analyzed from 1968 to the present. 1968 is the year in which the first federal Bilingual Education Act was passed authorizing the allocation of funds for the establishment of bilingual programs. Data will also be analyzed from a sample of states and from a sample of representative school districts throughout the country. Data on all levels will be separated into "factual" information as opposed to the perceptions of individuals. The roles of local bilingual/ESL directors will be contrasted with those of SEA coordinators of bilingual/ESL education and those of directors of federal- and state-funded technical assistance agencies created especially to serve the needs of various bilingual/ESL constituencies.

When all these data have been gathered and analyzed, the brief history will be written from the point of view of analyses and trends over time in

Illustrative Information Flow Diagram

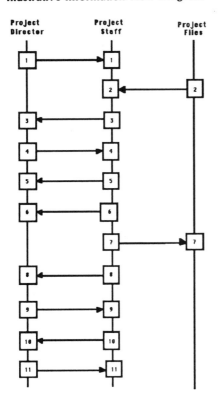

NOTES

1. Task

2. Data for Protocol Construction

3. Draft Interview

4. Revisions

5. Revised Protocol

6. Authorization

7. Pilot

8. Revised

9. Final

10. Final

11. Authorization to Reproduce and Administer the Protocol

various significant geographical regions including the New York area, Texas, California, Chicago, and the Midwest, Florida, the Southwest, New England, and the Washington, D.C. area.

The writing of this short history will involve the production of a first draft with feedback and corrections by other project staff leading to several more drafts, approval of the final draft by the project director, and final proof reading and production.

Activity Outputs

When complete, the short history will present an insightful picture of the evolution of the role of local bilingual/ESL director from its inception, which resulted from the enactment of Title VII of the Elementary and Secondary Education Act of 1968, and from the enactment of various state laws beginning with the first, Chapter 71A, passed in Massachusetts in 1971. The history will examine the role of local director as a manager of staff and the status of the role within the school district. In addition will be examined the director's role in the local community and on the state and federal levels. The short history will examine the professional status of bilingual/ESL directors in terms of their own perceptions, state certification, and professional organizations and activities on national and regional levels

Required Input Conditions

1. Information on the history of bilingual/ESL education in the United States (700 Subsystem)
2. Research specifically focused on the evolution of the role of the bilingual/ESL director (700 Subsystem)
3. Documentation from the literature and legal documents (600 Subsystem)
4. Data and research from the field (800, 1100, and 1200 Subsystems)
5. Information on bilingual/ESL certification (900 Subsystem)

Resources Required

1. Staff and staff time (1–4 weeks). Cost: $635–2,725.
2. Computer search capability. Cost: $50 per month.
3. Access to libraries and other document collections. Cost: indirect.
4. Word-processing capability. Cost: $100 per month.
5. Telephone time. Cost: $150 per month.
7. Secretarial support. Cost: $400–$1,720 per month.
8. Acquisition of print materials. Cost: $75.
9. Desk, space, ordinary supplies. Cost: indirect.
10. Proofreaders. Cost: $10 per hour.

Management Responsibility

The project manager and his/her superordinates are responsible for overall management of resources needed to complete this activity. The manager must see that one or more staff persons are assigned to the task with sufficient time to complete it; that financial resources are on hand to purchase computer searchers or computer search capability; that word processing and secretarial support are available; that monies and a process for ordering print materials are available; and that space and ordinary equipment (desk, chairs, etc.) are provided for staff assigned to the activity.

Input for this activity is required from Subsystems 600, 800, 900, 1100, and 1200. The project manager is responsible for seeing that staff assigned to these activities are performing effectively and according to schedule and that reports generated by these activities are made available to staff assigned to activity 730-740 in a timely fashion.

Other activities in the 700 Subsystem that feed into activity 730-740 will be performed by the same staff or staff person. The project manager must see that these staff are assigned to the other 700 Subsystem activities and that they are performed effectively and according to schedule.

H. Illustrative Internal Interface Analysis

Since this project involves the production of several reports that are then synthesized into one document through a process of meta-analysis, it is important to determine a common format for all of the reports to allow for effective fusion. It became important, therefore, to determine which activities provide both a format as well as prerequisite data for subsequent reports, to schedule activities accordingly, and thereafter to determine which activities could be scheduled simultaneously.

Consequently, the devising of an initial taxonomy or classification system for the collecting, organizing, storing, and retrieving of data takes place in the 500 Subsystem and precedes all research work. the next and only set of activities to take place is the 600 Subsystem: Survey of the Literature, which will provide the basis for all further research in the project with the exception of the 700 Subsystem: Introduction to the Syllabus, for which it will provide only partial information. The data collected during the implementation of the 600 Subsystem will also suggest changes in the initial organizing taxonomy. These changes will be integrated into the survey of literature report itself and will determine the course of the next piece of research, the 800 Subsystem: Interview of Experts, which will also provide a basis for the subsequent research subsystems. Again, the data collected from interviewing experts will suggest further changes in the taxonomy. These are to be integrated into the report on the Interview of Experts and will determine the format of the subsequent four research reports coming out of Subsystems 900, 1000, 1100, and 1200, which are implemented simultaneously.

The sequencing of the above subsystems not only will produce data in a format and sequence that are needed, but will provide the basis of an orderly scheduling of tasks and assignments for staff. All project staff can be assigned to work on Subsystems 600 and 700 in sequence and, upon their completion, divide up the work of the four subsystems to follow.

Index